ZEN, DRUGS
AND MYSTICISM

BY THE SAME AUTHOR

The Catholic Church and World Religions
Concordant Discord
The Convergent Spirit
The Dawn and Twilight of Zoroastrianism
Dialectical Christianity and Christian Materialism
Evolution in Religion
Hindu and Muslim Mysticism
Hinduism
Mysticism Sacred and Profane
At Sundry Times

ZEN, DRUGS AND MYSTICISM

by

R. C. ZAEHNER

PANTHEON BOOKS
A Division of Random House, New York

FIRST AMERICAN EDITION

Copyright © 1972 by R. C. Zaehner

All rights reserved under International and Pan-American Copyright Conventions. Published in the United States by Pantheon Books, a division of Random House, Inc., New York.
Originally published in England as *Drugs, Mysticism and Makebelieve* by William Collins Sons & Co. Ltd., London, England.

Library of Congress Cataloging in Publication Data
Zaehner, Robert Charles.
Zen, Drugs and Mysticism.

British ed. published under title: Drugs, Mysticism and Makebelieve.
   Includes bibliographical references.
   1. Hallucinogenic drugs and religious experience.
2. Mysticism. I. Title. [DNLM: 1. Buddhism.
2. Drugs. 3. Mysticism. B 828 Z17z 1972]
BL65.D7Z3 1973   200'.19   72-11871
ISBN 0-394-48540-8

Manufactured in the United States of America

2 4 6 8 9 7 5 3

FOR
ANNE PETER
NICKIE 'DOODIES'
LUCY AND CHRISTOPHER

CONTENTS

	Foreword	*page* 9
1	The Climate of our Unbelief	13
2	The Vitalist Heresy	35
3	Mysticism and LSD	66
4	LSD and Zen	112
5	Beyond Good and Evil	136
6	Salvation through Death	172
7	Make-believe	195
	Index	213

FOREWORD

This book is an expansion of a series of three talks delivered on BBC3 and subsequently printed in *The Listener* on 5, 12 and 19 November 1970 under the title of 'Theology, Drugs and Zen'. I have added nothing to my original comments on modern theology, but have expanded the sections on drugs and Zen considerably and added long sections on Richard Jefferies, Bernanos, Teilhard de Chardin, and Bonhoeffer which were totally absent from the original talks.

It may be (rightly) objected that there is little in this 'new' material which has not appeared in my earlier works. This is true but, I am afraid, inevitable since, as Ecclesiastes says, 'There is nothing new under the sun', and the best of us repeat ourselves. To those already familiar with my earlier work on mysticism and Hinduism I would apologize if I seem to repeat myself unbearably. My excuse is that this book is aimed at a wider public which, I hope, will be unfamiliar with my earlier work.

I would especially thank Miss Jennette Bowling for typing out at least half of the book when she had better and more urgent things to do in this illustrious college, and Miss Judy Todd and all concerned in Messrs Collins's office with seeing the British book through the press. Between them they have saved me many maddening man-hours.

I have also to thank Editions du Seuil of Paris for their kind permission to include extracts from the works of Teilhard de Chardin in a translation of my own which sometimes differs from the English versions published by Messrs Collins, and also Messrs Collins for concurring in this permission. Librairie Plon of Paris have kindly given me permission to make my own translations of passages from the novels of George Bernanos, and from the first volume of the same author's *Correspondance*.

Finally I must acknowledge my gratitude for permission to quote from the following books: The Jerusalem Bible, copyright © 1966 by Darton, Longman & Todd, Ltd., and Doubleday and Company, Inc., used by permission of the publishers; *Psychedelics* by Bernard Aaronson and Humphrey Osmond, published by the Hogarth Press, London, and Doubleday and Company, Inc., New York; *The Confessions of St Augustine* in the translation of F. J. Sheed, copyright © 1943 Sheed & Ward Inc., New York; *Letters and Papers from Prison* by Dietrich Bonhoeffer, enlarged edition, copyright © 1953, 1967, 1971 by SCM Press Ltd., reprinted with permission of The Macmillan Company, New York, and SCM Press, London; *Between Man and Man* by Martin Buber, published by Routledge & Kegan Paul, London; Asian Institute Translation No. 3, *The Platform Scripture*, edited by Wing-Tsit Chan, and published by St John's University Press, New York; *LSD, Man & Society*, edited by R. C. DeBold and R. C. Leaf, copyright © 1967 by Wesleyan University, reprinted by permission of Wesleyan University Press, Middletown, and Faber and Faber, London: *The Doors of Perception* by Aldous Huxley, published by Chatto and Windus, London, and Harper & Row, New York, used by permission of Mrs Laura Huxley; *This Timeless Moment* by Laura Huxley, published by Chatto and Windus, London, and Farrar, Straus & Giroux, Inc., New York; *Journal of a Soul* by Pope John XXIII, copyright © 1965, Geoffrey Chapman Ltd., used with permission of McGraw-Hill Book Company, New York, and Geoffrey Chapman, London; *Answer to Job* in *The Collected Works of C. G. Jung*, edited by G. Adler, M. Fordham, and H. Read, and translated by R. F. C. Hull, Bollingen Series XX, volume 11, *Psychology and Religion: West and East*, Copyright © 1958 and 1969 by Bollingen Foundation, reprinted by permission of Princeton University Press, Princeton, and Routledge & Kegan Paul, London; *Memories, Dreams, Reflections* by C. G. Jung, © 1961, 1962, 1963, by Random House, Inc., published by Collins, and Routledge & Kegan Paul, London, and Pantheon Books/A Division of Random House, Inc., New York; *The Three Pillars of Zen* by Philip Kapleau, published by John Weatherhill, Inc., New York and Tokyo; *The Only Revolution* by J. Krishnamurti, published by Victor Gollancz, London, and Harper & Row, New York; *The Politics of Ecstasy* by Timothy Leary, copyright © 1968 by The League for Spiritual Discovery, Inc., published by G. P. Putnam's Sons, New York, and MacGibbon & Kee, London; *The Varieties of Psychedelic Experience* by R. E. L. Masters and Jean Houston, copyright © 1966 by R. E. L. Masters and Jean Houston, reprinted by permission of Holt, Rinehart and Winston, Inc., Publishers, New York; *Selected Poems from the Dīvāni Shamsi Tabrīz*, edited by R. A. Nicholson, and published by Cambridge University Press, Cambridge; *Remembrance of Things Past* by Marcel Proust, translated by C. Scott-Moncrieff and Stephen Hudson, reprinted by permission of Mr George Scott Moncrieff and the publishers, Chatto and Windus, London, and Random House, Inc., New York; *Following Darkness* by Forrest Reid, published by Edward Arnold, London; *A Flower Does Not Talk* by Abbot Zenkei Shibayama, published by Charles E. Tuttle, Tokyo; *Letters to Two Friends, 1926-1952*, by Pierre Teilhard de Chardin, published by Rapp & Whiting, London, and The New American Library, New York; *The Dead Sea Scrolls in English*, translated by G. Vermes, © G. Vermes, 1965, published by Penguin Books Ltd., Harmondsworth; *The Complete Works of Chuang Tzǔ*, translated by Burton Watson, and published by Columbia University Press, New York; *Hsün Tzǔ, Basic Writings*, translated by Burton Watson, and published by Columbia University Press, New York.

R. C. ZAEHNER

All Souls College
Oxford

1
THE CLIMATE OF OUR UNBELIEF

'The old house has collapsed behind our backs and when we came to take our place in the homes of the young, they hadn't yet found out how to build their own, and we found ourselves in an indeterminate sphere, among the stones and the rafters, in the rain.'[1]

These words were written by the French novelist Georges Bernanos in 1935. Even then, it seems, there was a generation gap. There is nothing new in this. The only difference is that it is now more stridently publicized. Hitherto there were plenty of other (and more important) things to shout about: there still are. The Vietnam war, no doubt; but protesting against this has by now become an empty ritual signifying nothing. The Soviet rape of Czechoslovakia roused practically no righteous indignation in our noble breasts, whether young, middle-aged, or old. The horrors perpetrated in East Pakistan in the name of a single Islamic state (which was in any case a geographical absurdity right from its inception) which drove between nine and ten millions from their homes because they had been deprived of everything except their lives and were old-fashioned enough to wish to preserve them – these horrors provoked little protest and no effective pressure on the perpetrators of this wholesale massacre and terrorism. None of this has really stirred the conscience of the world. Can the reason be that the world no longer has a conscience? Can it be that frightfulness has now become so commonplace that it is already being taken for granted? This may well be, for, if anyone really cared, the mass media, always sensitive to the public mood, would have sensed that mood and reflected it – they are very good at this. But no, the themes that are now eternally plugged are the generation gap and, of course, the 'sexual revolution' which is, in part, the

---

1. Georges Bernanos, *Un mauvais rêve*, in *Oeuvres romanesques* (Bibliothèque de la Pléiade, Gallimard, Paris, 1961, copyright Librairie Plon), p. 918.

result of it. Call it the 'generation gap' and everyone will think that because a new cliché has been coined, a new reality has been discovered. But the reality has always been there: the young mistrust the old and the old dislike the young if for no more substantial reason than that many of them prefer to wear their hair long and some of them have beards. There is nothing new in this. The old and ageing have always resented the innovations of the young simply because they themselves have 'made good' and have won, often by much hard work and self-sacrifice, a position of affluence that their fathers had never known and from which their children are the first to benefit. The young are ungrateful, but then they always have been. Have things ever been much different? The mass media are indeed hard put to it to find anything new or interesting to say. Like everyone else, they are spiritually bankrupt. The young look for guidance and find none, only blind guides chattering to dead souls. Dead souls longing to come to life. But who is to give them life?

The young do not turn to the Churches. But there is nothing new in this. Few intelligent young men have ever turned to the Churches since the eighteenth century. They had (and have) nothing new to offer except the same meaningless formulas, dressed up, maybe, in a more modern verbiage but none the less meaningless to a generation that has to a large extent openly done with religion. Indeed, 'one of the palliatives that modern Christianity has to offer is that it has managed to create a verbal jargon without meaning which is supposed to satisfy everything except reason.' The quotation is not from a modern writer distracted by the postures of a Christianity at bay: it was written in 1763 by a man in search of a living religion which he could not find either in the Protestantism or the Catholic Church of his day – Rousseau, who already was dismayed at the climate of unbelief that had settled on the Europe of his time and against which the religious establishments of the day were powerless because they too, supported as they were everywhere by the secular power, had, beneath the trappings of belief, succumbed internally to the forces of the new rationalism.

Has 'modern' Christianity succeeded in modernizing itself meanwhile? I would dearly like to think it had, but this particular religious establishment, like most establishments, is wonderfully good at deceiving itself. It no longer deceives others.

The vociferous young may be misguided – naturally so since their natural guides are blind – but they are not necessarily stupid. Nor is their rejection of Christianity stupid at all. After all, if the Christian offers you a diet of bread and fish and this simple fare tastes to you like stones and serpents, you have to be very stupid indeed not to notice the difference. 'He could save others, himself he cannot save', said the chief priests and scribes at the foot of the Cross. Perhaps. To the successors of these eminently respectable pillars of the religious establishment we might say: 'You can deceive yourselves, others you cannot deceive.' They can no longer get away with it, and no one takes them seriously. But –

There was a man called John – John XXIII, Supreme Pontiff of the Roman Catholic Church. But John was a miracle. And, of course, we no longer believe in miracles; so we will not talk about John – just yet.

But what is wrong with the young? Nothing at all, answer the middle-aged would-be with-it whiz-kids. Never, we are told, has there been such a splendid generation. I may be wrong, but I very much doubt whether the 'splendid generation' takes such a facile view of itself. If you are a dead soul groping around for some sort of life, you may be flattered by this unexpected, possibly unwelcome, and certainly grotesque adulation lavished on you by blind guides. At least it is a belated admission on their part that they *are* blind. But it is bleak comfort when you know that you have not 'found out how to build' your own house and when, despite all your efforts, you find yourself 'in an indeterminate sphere, among the stones and the rafters, in the rain'.

Man needs to believe in something, even if it is only make-believe: and religion is largely make-believe in that it makes you believe in something that your reason would not normally accept. This make-believe the religious-minded call faith – the acceptance of something which, if true, would make life on earth and death, from which life is inseparable, bearable. In the last few hundred years Christian man has received some pretty nasty shocks from the physical sciences. If one is convinced, as our forebears were, that the earth is the centre of the universe, then man himself, clearly the highest product and crown of the earth, must himself be the end-point and goal of the universe: the universe is for the earth, and the earth and all it contains is for man. This was a manageable perspective, but even this limited vision was marred by the inevitable end of it all – physical death. But then came the Gospel, the 'good news', that in Christ death itself had been conquered and that through Christ man was assured of immortality. All seemed to be right in a fundamentally intelligible world. Then came Copernicus and after him the discovery of the immensity of the universe and of the fact that from the point of view of the universe the earth is a tiny speck of star-dust whose existence or non-existence could not be of the slightest significance to the grand operations of the immeasurable whole. It was precisely the realization of man's insignificance in the universal context that drew from Pascal that anguished cry: '*Le silence eternel de ces espaces infinis m'effraie*' – 'the eternal silence of these infinite spaces appals me'. Even in the seventeenth century it was not easy to be a mathematician and a Christian at the same time. It is very much more difficult now. Pascal was a man of faith, but faith, though it may be make-believe, must also have the force to make you believe. From conventional faith to the kind of certainty that forces belief there is no way except through the most radical doubt. Before you commit yourself to any religion or faith, you have to face the hard facts of existence as science is revealing them ever more clearly. What Pascal said in the seventeenth century is far more frighteningly true today:

'When I consider how short a time my life lasts – absorbed as it is in the eternity that precedes it and that which follows it – and how small is the space that I occupy or even that I can see, lost as I am in the infinite immensity of spaces which I do not know and which do not know me, I am appalled and wonder that I should be here rather than there, for there is no reason why it should be here rather than there, now rather than then. Who has put me here? At whose orders and discretion have *this* place and *this* time been allotted me? . . .'

'The eternal silence of these infinite spaces appals me.'[2]

Even in the seventeenth century man had lost his bearings in a silent and indifferent universe in which his very existence seemed to be an anomaly and, so far from being the lord of creation, he saw himself to be of less account than an insect trapped in the enormous mechanism of space-time of which our world was only an infinitesimal part. Of this we shall have more to say later.

Already in the eighteenth century Christianity, as traditionally expounded, had ceased to be relevant. Despite Pascal's dismay at the silent immensity of space and the quantitative nothingness of man that that implied, scientific man was already flexing his muscles, and even Pascal, as a scientist and mathematician, could see that man's quantitative nothingness must be compensated for by his qualitative uniqueness which set him apart from every other form of creation known to exist in 'the eternal silence of these infinite spaces'.

'Man is but a reed', he said, 'the weakest one in all nature; but it is a thinking reed. It is quite unnecessary for the whole universe to be mobilized to crush him; a vapour or a drop of water is quite enough to kill him. But even if the universe were to crush him, man would still be more noble than what kills him because he knows he dies, and of the advantage that the universe has over him the universe knows nothing.'[3]

To know he knows no doubt sets man apart from and above all created things. But to know he *dies* can only mean that his knowledge must perish with him. This considerable limitation of his powers should always preserve man from intellectual pride; but man, the more completely he becomes master of his environment, tends to become increasingly proud and, at least until the twentieth-century cataclysm was inaugurated by the First World War, increasingly convinced that one day science will solve all our enigmas. Even now the myth of the perfectibility of man has not been shattered. This is certainly not the fault of the scientists, but it is the fault of those who claim to speak in the name of

---

2. Blaise Pascal, *Pensées*, in *Oeuvres complètes* (Bibliothèque de la Pléiade, Gallimard, Paris, 1957), pp. 1112–13.
3. Ibid., pp. 1156–7.

science, of whom in modern times Engels (on the Marxist side) and Teilhard de Chardin (on the Christian side) are perhaps the most notorious. Both Marxism and the ideas of Teilhard de Chardin owe much of their success to the fact that they claim to be scientifically based. For both, evolution, so far from diminishing the stature of man, shows him to be the apex and crown of the evolutionary process itself. The apparently 'dead' matter of the universe, given the right chemical and physical conditions, takes what Engels calls a qualitative leap, so far as we know, on this earth of ours and probably nowhere else. When once life has appeared the process of 'natural selection' takes over and out of this natural selection consciousness develops, then out of simple or diffused consciousness man is born. Consciousness, then, is the goal for the achievement of which all the countless galaxies in the universe have been striving.

With the birth of consciousness human history begins; but history is only the conscious prolongation on a human scale of the process of evolution which for millions of years has been operating on this planet, and the evolution on this planet is preconditioned by the evolution of the whole universe from which it proceeds. Man emerges not as the centre of the universe as he was in the old Aristotelian scheme of things but as the culmination of the whole evolutionary process – and this is even more flattering to human pride. But, according to the well-nigh unanimous verdict of the scientific establishment today, it is all wrong; and its wrongness has been most recently reaffirmed by the distinguished French biochemist, Jacques Monod, in a best-seller entitled *Chance and Necessity*.

I will not attempt to summarize Monod's account of the genetic code since this is now an established scientific fact which the non-scientist can only accept. What he emphasizes is that we are faced on the one hand with a 'chemical machinery' on the microscopic level which from bacteria to man is essentially the same and invariable:[4] 'the entire [genetic] system is totally, intensely conservative, locked into itself, utterly impervious to any "hints" from the outside world. . . . It is not Hegelian at all, but thoroughly

4. Jacques Monod, *Chance and Necessity* (E.T., Collins, London, 1972), p. 101.

Cartesian: the cell is indeed a *machine*.'[5] But however fixed and invariable the genetic code and its translation may be, this is to reckon without the element of pure chance that enters into the structure of living matter and without which there could be no evolution, no consciousness, no man. These 'mutations' are alone responsible for evolutionary advance, and they are totally unforeseeable and unpredictable. Life, and consciousness, and man are dependent on pure chance, what Monod calls 'essential' chance. Man, then, so far from being the result and end-product of some immanent will or vital principle working within Nature is quite literally a freak produced by pure chance operating on a microscopic machine which nevertheless determines his whole development. Man is finally dethroned and made the plaything of a mindless universe, 'alone in the unfeeling immensity of the universe, out of which he emerged only by chance'.[6] In case he should be misunderstood Professor Monod rubs in his point in no uncertain terms:

'We say that these events are accidental, due to chance. And since they constitute the *only* possible source of modifications in the genetic text, itself the *sole* repository of the organism's hereditary structures, it necessarily follows that chance *alone* is at the source of every innovation, of all creation in the biosphere. Pure chance, absolutely free but blind, at the very root of the stupendous edifice of evolution: this central concept of modern biology is no longer one among other possible or even conceivable hypotheses. It is today the *sole* conceivable hypothesis, the only one compatible with observed and tested fact. And nothing warrants the supposition (or the hope) that conceptions about this should, or ever could, be revised.'[7]

This, then, from the point of view of biochemistry, is the truth. It is a hard truth, for it appears to make human existence literally absurd and religion meaningless; for in a world which seems to be rigorously determined by scientific law on the one hand and to be at the mercy of blind chance on the other there seems to be no place for a personal God of any kind or for a purposeful and

---

5. Ibid., p. 108 (Monod's italics).   6. Ibid., p. 167.
7. Ibid., p. 110 (Monod's italics).

rational form of evolution on which both Marxism (at least as interpreted by Engels) and the philosophies of Bergson and Teilhard de Chardin are based. Their hopes are founded on a misreading of the scientific evidence and, whether their authors knew it or not, their vision of a perfected society in which all things will be made new is a lie founded on a lie. But man has always flourished on comforting lies and he is not likely to abandon the last of his illusions – the illusion that evolution tends towards a perfected society – without a struggle. This principle of chance and uncertainty which science now tells us is embedded in the very structure of matter was a medicine that the older generation of scientists themselves found very hard to swallow, and even Einstein said he could not accept that 'God plays at dice'.[8]

We have recently heard a great deal about 'alienation' – alienation from God, from the universe, from our fellow-men, and from ourselves. According to the whole pantheist tradition, starting in the West with Heraclitus and ending with Engels, Jung, and Teilhard de Chardin, and striking us again via the Indian religions through neo-Vedanta and Zen, man at his deepest level and the Universe or 'God' are in some way identical. To recognize this identity means to overcome alienation in every form, for if all things are One, then there is nothing from which to be alienated. According to modern physics this pantheistic dream is simply untrue; man and Nature are in no sense one – the old alliance and solidarity between man and Nature is broken and with it all the religions that would identify God with Nature.

Long ago Nietzsche announced that God was dead, and in the long run it was the consciousness of the truth of his words that must have driven him mad. Now we are told that the universe is dead and that life on this tiny planet of ours is due to pure chance – a mutation so utterly improbable as to be quite unforeseeable. The advances of science have indeed been so prodigious in the last three hundred years that what is not strictly in accordance with science as at present understood is brusquely ruled out of court. We have put science in the place of God: we fear its awful potentialities since, like the God it has replaced, it may destroy us

8. Ibid., p. 112.

at any moment, perhaps by pure chance. We use it and are grateful for the undoubted benefits it has brought us, but we do not take note of the frightening message with which it now confronts us. It is not the bomb or the population explosion or pollution or any of the side-effects of science that are ultimately terrifying, but the austere teaching on which all science is based, that is, according to Professor Monod, that the *only* source of authentic truth is knowledge objectively acquired.

In the *Communist Manifesto* Marx and Engels savagely attacked the nineteenth-century bourgeoisie for their overthrowing of all established values. 'Constant revolutionising of production,' they wrote, 'uninterrupted disturbance of all social conditions, everlasting uncertainty and agitation distinguish the bourgeois epoch from all earlier ones. All fixed, fast frozen relations, with their train of ancient and venerable prejudices and opinions, are swept away, all new-formed ones become antiquated before they can ossify. All that is solid melts into air, all that is holy is profaned, and man is at last compelled to face with sober senses his real conditions of life and his relations with his kind.'[9] But Marx and Engels were only scratching at the surface. It was not the bourgeoisie as such that was responsible for the overthrow of all hitherto accepted values, but the fact that the bourgeoisie represented and exploited the new science the discoveries of which were not only to shake Christianity to its foundations but all the religious and semi-religious ideas by which the world had lived and in the end, of course, the grandiose superstructure of dialectical materialism itself which Engels had imposed on Marx's economic foundations.

The enemy is not the bourgeoisie or any other convenient scapegoat but science itself which is at the basis of our confusion and alienation; and Professor Monod has rendered a great public service in pointing this out in no uncertain terms. As the Jews persistently rebelled against Yahweh, so too is modern man beginning to rebel against his newly-found all-powerful and apparently irrational God.

9. *Manifesto of the Communist Party*, in *Karl Marx: Selected Works*, Vol. I (E.T., Lawrence & Wishart, London, 1942), pp. 208-9.

'Behind [man's] protest is the refusal to accept the essential message of science. The fear is the fear of sacrilege: of outrage to values; and it is wholly justified. It is perfectly true that science attacks values. Not directly, since science is no judge of them and *must* ignore them; but it subverts every one of the mythical or philosophical ontogenies upon which the animist[1] tradition, from the Australian aborigines to the dialectical materialists, has based morality: values, duties, rights, prohibitions.

'If he accepts this message in its full significance, man must at last wake out of his millenary dream and discover his total solitude, his fundamental isolation. He must realize that, like a gipsy, he lives on the boundary of an alien world; a world that is deaf to his music, and as indifferent to his hopes as it is to his suffering or his crimes. . . . It is at this point that modern man turns towards science, or rather against it, now seeing its terrible capacity to destroy not only bodies but the soul itself.'[2]

The words of Bernanos now take on a more sinister meaning: 'The old house has collapsed behind our backs and when we came to take our place in the homes of the young, they hadn't yet found out how to build their own, and we found ourselves in an indeterminate sphere, among the stones and the rafters, in the rain.' 'The eternal silence of these infinite spaces appals me.'

We are trapped and it seems there is no way out. Our cry goes up to heaven, but since heaven and all its galaxies are indifferent and dead, there is no one to hear us.

Having destroyed our illusions and justified a total despair, however, Professor Monod goes on to sketch what he considers may be a viable and 'authentic' interpretation of man's predicament as seen by objective science. Having scornfully rejected the 'animistic' or 'vitalistic' vision of Engels and Teilhard de Chardin, he proceeds to introduce precisely such a 'teleological' principle via the genetic code itself and the genetically predetermined 'per-

1. 'Animism' defined by Monod (op. cit., p. 38) as the 'projection into inanimate nature of man's awareness of the intensely teleonomic functioning of his own central nervous system. It is, in other words, the hypothesis that natural phenomena can and must be explained in the same manner, by the same "laws", as subjective human activity, conscious and purposive.'
2. J. Monod, op. cit., pp. 160-1.

formance' of man which is quite unlike that of any other known living organism. For Teilhard de Chardin the 'noosphere' (that is, the sphere of ideas) develops out of the biosphere (the sphere of life), though how or why this should happen he does not (any more than Engels) attempt to explain. Teilhard's ideas are difficult and, no doubt, scientifically naïve; so too, no doubt, are his 'philosophy' and 'theology', but I cannot see that Monod's 'solution' of the human predicament is any more 'rigorous' than is Teilhard's, for in the last chapter of his book, entitled 'The Kingdom and the Darkness', he seems to be offering a basically optimist solution which scarcely differs from Teilhard's own. True, he does not represent man as the culminating point of *all* evolution, but he does, like Teilhard and Engels, regard a socialized humanity as being the ideal to which evolution (in his, no doubt, more strictly scientific sense) is in fact propelling man.

'For hundreds of thousands of years', he writes, 'a man's lot was identical with that of the group, of the tribe he belonged to, and outside which he could not survive. The tribe, for its part, could only survive and defend itself through its cohesion. Whence arose the extreme subjective power of the laws that organized and guaranteed this cohesion. A man might perhaps infringe them; it is unlikely that anyone ever dreamed of denying them. Given the immense selective importance such social structures perforce assumed over such vast stretches of time, it is difficult not to believe that they must have influenced the genetic evolution of the innate categories of the human brain. This evolution must not only have facilitated acceptance of the tribal law, but created the *need* for the mythical explanation which gave it a foundation and sovereignty. We are the descendants of these men, and it is probably from them that we have inherited the need for an explanation, the profound disquiet which forces us to search for the meaning of existence. That same disquiet has created all myths, all religions, all philosophies and science itself. I have very little doubt that this imperious need develops spontaneously, that it is inborn, inscribed somewhere in the genetic code. . . .

'The invention of myths and religions, the construction of vast philosophical systems – they are the price man has had to pay in order to survive as a social animal without yielding to pure automatism. But a cultural inheritance would not, all alone, have been strong or reliable enough to hold up the social structure. That heritage needed a genetic support to provide something essential to the mind. How else account for the fact that in our species the religious phenomenon is invariably at the base of social structure? How else explain that, throughout the immense variety of our myths, our religions and philosophical ideologies, the same essential "form" always recurs?'[3]

But surely the trouble is that the same essential form does *not* turn up, as we shall very soon see and as Professor Monod seems to admit in the sharp distinction he draws between mechanistic idealism (supported by the state of science today) and dialectical materialism (a scientific abortion). Are they both genetically based? And if so, which is validated by the 'principle of objectivity', and why? It may be that modern biochemistry has finally severed the umbilical cord between man and Nature; but if so, it leaves us with mysteries far more profound than those we have been forced to abandon. But Professor Monod is not only rigorously scientific in his insistence that modern man, now 'come of age', as Bonhoeffer said, must now face the profoundly inhuman fact that 'he is alone in the unfeeling immensity of the universe, out of which he emerged only by chance', he is also a human being haunted by the meaning of existence: he invites to despair, but he will not despair himself. Has he any more reason for not doing so than Teilhard de Chardin whom he so roundly berates? I do not think so. The essential mysteries of the emergence of life, consciousness, and thought, though they have now been accounted for in a way that can only scandalize any man-centred view of the universe, still remain mysteries. Science can explain the 'how' of things, it cannot explain the 'why'. Should it try to do so, it necessarily departs from its own principle of objectivity. True, Professor Monod is cautious and does not set himself up as a prophet of evolution as Teilhard sometimes seemed to do. But, given the reality of 'the eternal silence of these infinite spaces' with which he once again confronts us, is he cautious enough?

3. Ibid., pp. 155–6.

'For a biologist it is tempting', he says, 'to compare the evolution of ideas [Teilhard's "noosphere"!] and of the biosphere. For while the abstract kingdom transcends the biosphere by even more than the latter transcends the nonliving universe, ideas have retained some of the properties of organisms. Like these, they tend to perpetuate their structures and to multiply them; they too can fuse, recombine, segregate their content; in short, they too can evolve, and in this evolution selection certainly plays an important role. I shall not hazard a theory of the selection of ideas. But one may at least try to define some of the principal factors involved in it. This selection must necessarily operate at two levels; that of the mind (*l'esprit*) itself and that of performance.

'The performance value of an idea depends on the change it brings to the behaviour of the person or the group that adopts it. The human group upon which a given idea confers greater cohesiveness, greater ambition and greater self-confidence thereby receives from it an added power to expand which will insure the promotion of the idea itself. Its "promotion value" bears no relation to the amount of objective truth the idea may contain. The might of the powerful armament provided by a religious ideology for a society does not lie in its structure, but in the fact that this structure is accepted, that it gains command. So one cannot well separate such an idea's power to spread from its power to perform.'[4]

We seem to have moved some distance from the 'principle of objectivity' proclaimed by Professor Monod as the sole valid criterion of knowledge and are now faced with the 'performance value' of ideas and their 'promotion value' which 'bears no relation to the amount of objective truth the idea may contain'. We seem, once again as with Teilhard de Chardin, to be slipping into a terrain that is perilously slippery and imprecise. However, let us see where we go from here.

'The "spreading power" of an idea is much more difficult to analyse. Let us say that it depends upon pre-existing structures in the mind, among them ideas already implanted by culture, but also undoubtedly upon certain innate structures which are very

4. Ibid., pp. 154-5.

difficult for us to identify. What is very plain, however, is that the ideas having the highest invading potential are those that *explain* man by assigning him his place in an immanent destiny, a safe harbour where his anxiety dissolves.'

When authors, however distinguished they may be, stray outside their speciality and start introducing conclusions with words such as 'undoubtedly', you may be very sure that the author himself is very *un*sure of the 'objective truth' of what he propounds, and the reader will do well to be on his guard. Even so, when Professor Monod says that 'the ideas having the highest invading potential are those that *explain* man by assigning him his place in an immanent destiny, a safe harbour where his anxiety dissolves', he is saying no more than that man, incurably, will believe what he wants to believe. This is indeed the 'promotion value' of an idea irrespective of its objective truth with which hitherto Professor Monod has been exclusively and 'puritanically' concerned. But, he goes on to say, previous religious and philosophical systems (the last of which is Marxism) have been rooted in the 'animist' and 'vitalist' presupposition that man has his necessary (and honoured) place in Nature's plans, and this presupposition has now been proved by science to be false. And yet man's 'disquiet' which compels him to look for the meaning of existence is 'inscribed somewhere in the genetic code'. No solution, he implies, that is not sanctioned by the genetic code, can be true. But what have science, the genetic code, and, of course, pure chance (which seems to have been temporarily forgotten) got to offer that is both true and can still our genetic anguish? At first sight the prospect seems daunting enough, so daunting indeed that it took millennia for man to discover 'in the realm of ideas ... those presenting objective knowledge as the *only* source of real truth'.[5]

'Cold and austere, proposing no explanation but imposing an ascetic renunciation of all other spiritual fare, this idea could not allay anxiety; it aggravated it instead. It claimed to sweep away at a stroke the tradition of a hundred thousand years, which had become assimilated in human nature itself. It ended the ancient

5. Ibid., p. 158.

animist covenant (*ancienne alliance* = "Old Testament") between man and nature, leaving nothing in place of that precious bond but an anxious quest in a world of icy solitude. With nothing to recommend it but a certain puritan arrogance, how could such an idea be accepted? It was not; and it still is not. If it has commanded recognition, this is solely because of its prodigious powers of performance.'

That the 'performance' of science in the last three hundred years has not opened up before us an unlimited field of human progress but has landed us on the brink of an 'abyss of darkness', we no longer need Professor Monod to tell us. We all know that science has nothing to do with ethics, and from most of Professor Monod's book we can only conclude that he knows this too. Man is not only a rational animal: he is a depraved one, or, in the telling phrase of India's Teilhard de Chardin, the 'evolutionist' Sri Aurobindo, he 'is an abnormal who has not found his own normality'.[6] In the process of finding his normality, indeed, it would appear that man (if we may for a moment speak of him in ethical terms rather than in terms of performance) so far from transcending the beasts sank far below them. For, whereas war between different species of animals is almost unknown, it seems to have played a leading part in the evolution of *Homo sapiens*. 'It is quite possible', Professor Monod assures us, 'that the sudden disappearance of Neanderthal man was the result of genocide committed by our ancestor *Homo sapiens*.'[7] Is genocide, too, genetically inborn in the human brain? The disastrous history of the present century has done nothing to invalidate this depressing hypothesis.

'Where is the remedy?' Professor Monod asks with a very understandable anxiety. 'Must one claim once and for all that objective truth and the theory of values are eternally opposed, mutually impenetrable domains? This is the attitude adopted by many modern thinkers, whether writers, or philosophers, or indeed scientists. I believe that it is not only unacceptable to the vast number of men, whose anxiety it can only perpetuate and

6. Sri Aurobindo, *The Human Cycle* (Sri Aurobindo Ashram, Pondicherry, 1949), p. 290.
7. J. Monod, op. cit., p. 151.

worsen; I also believe it is absolutely mistaken, for two essential reasons.

'First, of course, because values and knowledge are always and necessarily associated in action as in discourse.

'Secondly, and above all, because *the very definition of "true" knowledge rests in the final analysis upon an ethical postulate.*'[8]

This is the language not of science but of faith pretending to be science: it is the language of make-believe. The usual signs that we are passing from the 'principle of objectivity' to the uncontrolled freedom of subjective fantasy are there – the use of such adverbs as 'of course' (*bien entendu*) in support of a highly debatable proposition, and the use of italics to bludgeon the reader into accepting something which not only contradicts the 'principle of objectivity' but which common sense also tells him is phoney. This more than dubious method is shown up for what it is on the very next page of Monod's book where the italicized dictum that 'the very definition of "true" knowledge rests in the final analysis upon an ethical postulate' is flatly contradicted. For on page 162 we read that 'knowledge in itself is exclusive of all value judgment (except that of "epistemological value") whereas ethics, in essence *nonobjective*, is forever barred from the sphere of knowledge'. Putting the two passages together we learn that all true knowledge which is necessarily objective is none the less based on an ethical postulate which is essentially subjective. From where, we may well ask, does the essentially subjective ethical postulate arise on which, it seems, the very 'principle of objectivity' is itself based? This seems to be dangerously close to the 'dialectical' thinking of Hegel, Engels, and Teilhard de Chardin; for we seem to be faced with yet another Hegelian pair of opposites – the principle of objectivity and a subjective ethical principle. And from all that he has said before, we can only assume that this subjective ethical principle is the result of 'essential' blind chance. In other words not only is the human brain, which is uniquely able to recognize and apply the principle of objectivity, due to blind chance, but in itself blind chance is the sole source of ethics and therefore of conscience. So be it, but this surely is a miracle far more astonish-

8. Ibid., p. 161.

ing than anything thought up by religion or 'vitalistic' philosophy. However, let us follow Professor Monod a little further in his 'scientific' argumentation.

'The postulate of objectivity . . . forbids any confusion of value judgments with judgments arrived at through knowledge. Yet the fact remains that these two categories inevitably unite in the form of action, discourse included. To abide by our principle we shall therefore take the position (*jugerons*) that no discourse or action is to be considered meaningful, *authentic*, unless – or only insofar as – it makes explicit and preserves the distinction between the two categories it combines. Thus defined, the concept of authenticity becomes the common ground where ethics and knowledge meet again; where values and truth, associated but not interchangeable, reveal their full significance to the attentive man alive to their resonance. In return, *inauthentic* discourse, where the two categories are jumbled, can lead only to the most pernicious nonsense, to the most criminal, even if unconscious, lies.'[9]

Once again the reader should be on his guard; for he may be quite certain that once an author starts speaking about 'authenticity' – whether it is 'authentic' Christianity, 'authentic' science, or what have you, he is simply proclaiming his own views as being alone valid and condemning all others as being 'inauthentic' and therefore bogus. The words 'authentic' and 'existential', through constant unthinking reiteration, have come to be almost meaningless. In practice 'authentic discourse' may be taken to mean 'what I am talking about', 'inauthentic discourse', 'what others are talking about'. In nine cases out of ten it is no more than a cheap verbal trick. In any case Professor Monod seems now to have left logical discourse far behind him and to have embarked on a kind of scientific theology reminiscent of the Athanasian Creed. Ethics and knowledge are 'distinct' as the three Persons of the Christian Trinity are distinct without 'confusing' the essence (in this case 'authenticity') which is their common ground. For 'Father, Son (Word), and Holy Spirit' read 'authenticity', 'objective knowledge (truth)', and 'ethics/value'. Modern theology may be barren enough,

9. Ibid., pp. 162–3.

but this kind of 'scientific' theology would appear to be even more barren. But clearly we have now left objective thinking far behind and, despite Professor Monod's lip-service to Descartes, we have now entered into the realm of 'existential' *Angst*.

Once again we are told that 'in an objective system ... any confusion of knowledge with values is unlawful, *forbidden* [italicized again, forbidden by whom?]. But – and this is the crucial point – the logical link which radically binds knowledge and values – this ban, this "first commandment" which ensures the foundation (*fonde*) of objective knowledge, itself is not, and cannot be, objective. It is a moral rule, a *discipline*. True knowledge is ignorant of values, but it has to be grounded on a value judgment, or rather on an *axiomatic* value. *It is obvious* [my italics this time] that the positing of the principle of objectivity as the condition of true knowledge *constitutes an ethical choice and not a judgment reached from knowledge (jugement de connaissance), since, according to the postulate's own terms, there cannot have been any "true" knowledge prior to this arbitral choice.* In order to establish the *norm* for knowledge the objectivity principle defines a *value*: that value is objective knowledge itself. To assent to the principle of objectivity is, thus, to state the basic proposition of an ethical system: *the ethic of knowledge*.'

I have read it in French and, to the best of my ability, translated it into English; but this time I see no alternative but to give up. Either Professor Monod is trying to describe what is essentially indescribable or he is simply talking nonsense and trying to pull the wool over our eyes with his repetitive italics and 'axioms' that seem rather to be paradoxes gone mad. In trying to describe the indescribable he joins the company of the mystics, and he might do well to reflect on what his 'animist' predecessors, Engels and Teilhard de Chardin, have said before him. Engels, in promulgating the (apparently non-existent) 'law' of the transformation of quantity into quality was denounced for his 'mysticism and incomprehensible transcendentalism',[1] while Teilhard made bold to say: 'Neither in its impetus nor its achievements can science go to

---

1. Frederick Engels, *Dialectics of Nature* (E.T., Moscow, 1954), p. 91.

its limits without becoming tinged with mysticism and charged with faith.'[2]

Whether Professor Monod would jib at the charge of mysticism I do not know, but he lays himself wide open to the charge of transcendentalism and idealism, and indeed rejoices in it in his justifiable indignation against the pseudo-scientific make-believe of the dialectical materialists whose founding father was Engels rather than Marx.

Professor Monod is a socialist and a scientist. His quarrel with Engels is not that he was seeking to discern a universal ideology into which historical materialism could be fitted, but that he was not prepared to modify his system in accordance with new scientific discoveries, notably the second law of thermodynamics according to which the universe is mathematically determined to end in a state of complete, irreversible, and changeless disorder. By refusing to face this most depressing of all scientific discoveries Engels put himself beyond the pale of orthodox science and forfeited all claim to conform to the principle of objectivity. As a topsy-turvy Hegelian he could scarcely do otherwise since he was caught in a machine of his own making, not in the great machine of the universe which modern science has rediscovered and in which man is seen to be a meaningless epiphenomenon lost in 'the eternal silence of these infinite spaces'.

But the old dream dies hard, and, for Professor Monod, it must, in the interests both of the objective principle and of socialism, be administered the *coup de grâce*. 'For the young in spirit that great vision of the nineteenth century still persists', he says, 'with grievous intensity. Grievous because of the betrayals this ideal has suffered, and because of the crimes committed in its name. It is tragic, but was perhaps inevitable, that this profound aspiration had to find its philosophical doctrine in the form of an animist ideology. Looking back, it is easy to see that, from the time of its birth, historical messianism based on dialectical materialism contained the seeds of all the dangers later encountered. Perhaps more than the other animisms, historical materialism is based on a total

---

2. Pierre Teilhard de Chardin, *The Phenomenon of Man* (E.T., Collins, London, and Harper, New York, 1959), p. 284.

confusion of the categories of value and knowledge. This very confusion permits it, in a travesty of authentic discourse, to proclaim that it has "scientifically" established the laws of history, which man has no choice or duty but to obey if he does not wish to sink into oblivion.

'This illusion, which is merely puerile when it is not fatal, must be given up once and for all. How can an authentic socialism ever be built on an essentially inauthentic ideology, a caricature of that very science whose support it claims (most sincerely, in the minds of its followers)? Socialism's one hope is not in a "revision" of the ideology that has been dominating it for over a century, but in completely abandoning that ideology.'[3]

So far so good. Professor Monod has destroyed the last of the animist ideologies, but what 'authentic' ideology has he to put in its place? Well of course *only* [my italics again] the ethic of knowledge could lead to socialism'. Has he anything more positive to say? He does his best:

'Understood and accepted – could [the ethics of knowledge] ever be? If it is true, as I believe, that the fear of solitude and the need for a complete and binding explanation are inborn – that this heritage from the remote past is not only cultural but probably genetic too – can one imagine such an austere, abstract, proud ethic calming that fear, satisfying that need? I do not know. But it may not be altogether impossible. Perhaps, even more than an "explanation" which the ethic of knowledge cannot supply, man needs to rise above himself, to find transcendence. The abiding power of the great socialist dream, still alive in men's hearts, would indeed seem to suggest it. No system of values can claim to constitute a true ethic unless it proposes an ideal transcending the individual self to the point even of justifying self-sacrifice, if need be.'[4]

So here we are again back to Engels' 'mysticism and incomprehensible transcendentalism' and Teilhard's 'hyper-personalisation',[5] the transcendence of self in a greater whole so typical of most forms of mysticism. Like all these the 'ethic of knowledge'

3. J. Monod, op. cit., p. 166.   4. Ibid., pp. 164–5.
5. P. Teilhard de Chardin, op. cit., p. 259, etc.

'puts forward a transcendental value, true knowledge, not for the use of man, but for man to serve from deliberate and conscious choice'.[6] In other words, man, after having witnessed the destruction of all his gods, is asked to sacrifice himself, if necessary, to the 'transcendental value of pure knowledge' of which he knows absolutely nothing except that it is 'authenticity'(!) itself. The bait is good enough no doubt for the idealist young for whom Professor Monod seems to be writing, for it is in the nature of the young to sacrifice themselves or rather to be sacrificed by their mentors on the altar of self-transcendence. In the recent past they have done it for Hitler, for Stalin, for democracy, for Mao. In the remote past they have done it for what they believed to be God. Now with their eyes opened by the second law of thermodynamics and by the twin scientific certainties of the determinism of the genetic code and of pure chance, they are to be summoned to sacrifice themselves for the 'pure' ideal of the 'ethic of knowledge', since transcend themselves they must!

But the new 'scientism', if it is to keep in step with the humane (pseudo-) sciences, must also be a humanism. It is: for 'it respects man as the creator and repository of that transcendence'. Just how anthropocentric can one get? Man, having been excluded from all meaningful participation in the immensities of space, now defends himself by ignoring these immensities as being irrelevant to him. Though his kingdom may be reduced to a speck of dust, it is still *his* humanistic, human kingdom of which *he* remains undisputed lord.

Self-transcendence and humanism, however, are not enough. We must never forget the 'principle of objectivity' as applied to our own biological origins. And here we come to what is presumably the quintessence of this empty 'system':

'The ethic of knowledge is also in a sense "knowledge of ethics" [how dialectical it all is!], that is, of the urges and passions, the needs and limitations of the biological being. It is able to confront the animal in man, to see him not as absurd but strange, precious in his very strangeness: the creature who, belonging simultaneously to the animal kingdom and the kingdom of ideas

6. J. Monod, op. cit., p. 165.

[that is, precisely, Teilhard's "noosphere"!], is both torn and enriched by this agonizing duality, expressed alike in art and poetry and in human love. ... The ethic of knowledge ... encourages [man] to honour and assume this [biological] heritage, while knowing how to dominate it when necessary. As for the highest human qualities, courage, altruism, generosity, creative ambition, the ethic of knowledge both recognizes their sociobiological origin and affirms their transcendent value in the service of the ideal it defines.'[7]

Who has been taken in? And what *is* the ideal? I have quoted Professor Monod at considerable length as, in fairness, I was bound to do in order to try to extract some meaning from all those heartfelt italics, 'of courses', 'undoubtedlys', and so on. Nothing at all has emerged, at any rate for me, except an 'existential' and 'authentic' void and a similarly qualified Trinity of 'authenticity', 'objective knowledge/truth', and 'ethics/value'. To these essentially religious concepts we may have to return. Meanwhile, appalled as never before by 'the eternal silence of these infinite spaces', we still have no choice but to drift in our still 'indeterminate sphere, among the stones and the rafters, in the rain'.

7. Ibid., p. 165.

2
THE VITALIST HERESY

'Wishing henceforward to know my individual place among my own kind, and contemplating the various orders [of existence] and the men that constitute them, what happens to me? What do I see? What has happened to the order I had previously observed? Nature had once shown me a picture in which there was harmony and due proportion; but in the picture of the human race I saw only confusion and disorder! Among the elements concord reigns supreme, but men live in chaos. The animals are happy, only their king is wretched! Wisdom, where are your laws? Providence, is it thus that you govern the world? O beneficent Being, what has happened to your power? I see evil on the face of the earth.'[8]

These words were penned by Rousseau in the eighteenth century, but every preceding and successive generation in the Christian West has at some stage been brought face to face with the fact of evil, and no generation more than our own. So too, Dietrich Bonhoeffer, the almost saintly Protestant pastor, liquidated by the Nazis for his part in a conspiracy against what he regarded as an almost Satanic power, wrote from his prison shortly before he was executed:

'One may ask whether there have ever before in human history been people with so little ground under their feet – people to whom every available alternative seemed equally intolerable. . . . The great masquerade of evil has played havoc with all our ethical concepts. For evil to appear disguised as light, charity, historical necessity, or social justice is quite bewildering to anyone brought up on our traditional ethical concepts, while for the Christian

---

8. Jean-Jacques Rousseau, *Émile* (Garnier-Flammarion, Paris, 1966), pp. 361–2; in *Oeuvres complètes*, Vol. IV (Bibliothèque de la Pléiade, Gallimard, Paris, 1969), p. 583.

who bases his life on the Bible it merely confirms the fundamental wickedness of evil.'[9]

The fundamental wickedness of evil. There it is, and we have all seen it. No longer, in this century of insane injustice, can we close our eyes to this awful thing: no longer can we accept the glib philosophic dismissal of evil as simply a 'deprivation of good' with which Christianity and the Roman Catholic Church in particular has been lulled into a comfortable acceptance of the unacceptable since Augustine proclaimed this facile doctrine in the West and Aquinas stamped it with an authority that was to become normative in the Roman Church for some six centuries.

In this century we have woken up to two inescapable facts – the littleness of man produced by pure chance in a universe of infinite space-time in which he is but a passing and insignificant speck of living dust, and the evilness of man which seems to become more evil the more scientific knowledge is accumulated. And so man, always ready to shirk his responsibilities, finds a new scapegoat: and this time it is science. And so 'modern man turns towards science, or rather against it, now seeing its terrible capacity to destroy not only bodies but the soul itself'.[1] Science, like the matter it studies, however, is dumb, or, when it offers solutions, speaks in riddles, and no one understands. What of religion? Oh, of course we all know that Christianity has been discredited, but Christianity is not the only religion. Can we not find in India or China with their very different religious traditions some answer that will ease our double predicament of insignificance and evil? Perhaps.

But after all there *was* a man called John, and for four unforgettable years not only the Roman Catholic Church but the whole world was alive with hope, for here at last was a *good* man. And not only was he a good man: he was also Pope, the supreme head of the largest organized religious body in the world. On the Protestant side there was also a man called Dietrich Bonhoeffer. He too was good. In the words of an English fellow-prisoner who was with him till the end: 'Bonhoeffer was all humility and sweet-

---

9. Dietrich Bonhoeffer, *Letters and Papers from Prison*, enlarged edition (E.T., SCM Press, London, and Macmillan, New York, 1971), pp. 3–4.
1. Above, p. 22.

ness; he always seemed to diffuse an atmosphere of happiness, of joy in every smallest event in life, and of deep gratitude for the mere fact that he was alive.... He was one of the very few men I have ever met to whom his God was real and ever close to him.'[2]

But John is dead and Bonhoeffer is dead: and their successors have played havoc with their inheritance. On the one hand you have progressives and conservatives assailing each other with all the zestful uncharitableness that was formerly directed against heretics or rather (as one is now encouraged to say) the 'separated brethren'. On the other the theologians have seized upon Bonhoeffer's last thoughts which he never lived to develop in order to bombard us with such vacuous irrelevancies as the 'death of God' theology and 'Christian atheism'. It would appear that in human affairs, as in physics, there is a law corresponding to the second law of thermodynamics: Every 'good' seems to increase its entropy – its evil. How much cosier the world would be had Pope John and Dietrich Bonhoeffer never shown us what goodness is! Is there any point in even trying to be good in a world not only meaningless but dominated, it would seem, by an evil power we can neither restrain nor even define?

For a long time now we have known that there is a thing called Zen. Perhaps the wave of Zen has passed its peak, but like analytical philosophy it seems to have unsuspected stamina. What, then, has Zen got that the Christian Churches seem helpless to supply? With one voice the Zen people reply, 'Experience – a living experience of the truth.' What they mean by truth we will not discuss for the moment, and in this we merely follow their example. The 'truth' cannot be put into words: it can only be experienced. This they repeat again and again. Institutional Christianity (apart from the turmoils of the Catholic Church) has reduced itself to a vain formalism and an outdated morality: Zen is a living experience of ultimate reality which, in the last resort, is open to all, irrespective of race, colour, or creed. Yes, *creed*: since you can and do have Zen Taoists and now Zen Catholics – and, who knows, perhaps

2. Eberhard Bethge, *Dietrich Bonhoeffer* (E.T., Collins, London, and Harper & Row, New York, 1970), p. 823.

somewhere tucked away in Chairman Mao's China you have Zen Communists too.

Of course, no serious Zen master will tell you that it is actually possible for the vast majority of the human race in its present stage of development to achieve unmediated contact with reality, in this life at least: but the promise is there. 'There *is*', indeed, the Buddha himself is alleged to have said, 'something unborn, not become, not made or compounded, and were it not for this something unborn, not become, not made or compounded, no escape could be shown from what is born, has become, is made and compounded. But since there is an unborn, not become, not made or compounded, therefore an escape *can* be shown from what is born, has become, is made and compounded.'[3] And the guarantee of this 'something' that is not subject to change is the Buddha's own experience of what the Buddhists call 'enlightenment' – or more literally 'awakening' – which means, among other things, the conquest of death by transcending everything that binds us to this world of space and time. It means final release from the whole vertiginous world of matter and energy into a peace so profound that it cannot be named. What Zen offers is nothing more nor less than the eternal – not God, 'the eternal, the ancient of days', and all that kind of thing, but the eternal, though heavily disguised, in you and me. To anyone at all familiar with the Catholic mystics there is nothing particularly strange in this, but even Catholics do not read the Catholic mystics, let alone expound them, and so they leave the field wide open to Zen, to the Vedanta, and to the purveyors of 'instant' Zen and 'instant' Vedanta through the God-given agency of psychedelic drugs, or so they would have us believe.

Christianity, which should have known better, has been completely taken off its guard by this new movement among the young. Certainly the movement is chaotic enough, and our latter-day scribes and Pharisees, purblind as ever, seize upon its negative aspects in panic-stricken and not very dignified alarm. It is, they say, a movement of nihilistic and wholly unconstructive revolt. Perhaps this is true of a minority more sizeable than most of our

3. *Udāna*, pp. 80–1.

The Vitalist Heresy

self-appointed pundits are prepared to admit, but it is only a half-truth, and the less interesting half at that. In fact there seem to be two movements, not one: a Buddhist one and a Marxist one – the 'drop-outs', whose sole aim would seem to be to escape from this wicked world, and the radical Left which wants to change it, or rather to destroy it first so that someone or other may descend and create a new order out of chaos. Well, this is all as old as Jeremiah and probably much older, for Jeremiah was bidden by that odious God 'out there' whom Dr John Robinson so cordially dislikes 'to tear up and to knock down, to destroy and to overthrow, to build and to plant'. Well, the Lord God or whatever you want to call him gave the same message to Marx, and we are not through with the Lord God yet, however heavily he may be disguised. It all follows a well-known pattern, and it happens, alas, to be a religious pattern playing itself out under the eyes of the Churches which have no eyes to see, or seeing do not understand.

Religions, it seems to me, can be classed as either prophetic or mystical. Prophets for the moment are very much out of fashion but the mystics (unless, of course, they are Christian) are still 'in'. True, the so-called neo-orthodox among the Protestants still talk a great deal about prophecy, about Barth, Brunner, and Bultmann (I wonder why they all begin with B), but does anyone listen to them? Oh yes, the neo-orthodox, and, of course, the dear theologians, whose quantitative output continues to be prodigious but whom nobody ever reads except theology students (they have to) and the theologians themselves, who have to keep abreast of the latest theological fashion because that, apparently, is what they are paid to do. So they write about Barth and Brunner and Bultmann – and, I am afraid, Bonhoeffer too – and this seems to keep the little circle perfectly happy. They love their crisis theology but seem quite unable to cope with the perfectly genuine prophetical crisis represented by the radical Left. 'The dog barks but the caravan passes on', as a Turkish proverb says. The day of theology was already over in the eighteenth century except, of course, among the Germans who, as Charles Péguy rightly pointed out, 'delight in confusion. That is what they call depth.' Oh, German depth, will it never stop plaguing us? And it plagues the radical

Left too, not in the shape of Barth and Co. (of whom they have probably never heard) but in the shape of the early Marx and the unreadable Marcuse.

Thus on the one side we have our prophets, the radical Left, who idolize Mao not so much, one suspects, for his writings as because even now it is extremely difficult to find out anything about what is actually going on in China and because the god you do not know is usually preferable to the one you do. On the other side you have the drop-outs and they are a more obviously religious group, for, though they probably have no use for Christianity of any kind, they are at least interested in Buddhist and Hindu mysticism – because mysticism in any shape or form is no longer a commodity in which the Christian Churches deal.

It may be difficult to classify the drop-outs, but the cult seems to include four ingredients in varying degrees: Eastern mysticism, drugs, pop music, and, of course, sex. Again there is nothing particularly new in this: both in the Hindu-Buddhist East and throughout the Muslim world you will find the same apparently incongruous alliance between drugs, music, dance, and sex, on the one hand, and mystical ecstasy on the other. In Islam, of course, such goings-on have always been rather more than suspect to the orthodox, and even in Hinduism and Buddhism the combination of human sexuality with divine love has been a fringe activity at best, while the taking of drugs (notably hashish, that is, pot) has been used throughout the East to produce ecstasy – whether you wish to call it religious or not is very much a matter of taste.

In modern times it was Aldous Huxley who first connected the effects of psychedelic drugs with what he conceived to be the *satori* of the Zen Buddhists and the beatific vision of the Christian mystics. In fact, William James had made the same comparison some fifty years before, except that he preferred to speak of the Hegelian philosophy in which all discordant opposites are reconciled in one ineffable synthesis. No matter. Since the ultimate synthesis is by all accounts ineffable, why quibble? In any case, the mystics of all religious traditions and of none are remarkably prolific in their description of what cannot be described; and these descriptions, as often as not, seem to fit in remarkably well with

The Vitalist Heresy

the 'positive' or 'beatific' as opposed to the 'negative' and terrifying reactions that LSD and kindred drugs undoubtedly produce.

In the past a man aspiring after a mystical experience was told with a singular unanimity that no such experience could be hoped for without a rigorous ascetic training lasting maybe several lifetimes. Now not many people are prepared to face these gruelling austerities, least of all the 'drop-out' young. But, Aldous Huxley has assured us, this was all quite out of date and needlessly tiresome and tiring: for what asceticism had done for the mystics of the past, drugs could do for the mystics of the present. When still writing under the influence of mescalin he was quite sure of it:

'*Istigkeit* – wasn't that the word Meister Eckhart liked to use? "Is-ness". The Being of Platonic philosophy – except that Plato seems to have made the enormous, the grotesque mistake of separating Being from becoming, and identifying it with the mathematical abstraction of the Idea. He could never, poor fellow, have seen a bunch of flowers shining with their own inner light and all but quivering under the pressure of the significance with which they were charged; could never have perceived that what rose and iris and carnation so intensely signified was nothing more, and nothing less, than what they are – a transience that was yet eternal life, a perpetual perishing that was at the same time pure Being... Words like Grace and Transfiguration came to my mind, and this of course was what, among other things, they stood for... The Beatific Vision, *Sat Chit Ananda*, Being-Awareness-Bliss – for the first time I understood, not on the verbal level, not by inchoate hints or at a distance, but precisely and completely what those prodigious syllables referred to.'[4]

What, then, had Huxley found? Not Dr Robinson's God 'out there' – who, as Jung sensibly said, if he is indeed absolute and beyond all human experience, 'leaves me cold'[5] – but the Kingdom of God within you. This is the God that the Christian Churches have consistently neglected, and all the avant-garde theologians

---

4. Aldous Huxley, *The Doors of Perception* (Chatto & Windus, London, and Harper & Row, New York, 1954), pp. 12–13.
5. Richard Wilhelm and C. G. Jung, *The Secret of the Golden Flower* (Kegan Paul, Trench, Trubner, London, 1938), p. 129.

can do is, taking their cue from ideas Bonhoeffer had been unable to develop before his death, to blather about the 'death of God' theology, 'religionless Christianity', 'Christian atheism', and so on. Of course, it does no harm, nor, for that matter, does it do any manner of good: and in any case who cares? Certainly not the drop-outs who are looking for a quite different type of God – a God whom they can actually experience, or, better still, a God who is no longer a god at all but a *state* of timeless bliss which the Buddhists call Nirvana. This, the devotees of what is sometimes called 'beat' Zen maintain, can be brought on by taking LSD, which they claim can help you transcend your ordinary everyday humdrum self-consciousness into what is sometimes called 'cosmic consciousness', what Freud called the 'oceanic feeling'. This is the feeling to which Tennyson attested when he wrote:

'I have never had any revelations through anaesthetics, but a kind of waking trance – this for lack of a better word – I have frequently had, quite up from boyhood, when I have been all alone. This has come upon me through repeating my own name to myself silently, till all at once, as it were out of the intensity of the consciousness of individuality, individuality itself seemed to dissolve and fade away into boundless being, and this not a confused state but the clearest, the surest of the surest, utterly beyond words – where death was an almost laughable impossibility – the loss of personality (if so it were) seeming no extinction, but the only true life.'[6]

There are two points to be noted here. The first and most important is surely that in this state of expanded consciousness Tennyson felt that 'death was an almost laughable impossibility'. This seems to have been the result of the loss of any sense of personality as normally understood, the loss of the 'ego' which, according to Jung, is the centre of our conscious personality but not of the whole personality of which normal waking consciousness only forms a small part. It is this conscious individuality that is the subject of death not the 'boundless being' into which it merges, since this boundless being transcends both space and time. This is

6. Quoted in William James, *The Varieties of Religious Experience* (Longmans, Green, London, 1902), p. 384.

The Vitalist Heresy

usually called 'nature mysticism' or 'cosmic consciousness'. It appears in practically all types of mysticism and is essential to most of the experiences described in the Hindu sacred books. It occurs very early in those works and perhaps one of its most typical manifestations is also one of the earliest. It runs as follows:

'This whole universe is Brahman. . . .

'He who consists of mind, whose body is the breath of life, whose form is light, whose idea is the real, whose self is space, through whom are all works, all desires, all scents, all tastes, who encompasses all this universe, who does not speak and has no care – he is my Self within the heart, smaller than a grain of rice or a barley-corn, or a mustard-seed, or a grain of millet, or the kernel of a grain of millet; this is my Self within the heart, greater than the earth, greater than the atmosphere, greater than the sky, greater than all these worlds.

'All works, all desires, all scents, all tastes belong to it: it encompasses all this universe, does not speak and has no care. This my Self within the heart is that Brahman. When I depart from hence I shall merge into it. He who believes this will never doubt.'[7]

Here, in a passage composed probably about 600 B.C., we find an experience that seems almost identical with Tennyson's: 'individuality itself seemed to dissolve and fade away into boundless being' – 'greater than all these worlds' but even so the true '*Self* within the heart'. Death is not the final end – except for the little individual ego – it is rather to merge into the life of the All which 'does not speak and has no care'. Brahman is not God in the Christian sense of the word since it is not interested in human affairs: it is rather 'boundless being' which is yet the base of all becoming. It 'does not speak and has no care', and as such it could scarcely be more different from the God of the Bible and the Koran. It is this 'principle of eternity' rather than any personal God that the takers of psychedelic drugs claim to experience. It is 'vitalist' since its body is the 'breath of life' and is therefore, according to Professor Monod's scientific view, totally unaccept-

7. *Chāndogya* Upanishad, 3.14, based on the still earlier *Shatapatha* Brāhmana, 10.6.3.

able to modern science. It is at the source of the age-old dream that dies so hard and must, then, according to him, be abandoned. And yet how pertinacious it is!

To transcend death: what is religion about if not that? The solutions offered may vary greatly, but this seems to be at least one of the great themes of the world religions. And it is precisely because LSD and similar psychedelic drugs are alleged to be able to reproduce such a deathless and timeless *state* that their users attach to them a specifically religious value.

Among the moderns Proust too had had the experience and, for those who have eyes to see, this recovery of a *timeless* state of being constitutes salvation, for, although his whole great novel may be regarded as one vast essay in disillusion, the dénouement so minutely described in the opening section of *Le temps retrouvé* (*Time Regained*) is an escape from time into timelessness, from all the frustrations and pettiness of earthly life into a life that is quite outside time and in which death is therefore an 'almost laughable impossibility'. As another Upanishad puts it:

> From the unreal lead me to the real!
> From darkness lead me to the light!
> From death lead me to immortality![8]

It was this reality and this immortality that invaded Proust as if quite by chance as he returned tired and dispirited from an afternoon walk and was offered a cake and a cup of tea. Then, miraculously, 'no sooner had the warm liquid, and the crumbs with it, touched my palate than a shudder ran through my whole body, and I stopped, intent upon the extraordinary changes that were taking place. An exquisite pleasure had invaded my senses, but individual, detached, with no suggestion of its origin. And at once the vicissitudes of life had become indifferent to me, its disasters innocuous, its brevity illusory ... filling me with a precious essence; or rather this essence was not in me, it was myself. I had ceased now to feel mediocre, accidental, mortal. Whence could it have come to me, this all-powerful joy? I was conscious that it was connected with the taste of tea and cake, but that it infinitely

8. *Brihadāranyaka* Upanishad, 1.3.28.

The Vitalist Heresy

transcended those savours, could not, indeed, be of the same nature as theirs. Whence did it come? What did it signify? How could I seize upon and define it?'[9]

The occasion for the strange experience was trivial as it so often is. And in many cases of Zen enlightenment we find that the experience coincides with some equally trivial circumstance like the striking of the temple gong. The difference is that, in the case of Proust as with many other 'nature mystics', the experience of the 'immortal' and the 'real' ('I had ceased now to feel mediocre, *accidental, mortal*') comes totally unheralded and without any prior knowledge that such states exist or even can exist, whereas the student of Zen accepts on the authority of his master that there *is* 'something unborn, not become, not made or compounded' and that this 'something' not only can be experienced but was experienced, not only by the Buddha himself but by all genuine Zen masters in the past and the present. He has heard about the experience, has been striving to attain it, maybe for years, and once he has attained it, he can recognize it for what it is; and should he be unsure, his master is always there to guide him.

In Proust's case there was no such previous faith or knowledge. He seems to have had the experience four times and in each case he was transported from the unreal, from death and the fear of death, to immortality. In the last volume of his monumental work he tries to analyse what had happened to him:

'But let a sound, a scent already heard and breathed in the past be heard and breathed anew, simultaneously in the present and in the past, real without being actual, ideal without being abstract, then instantly the permanent and characteristic essence hidden in things is freed and our true being which has for long seemed dead but was not so in other ways awakes and revives, thanks to this celestial nourishment. An instant liberated from the order of time has recreated in us man liberated from the same order, so that he should be conscious of it. And indeed we understand his faith in his happiness even if the mere taste of a madeleine does not logically seem to justify it; we understand that the name of death

9. Marcel Proust, *Remembrance of Things Past, Swann's Way*, Vol. One (Chatto & Windus, London, 1941), p. 58.

is meaningless to him for, placed beyond Time, how can he fear the future?'[1]

In the case of both Tennyson and Proust the experience is one of release from time into timelessness and from place into 'boundless Being'. Essentially it is a release from this conditioned, phenomenal world defined by the Buddhists as being un-ease (anxiety, distress, Pali *dukkha*), impermanence, and insubstantiality into a world that is serene, abiding, and real. In both cases this meant what appeared to be a loss of individuality in the 'permanent essence of things' which is also 'the only true life'. In Proust's case the experience, 'so far from giving me a more flattering notion of my personality, had, on the contrary, almost made me doubt its very existence'.[2] As the Upanishads would say, he had 'merged into Brahman'. Discarding the ego he had discovered what Jung calls the 'self', that second personality of which he speaks in his *Memories, Dreams, Reflections* and which inhabits a different world, for 'besides [this] world there existed another realm, like a temple in which anyone who entered was transformed and suddenly overpowered by a vision of the whole cosmos, so that he could only marvel and admire, forgetful of himself'.[3] And this as the Upanishad says 'does not grow old with [the body's] ageing, nor is it slain when [the body] is slain. This is the true city of Brahman; in it are concentrated [all] desires. This is the Self, exempt from evil, untouched by age or death or sorrow, untouched by hunger or thirst; [this is the Self] whose desire is the real, whose idea is the real.'[4]

All this can be classified as nature mysticism and it seems to be of the essence of Zen as we shall see. But the cases of Tennyson and Proust are not wholly typical since Proust's experiences were triggered off not by the contemplation of Nature so much as by what seemed to be trivial accidents the connection of which with the tremendous experience seemed hard to explain, whereas Tennyson seems to have been able to recall the experience almost at will by the simple process of repeating his own name to himself.

1. Ibid., *Time Regained*, p. 218.   2. Ibid., p. 219.
3. C. G. Jung, *Memories, Dreams, Reflections* (Collins and Routledge & Kegan Paul, London, and Random House, New York, 1963), p. 55.
4. *Chāndogya* Upanishad, 8.1.5.

The Vitalist Heresy

This he called 'a kind of waking trance – this for lack of a better word'. The word, however, is probably quite apposite, for the technique of repeating sacred words over and over again in order to produce what seems to be a kind of self-hypnosis is well known in the East: the Hindus call it *japa*, the Muslims *dhikr*. In the case of the Hindus the word or words (*mantra*) repeated are usually laid down by a spiritual director, in the case of Muslims the word repeated is either 'Allah' ('God') or simply '*hūwa*' ('He'). The repetition of the Roman Catholic rosary may be presumed to have the same effect. The typical nature mystic, however, will attribute his expanded consciousness to contact with Nature – the sun, the sea, trees, mountains, the earth – which his consciousness seems to drink in so that all distinction between subject and object seems to fade away. As the Upanishad again says: 'Whoso thus knows that he is Brahman becomes this All.'[5] This melting of our every-day self-consciousness into 'cosmic' consciousness has been beautifully expressed by the Irish novelist, Forrest Reid. Typically it is the sheer beauty of unsullied nature that triggers off the experience:

'It was as if I had never realized how lovely the world was. I lay down on my back in the warm, dry moss and listened to the skylark singing as it mounted up from the fields near the sea into the dark clear sky. No other music gave me the same pleasure as that passionately joyous singing. It was a kind of leaping, exultant ecstasy, a bright, flame-like sound, rejoicing in itself. And then a curious experience befell me. It was as if everything that had seemed to be external and around me were suddenly within me. *The whole world seemed to be within me.*[6] It was within me that the trees waved their green branches, it was within me that the skylark was singing, it was within me that the hot sun shone, and that the shade was cool. A cloud rose in the sky, and passed in a light shower that pattered on the leaves, and I felt its freshness dropping into my soul, and I felt in all my being the delicious fragrance of the earth and the grass and the plants and the rich brown soil. I could have sobbed for joy.'[7]

5. *Brihadāranyaka* Upanishad, 1.4.10.   6. My italics.
7. Forrest Reid, *Following Darkness* (Arnold, London, 1902), p. 42.

At approximately the same time that Forrest Reid was writing the novel from which these words are taken William James was delivering his now classic Gifford Lectures before the University of Edinburgh which subsequently appeared as *The Varieties of Religious Experience*. Interested as he was, from a purely empirical and objective point of view, in every form of religious experience, he had sooner or later to come to grips with the subject of mysticism. This he did in his sixteenth and seventeenth lectures for which he had collected a wide variety of material both from the mystical traditions of the world religions and from persons who had no religious allegiance in particular. He had not been lucky enough himself to have had the kind of experience described by Forrest Reid. So he did what Aldous Huxley was to do some fifty years later. Well aware that mystics often referred to their states as 'intoxication', he was not afraid to write: 'The sway of alcohol over mankind is unquestionably due to its power to stimulate the mystical faculties of human nature, usually crushed to earth by the cold facts and dry criticisms of the sober hour. Sobriety diminishes, discriminates, and says no; drunkenness expands, unites, and says yes. It is in fact the great exciter of the *Yes* function in man. It brings its votary from the chill periphery of things to the radiant core. It makes him for the moment one with truth.'[8] To the average frequenter of cocktail parties this may come as a revelation. That there is a grain of truth in it may be conceded, but to state that by drinking three or four gin-and-tonics the drinker becomes 'one with truth' would surprise no one more than the drinker himself. The Muslim mystics, however, make a clear distinction between the 'drunken' ones among their number and the 'sober' variety with which they are contrasted, usually to the advantage of the latter. The study of mysticism in James's time, however, was still in its infancy, and these distinctions made by the mystics themselves were little known. James, however, wanted something better than alcohol, so he turned to nitrous oxide, the humble precursor of LSD, unaware, as in the nature of things he was bound to be, that in less than seventy years a new exponent of the mystical potentialities of drugs, Dr Timothy Leary, would arraign the

8. W. James, *The Varieties of Religious Experience*, p. 387.

brutalizing cult of alcohol as a detestable pseudo-alternative to the alleged mystical qualities of LSD. However, even nitrous oxide, so far as preternatural experience was concerned, utterly disposed of the pretensions of the fruit of the vine. After taking the drug James wrote:

'One conclusion was forced upon my mind at that time, and my impression of its truth has ever since remained unshaken. It is that our normal waking consciousness, rational consciousness as we call it, is but one special type of consciousness, whilst all about it, parted from it by the filmiest of screens, there lie potential forms of consciousness entirely different. We may go through life without suspecting their existence; but apply the requisite stimulus, and at a touch they are there in all their completeness, definite types of mentality which probably somewhere have their field of application and adaptation. No account of the universe in its totality can be final which leaves these other forms of consciousness quite disregarded. . . . Looking back on my own experiences, they all converge towards a kind of insight to which I cannot help ascribing some metaphysical significance. The keynote of it is invariably a reconciliation. It is as if the opposites of the world, whose contradictoriness and conflict make all our difficulties and troubles, were melted into unity. . . . to me the living sense of its reality only comes in the artificial mystic state of mind.'[9]

James, like other drug-takers who have enjoyed similar experiences, sees no reason to draw any distinction between what he calls 'the artificial mystic state of mind' and mystical states which occur naturally or even the more traditional currents of religious mysticism. To him the main characteristic of this state was the reconciliation of the opposites in which all things are 'melted into unity'. This is the merging into Brahman of the Indian Upanishads, and it would seem to be for this reason that people who have enjoyed these paranormal states through drugs instinctively turn to the Indian religious traditions, whether Hindu or Buddhist, rather than to the Christian or Muslim types of mysticism which, even when they tend to slip over into monism, rarely lose sight of a personal God with whom a relationship of love rather than a

9. Ibid., pp. 388–9.

merging into him remains essential. Nor does he draw a clear enough distinction between nature mysticism (Freud's 'oceanic feeling' and R. M. Bucke's 'cosmic consciousness'), in which the distinction between subject and object seems to melt away and one is merged into and in a sense becomes the 'All' (a very 'vitalist' All, it should be noted, and therefore anathema to orthodox science), and the total *transcendence* of the 'All', that is, of what Christian mystics call 'creatures', into an unconditioned state which the early Buddhists call Nirvana.

In the drug-induced state all things are merged into the One as they are so often in the Upanishads. As James says: 'I just now spoke of friends who believe in the anaesthetic revelation. For them too it is a monistic insight, in which the *other* in its various forms appears absorbed into the One.'[1] This is characteristic of nature mysticism and, when the state occurs naturally, it is usually brought about through the contemplation of Nature itself as in the case of Forrest Reid. Sometimes the word 'God' will be introduced, but this God is clearly not the biblical God one had learnt about at school but the all-pervading essence, the Brahman, of which the Upanishads speak. It is the God whom Spinoza identified with Nature, not the Law-giver of the Old Testament and the Koran. As typical of this 'artificial mystic state of mind' James quotes one of his friends who described it in these words: 'Into this pervading genius we pass, forgetting and forgotten, and thenceforth each is all, in God. . . . "The One remains, the many change and pass;" and each and everyone of us *is* the One that remains.'[2] 'God' here is clearly not the God of the Bible but the pantheistic God against which Protestant Christians instinctively react.

No one perhaps had a clearer impression and deeper experience of this 'God' than did Richard Jefferies and it is rather surprising that James does not quote him since, intense though his experiences were, he never pretended that they were other than purely subjective. Nature as experienced in a 'waking trance' is an inexplicable subjective revelation, but it bears no relationship to Nature as seen objectively. This was Jefferies' problem. His experiences as written down in *The Story of my Heart* seemed absolutely real

1. Ibid.   2. Ibid.

The Vitalist Heresy

to him, but in the sober light of rational reflection they did not correspond to the realities of the cosmos as science was beginning to reveal them nor to life as it must be lived on earth. Yet the feeling of this communion and union with all natural things and beyond these with a spiritual reality he could not describe or even attain to had stayed with him ever since he became aware of them at the early age of eighteen.

'I was not more than eighteen when an inner and esoteric meaning began to come to me from all the visible universe, and indefinable aspirations filled me. I found them in the grass fields, under the trees, on the hill-tops, at sunrise, and in the night. There was a deeper meaning everywhere. The sun burned with it, the broad front of morning beamed with it; a deep feeling entered me while gazing at the sky in the azure noon, and in the star-lit evening.

'I was sensitive to all things, to the earth under, and the star-hollow round about; to the least blade of grass, to the largest oak. They seemed like exterior nerves and veins for the conveyance of feeling to me. *Sometimes a very ecstasy of exquisite enjoyment of the entire visible universe filled me. I was aware that in reality the feeling and the thought were in me, and not in the earth or sun*;[3] yet I was more conscious of it when in the company of these. A visit to the sea increased the strength of the original impulse. I began to make efforts to express these thoughts in writing, but could not succeed to my own liking.'[4]

Jefferies was obsessed by his vision, but so disconcerting was it that he had the greater difficulty in committing it to paper. This seems to be typical of all mystics who have these strange experiences unheralded. It is not so much that the experience cannot be put into words, for this is not necessarily true. On the other hand what one puts into words is for the mystic factual truth. When the author of the Upanishad says, 'I am this all' or 'Death beyond death is all the lot of him who sees in This what seems to be diverse',[5] he is saying what he means, he is describing an

---

3. My italics.
4. Richard Jefferies, *The Story of my Heart* (reprint, Macmillan, London, 1968), pp. 140–1.
5. *Brihadāranyaka* Upanishad, 4.4.19.

experience in terms that for him are literally true. For anyone brought up in the Western tradition such words can at best be paradox, at the worst lunatic nonsense. Hence (until quite recently) the extreme reluctance of mystics to describe what they have experienced. They are reluctant to do so for fear of being thought mad. In the East, on the other hand, the madman is often regarded with reverence for he is thought to be in touch with the unseen world. This partly explains Jefferies' reluctance to write of his experience, but he was also restrained from writing because it took him some time to realize that the identity he felt with sea and sun and earth was only the symbol of a higher spiritual reality which he continued to approach but never fully realized. And yet his experiences were very diverse. Like all the nature mystics he had experienced a sense of identity with nature, but he had also, like Meister Eckhart and Proust, experienced what he called the eternal Now in which time is transcended and death becomes an 'almost laughable impossibility'. His starting point, however, was a sense of being at one with all natural things. He was not a Christian: rather the reverse since he avoids, if possible, all Christian terminology, and if he uses it, he makes it clear that he is using it in a specialized sense. Thus from Nature he passes to prayer, but it is not at all what conventional Christians of the nineteenth century understand by that word.

'I was utterly alone', he writes, 'with the sun and the earth. Lying down on the grass, I spoke in my soul to the earth, the sun, the air, and the distant sea far beyond sight. I thought of the earth's firmness – I felt it bear me up; through the grassy couch there came an influence as if I could feel the great earth speaking to me. I thought of the wandering air – its pureness, which is its beauty; the air touched me and gave me something of itself. I spoke to the sea: though so far, in my mind I saw it, green at the rim of the earth and blue in deeper ocean; I desired to have its strength, its mystery, and glory. Then I addressed the sun, desiring the soul equivalent of his light and brilliance, his endurance and unwearied race. I turned to the blue heaven over, gazing into its depth, inhaling its exquisite colour and sweetness. The rich blue of the unattainable flower of the sky drew my soul towards it, and there it rested, for pure colour is rest of heart. By all these I prayed; I felt an emotion of the soul beyond all definition; prayer is a puny thing to it, and the word is a rude sign to the feeling, but I know no other ... Breathing the earth-encircling air, thinking of the sea and the sky, holding out my hand for the sunbeams to touch it, prone on the sward in token of deep reverence, thus I prayed that I might touch to the unutterable existence infinitely higher than deity.'[6]

'Prayer', for Jefferies, is an aspiration of all his being, which in some mysterious way partakes of 'the earth, the sun, the air, and the distant sea' but is not identical with them, towards something far beyond all these, something to compare which to the Christian God of conventional religion would be ludicrous, and hence it has to be called, for lack of a better term, 'unutterable existence infinitely higher than deity'. For whatever it is, it is utterly other than matter; it is a 'fulness of soul till now unknown, and utterly beyond my own conception'.[7] It is beyond the universe of space and it is also beyond time but in the early stages of Jefferies' 'prayer' it seems to shimmer, darkly, behind all natural things. Thus, 'having drunk deeply of the heaven above and felt the most glorious beauty of the day, and remembering the old, old sea, which (as it seemed to me) was but just yonder at the edge, I now became lost, and absorbed into the being or existence of the universe. I felt deep into the earth under, and high above into the sky, and farther still to the sun and stars. Still farther beyond the stars into the hollow of space, and losing thus my separateness of being came to seem like a part of the whole. ... By all those things which are most powerful known to me, and by those which exist, but of which I have no idea whatever, I pray. Further, by my own soul, that secret existence which above all other things bears the nearest resemblance to the ideal of spirit, infinitely nearer than earth, sun, or star. Speaking by an inclination towards, not in words, my soul prays that I may have something from each of these, that I may gather a flower from them, that I may have in myself the secret and meaning of the earth, the golden sun, the light, the foam-flecked sea.'[8]

6. R. Jefferies, op. cit., pp. 3–4.   7. Ibid., p. 12.   8. Ibid., pp. 6–8.

Nature, in its way, is like the human soul, created in the image of God, or perhaps it would be better to say that it *is* the image of God, for without human consciousness there would be nothing into which it could be reflected. What Jefferies seems to be trying to express here is the thought long ago formulated in the Upanishads.

'He who, abiding in the earth, is yet other than the earth, whom the earth does not know, whose body is the earth, who controls the earth from within – he is the Self within you, the Inner Controller, the Immortal.' And as this 'Inner Controller' controls the earth, so does it control water, fire, the atmosphere, wind and sky, sun, moon and stars, space and darkness and light. And just as he controls all these cosmic phenomena, so does he control all man's inner faculties – breath, voice, eye and ear, mind and understanding, skin and semen. And so of this 'unutterable existence infinitely higher than deity' it can be said:

'As bees, dear boy, make honey by collecting the juices of many trees and reduce the juice to a unity, yet [those juices] cannot perceive any distinction there [so that any of them might know:] "I am the juice of this tree", or "I am the juice of that tree", [so too,] my dearest boy, all these creatures [here], once they have merged into Being do not know that they have merged into Being. ... This finest essence – the whole universe has it as its Self: That is the Real: That is the Self: That *you* are.'[9]

All this is implied in Jefferies' prayer 'that my soul might be more than the cosmos of life';[1] but he will not rest content until he passes from the symbols of eternity – from earth, and sky and sun and sea – to what these symbols represent.

'Full to the brim of the wondrous past, I felt the wondrous present. For the day – the very moment I breathed, that second of time then in the valley, was as marvellous, as grand, as all that had gone before. Now, this moment was the wonder and the glory. Now, this moment was exceedingly wonderful. Now, this moment give me all the thought, all the idea, all the soul expressed in the cosmos around me. Give me still more, for the interminable universe, past and present, is but earth; *give me the unknown soul,*

---

9. *Brihadāranyaka* Upanishad, 3.7.3–23; *Chāndogya* Upanishad, 6.9.
1. R. Jefferies, op. cit., p. 11.

The Vitalist Heresy

wholly apart from it,[2] the soul of which I know only that when I touch the ground, when the sunlight touches my hand, *it is not there*.[3] Therefore the heart looks into space to be away from earth.'[4]

The symbols have served their purpose, and Jefferies' prayer coincides with the Upanishadic prayer we have already quoted:

> From the unreal lead me to the real!
> From darkness lead me to the light!
> From death lead me to immortality!

To which might be added: 'From time lead me to the Timeless', as the *Maitrī* Upanishad (6.15) suggests: for the inmost soul of man has nothing in common with time which is merely a human invention 'mutually agreed upon for artificial purposes'.[5] And so Jefferies can say:

'Realizing that spirit, recognizing my own inner consciousness, the psyche, so clearly, I cannot understand time. It is eternity now. I am in the midst of it. It is about me in the sunshine; I am in it, as the butterfly floats in the light-laden air. Nothing has to come; it is now. Now is eternity; now is the immortal life ... The years, the centuries, the cycles are absolutely nothing. ... My soul has never been, and never can be, dipped in time. Time has never existed, and never will; it is a purely artificial arrangement. It is eternity now, it always was eternity, and always will be. By no possible means could I get into time if I tried. I am in eternity now and must there remain.'[6]

But what does Jefferies understand by 'I'? Probably it is what Jung calls his 'personality no. 2' – a personality that is 'outside time'[7] and for whom 'everything that happens in time had been brought together into a concrete whole',[8] in which 'one is interwoven into an indescribable whole and yet observes it with complete objectivity'.[9] So, too, Jefferies says:

'Sometimes I have concentrated myself, and driven away by continued will all sense of outward appearances, looking straight with the full power of my mind inwards on myself. I find "I" am

2. My italics.   3. My italics.   4. R. Jefferies, op. cit., pp. 14–15.
5. Ibid., p. 30.   6. Ibid., pp. 30–1.
7. C. G. Jung, *Memories, Dreams, Reflections*, p. 57.
8. Ibid., p. 275.   9. Ibid., p. 276.

there; an "I" I do not wholly understand, or know – something is there distinct from earth and timber, from flesh and bones. Recognizing it, I feel on the margin of a life unknown, very near, almost touching it: on the verge of powers which if I could grasp would give me an immense breadth of existence, an ability to execute what I now only conceive; most probably of far more than that. To see that "I" is to know that I am surrounded with immortal things. If, when I die, that "I" also dies, and becomes extinct, still even then I have had the exaltation of these ideas.'[1]

Of course Jefferies is inconsistent. At one moment (in time!) he says that by no possible means could he get into time if he tried; at another he faces the possibility that physical death may entail the death of the timeless 'I' too, yet even so it will have been enough to 'have had the exaltation of these ideas'. Unlike Tennyson, Proust, and Jung, he could not make a clear distinction between 'personality no. 1', which is our everyday self with all its cares and troubles, and 'personality no. 2', which lives at peace in what Jung calls 'God's world'. Like the Indian Yogis he uses matter and the material world to reach forth to the world of spirit (and here he follows in the footsteps of Thomas Traherne), but seen from the vantage-point of spirit 'a little spirit is equal to the entire cosmos, to earth and ocean, sun and star-hollow'.[2]

When he is in the 'eternal Now', it is matter, not spirit, that is incomprehensible. 'Why this clod of earth I hold in my hand?' he asks. 'Why this water which drops sparkling from my fingers dipped in the brook? Why are they at all? When? How? What for? Matter is beyond understanding, mysterious, impenetrable; I touch it easily, comprehend it, no. Soul, mind – the thought, the idea – is easily understood, it understands itself and is conscious. ... Except when I walk by the sea, and my soul is by it, the sea is dead. Those seas by which no man has stood – by which no soul has been – whether on earth or the planets, are dead. No matter how majestic the planet rolls in space, unless a soul be there it is dead.'[3]

Matter without spirit is dead, but once allied with spirit in a human body, the body itself becomes almost divine. Here Jefferies

1. R. Jefferies, op. cit., pp. 34–5.   2. Ibid., p. 82.   3. Ibid., pp 32–3.

The Vitalist Heresy

parts company with the whole 'orthodox' religious mystical tradition whether it be Christian, Muslim, Hindu, or Buddhist. He aligns himself rather with the Taoists in China, with the Zen Buddhists, with Traherne and Walt Whitman, and, in some respects, with the Upanishads too. For in the 'orthodox' religious traditions mystical experience is based on detachment from all things temporal: in the words of the greatest of the 'orthodox' mystics of Islam who flourished in the ninth and tenth centuries A.D., the essence of mysticism is to 'isolate the eternal from the originated'. This, of course, implies a measure of asceticism, but this, for Jefferies quite as much as for Whitman, is anathema.

'I believe', he says, 'all manner of asceticism to be the vilest blasphemy – blasphemy towards the whole of the human race. I believe in the flesh and the body, which is worthy of worship ... The ascetics are the only persons who are impure. Increase of physical beauty is attended by increase of soul beauty. The soul is the higher even by gazing on beauty. Let me be fleshly perfect.'[4]

Yes, but there is another side to the picture. Quite as much as for modern science, human consciousness is for Jefferies the result of pure chance, and without consciousness there can be no beauty, no ecstasy, in a mechanistic universe that is absolutely indifferent to human suffering, for, like the Hindu Brahman, 'it does not speak and has no care'.[5] Nature may have the power to invade human consciousness and to expand it so that man and Nature seem to form but one thing, but nonetheless 'there is nothing human in Nature. The earth, though loved so dearly, would let me perish on the ground, and neither bring forth food nor water. Burning in the sky the great sun, of whose company I have been so fond, would merely burn on and make no motion to assist me. Those who have been in an open boat at sea without water have proved the mercies of the sun, and of the deity who did not give them one drop of rain, dying in misery under the same rays that shine so beautifully on the flowers ... As for the sea, it offers us salt water which we cannot drink. The trees care nothing for us ... The sun scorches man, and will in his naked state roast him alive. The sea and the fresh water alike make no effort to uphold him if his vessel founders; he

4. Ibid., p. 88.   5. *Chāndogya* Upanishad, 3.14.3.

casts up his arms in vain, they come to their level over his head, filling the spot his body occupied. If he falls from a cliff the air parts; the earth beneath dashes him to pieces.'[6]

Earth, sky, sun, sea, trees, the air, and 'the deity', which can invade human consciousness 'as if they were the keys of an instrument, of an organ, with which I swelled forth the notes of my soul',[7] and fill it with rapture and ecstasy, are at the same time the implacable and remorseless enemies of man. In this Jefferies is more realistic than William James and most nature mystics and devotees of psychedelic drugs: he stands much nearer to Professor Monod for whom 'ethics and knowledge . . . values and truth, associated but not interchangeable, reveal their full significance to the attentive man alive to their resonance'.[8]

For Professor Monod 'ethics' and 'knowledge' are for ever distinct but always associated. Richard Jefferies too sees an unbridgeable dualism in man, but in his case the dualism is not so much between ethics and objective knowledge as between man's mystical (and therefore subjective) reaction to the universe and the scientific and objective judgment he passes on the universe. Subjective is mystical experience and ethical judgment, objective is the universe as seen and interpreted by science. This is what Teilhard de Chardin calls the 'inner' and 'outer' aspects of evolution, and this again is prefigured in the Upanishads, where we are told:

'As wide as is this space [around us], so wide is this space within the heart. In it both sky and earth are concentrated, both fire and wind, both sun and moon, lightning and the stars, what a man possesses here on earth and what he does not possess: everything is concentrated in this [tiny space within the heart].

'If they should say to him: "If all this is concentrated within this city of Brahman – all beings and all desires – what is left of it when old age overtakes it and it falls apart?"

'Then should he say: "It does not grow old with [the body's] ageing nor is it slain when [the body] is slain. This is the true city of Brahman; in it are concentrated [all] desires." '[9]

6. R. Jefferies, op. cit., pp. 43–4.   7. Ibid., p. 5.   8. Above, p. 29.
9. *Chāndogya* Upanishad, 8.1.3–5.

The Vitalist Heresy 59

This is the answer to Jefferies' 'prayer'; this is 'the inexpressible entity infinitely higher than deity' that has its being in an eternal Now. As to the 'deity' he associates with sun and sky, air, earth and sea, this may well be the Gnostic demiurge whom the second-century Gnostic heretic Marcion identified with the God of the Old Testament in whom, as Jung has pointed out,[1] good and evil are inextricably mixed. It is certainly not the 'higher than deity' to which Jefferies aspires. All Christian and theistic assumptions which proclaim a merciful God he dismisses with furious contempt. 'How can I adequately express my contempt for this assertion that all things occur for the best, for a wise and beneficent end, and are ordered by a humane intelligence!' he says. 'It is the most utter falsehood and crime against the human race.'[2] As for modern science man remains alone and left to his own devices in a universe that is not only indifferent to him but malignantly hostile.

'A great part, perhaps the whole, of nature and of the universe is distinctly anti-human. The term inhuman does not express my meaning, anti-human is better; outre-human, in the sense of beyond, outside, almost grotesque in its attitude towards, would nearly convey it. Everything is anti-human.'[3]

'Centuries of thought have failed to reconcile and fit the mind to the universe, which is designless, and purposeless, and without idea. . . . As these natural things have no connection with man, it follows again that the natural is the strange and mysterious, and the supernatural the natural.

'There being nothing human in nature or the universe, and all things being ultra-human and without design, shape, or purpose, I conclude that no deity has anything to do with nature. There is no god in nature, nor in any matter anywhere, either in the clods on the earth or in the composition of the stars. For what we understand by the deity is the purest form of Idea, of Mind, and no mind is exhibited in these. That which controls them is distinct altogether from deity. It is not force in the sense of electricity, nor a deity as god, nor a spirit, nor even an intelligence, but a power quite different to anything yet imagined. I cease, therefore, to

1. Particularly in his *Answer to Job*.   2. R. Jefferies, op. cit., p. 103.
3. Ibid., p. 45.

look for deity in nature or the cosmos at large, or to trace any marks of divine handiwork. I search for traces of this force which is not god, and is certainly not the higher than deity of whom I have written. *It is a force without a mind.*[4] I wish to indicate something more subtle than electricity, *but absolutely devoid of consciousness*,[5] and with no more feeling than the force which lifts the tides.'[6]

For one who has communed so intensely with sun and sea, earth and air and all natural things, these are strong words indeed, but they do seem to fit in with Professor Monod's destruction of the 'ancient covenant' between man and Nature which modern science, he says, has for ever shattered. Moreover, despite his mystical experience of the eternal Now and of 'losing his separateness of being' in the 'whole', Jefferies remains firmly dualistic – and pessimistic. The raptures induced by nature mysticism are not enough, for what the mystic understands by Nature (identified with God by Spinoza and the great majority of nature mystics) is not really Nature at all but the subjective experience of light and beauty and the interconnection of all things in the human consciousness which has its being outside time. The universe itself is mindless, devoid of consciousness, and amoral. If it has a ruler, then that ruler must be amoral too. Like the God of Lamentations 3:38 it is from this 'Most High' that evil and good come. 'Deity' is, it would seem, mathematics without consciousness, let alone conscience, while 'the unutterable existence infinitely higher than deity' is unknowable and unknown. 'Cosmic consciousness' is a purely subjective state that has nothing to do with the cosmos as objectively known.

After reading Richard Jefferies, how fatuous do the apostles of 'cosmic consciousness' and those who equate it with every form of mysticism appear! R. M. Bucke, a psychologist who lived at the turn of this century, seems to have coined the term and it seems appropriate enough. But his *interpretation* of it, which the apostles of LSD in the main follow, is totally subjective and glibly renounces any consideration of 'objective truth'.

'This consciousness', Bucke writes, 'shows the cosmos to consist

---

4. My italics.   5. My italics.   6. R. Jefferies, op. cit., pp. 49-50.

The Vitalist Heresy

not of dead matter governed by unconscious, rigid, and unintending law; it shows it on the contrary as entirely immaterial, entirely spiritual and entirely alive; it shows that death is an absurdity, that everyone and everything has eternal life; it shows that the universe is God and that God is the universe, and that no evil did or ever will enter into it.'[7]

This extraordinary assessment of the nature of 'cosmic consciousness' is based on one single experience whereas Jefferies assesses and judges a whole lifetime of mystical experience; and his conclusions, as we have seen, were very different. The devotees of psychedelic drugs, like Bucke, all too often base their interpretations on a single experience and must therefore be treated with the greatest reserve. Since Bucke's book has, directly or indirectly, influenced writers on 'mysticism' from James to the present day, we must quote his account of his own experience in his own words. This is what he says:

'He [i.e. Bucke] and two friends had spent the evening reading Wordsworth, Shelley, Keats, Browning, and especially Whitman. They parted at midnight... His mind, deeply under the influence of the ideas, images and emotions called up by the reading and talk of the evening, was calm and peaceful. He was in a state of quiet, almost passive enjoyment. All at once, without warning of any kind, he found himself wrapped around as it were by a flame-coloured cloud. For an instant he thought of fire, some sudden conflagration in the great city; the next, he knew that the light was within himself. Directly afterwards came upon him a sense of exultation, of immense joyousness accompanied or immediately followed by an intellectual illumination quite impossible to describe. Into his brain streamed one momentary lightning-flash of Brahmic Splendor which has ever since lightened his life; upon his heart fell one drop of Brahmic Bliss, leaving thenceforward for always an aftertaste of heaven.'[8]

So much for the *description* of the experience, but even this mere description is already tinged with interpretation. The

7. R. M. Bucke, *Cosmic Consciousness* (23rd ed., E. P. Dutton, New York, 1966), p. 17.
8. Ibid., pp. 9–10.

experience consisted of an inner light, joy, a flash of 'Brahmic' splendor, plus a 'drop' of 'Brahmic' bliss. In other words Bucke had an intense sensation of light and joy. To qualify these as '*Brahmic* Splendor' and '*Brahmic* Bliss' is already interpretation based either on reading some Hindu text or, more likely, a book on Hinduism or perhaps Emerson's poem 'Brahma'. In any case the tendency to identify or 'explain' these natural mystical experiences in terms of Upanishadic Hinduism was already in vogue – and rightly so since both Bucke's experience and most of the Upanishadic writings are not concerned with a *personal* God – but to qualify the experience as 'Brahmic' is still not direct experience but an interpretation, however vague, of that experience. Besides all this, however, there was 'an *intellectual* illumination quite impossible to describe'. Undeterred by this impossibility Dr Bucke proceeds to describe it in no uncertain way:

'Among other things he did not come to believe, he saw and knew that the Cosmos is not dead matter but a living Presence, that the soul of man is immortal, that the universe is so built and ordered that without any peradventure all things work together for the good of each and all, that the foundation principle of the world is what we call love and that the happiness of everyone is in the long run absolutely certain. He claims that he learned more within the few seconds during which the illumination lasted than in previous months or even years of study, and that he learned much that no study could ever have taught.'[9]

The reader will no doubt ask: 'Is the man serious?' Unfortunately he is, for it is a characteristic of the great majority of nature mystics (whether their experience has been spontaneous or drug-induced) that what they experience strikes them as being absolutely true. They do not just think they have seen Reality: they *know* they have. Though the experience is by all accounts ineffable and cannot be put into words that make sense to anyone who has not had such an experience, it strikes the subject as being far more real than the humdrum reality of their everyday lives where evil, so far from never having entered the universe, is experienced as being everywhere nauseatingly present. Only

9. Ibid., p. 10.

Jefferies among the examples we have quoted attempts to explain his 'beatific' experiences against the objective background of an indifferent universe and a suffering humanity. He makes no metaphysical claims on the basis of a whole series of experiences in which he transcended time and in which he became merged in Nature's beauty in 'an emotion of the soul beyond all definition': he merely describes as best he can, after years of hesitation about whether or not it was even possible to write the 'story of his heart' at all, the sensations which were certainly preternatural and carried utter conviction of their truth *at the time*. Like Proust and Tennyson he had dropped out of time into timelessness, but he necessarily dropped back into time again. He had tasted 'timeless' immortality but this did not mean that he would necessarily rejoin the timeless at the moment of his physical death. All he says is this: 'At least while I am living I have enjoyed the idea of immortality, and the idea of my own soul. If then, after death, I am resolved without exception into earth, air, and water, and the spirit goes out like a flame, still I shall have had the glory of the thought.'[1] This is very different from Bucke's extravagantly silly claims and is indeed far more modest and factual than what both William James and Aldous Huxley claimed for psychedelic drugs.

Despite Jefferies' reserve, however, it would seem that in the case of James and Huxley and other cases cited by James, and more recently in the ever-expanding literature on psychedelic drugs, the drug-induced experience – what is commonly called a 'successful trip' – can and often does induce a condition which seems to be indistinguishable from much, if not all, of what Jefferies describes. The essence of the experience is perhaps the feeling of infinity beyond space and time and the interconnectedness of all things, the latter sometimes appearing as 'love', by which Dr Timothy Leary rather crudely understands sex. The experience is almost always one of ecstatic joy because death and time are transcended and all the opposites are melted into One – the One of the Neo-Platonists and Meister Eckhart, and that One is the Self of all things –

1. R. Jefferies, op. cit., p. 28.

> Vast heavenly, unthinkable its form,
> More subtle than the subtle, forth it shines:
> More distant than the distant, it is yet here, right near;
> For those who see, it's even here, hidden in a secret place.'[2]

This is not the God that Christians claim to know: it is the other 'God' whom the Upanishads proclaim. Nothing is lacking in him – not even sex. For 'just as a man, closely embraced by his loving wife, knows nothing without, nothing within, so does this "person", closely embraced by the Self that consists of wisdom, know nothing without, nothing within. This is his [true] form in which all his desires are fulfilled, in which Self [alone] is his desire, in which he has no desire, no sorrow.'[3]

Of all the nature mystics perhaps Walt Whitman is the most thoroughgoing. Like Jefferies he is the poet of the body as well as of the soul,[4] and the body means sexuality and procreation: and sex means the union of the opposites, identity in distinction. There is nothing prudish about Whitman. Indeed he is an even more passionate opponent of asceticism in any shape or form than Jefferies himself:

> Urge and urge and urge,
> Always the procreant urge of the world.
> Out of the dimness opposite equals advance, always substance and increase, always sex,
> Always a knit of identity, always distinction, always a breed of life.[5]

As he himself says: '*Leaves of Grass* is avowedly the song of Sex and Amativeness, and even Animality – though meanings that do not usually go along with those words are behind all, and will duly emerge; and all are sought to be lifted into a different light and atmosphere.'[6] This is equally true of the Upanishads. This other God both transcends sex and, like the later Shiva, *is* sex – the union of the male and female principles, ever chaste, yet ever productive.

This is that other God – and 'that *you* are'. You do not know

2. *Mundaka* Upanishad, 3.1.7.
3. *Brihadāranyaka* Upanishad, 4.3.21.
4. Walt Whitman, *Song of Myself*, 21.
5. Ibid., 3.
6. *A Backward Glance* (Nonesuch edition, London, 1938), p. 871.

him, but Jefferies knew him and Whitman knew him, as have many others. You too can know him, and the LSD enthusiasts will tell you, you can, if your dispositions are right, know him by taking LSD. In this magic potion you can find ecstasy the likes of which you have never dreamt of, because not only will your consciousness have expanded to such an extent as to include the whole universe, but you will enjoy an ecstatic union with the Great Self of all things. All this had of course been said thousands of years ago in the Upanishads, the fount and origin of all nature mysticism, for here too we find the perfect expression of 'Whitmanism' in all its preposterous defiance of logic and common sense. Here is what the Upanishad[7] has to say about this other 'God' who permeates all things, controls all things, is other than, yet the same as, all things and for whom the Lord God Yahweh of the Old Testament has about as much relevance as a bunch of straw:

'This [Infinite] is below, it is above, it is to the west, to the east, to the south, to the north. Truly it is this whole universe.

'Next the teaching concerning the ego.

'I am below, I am above, I am to the west, to the east, to the south, to the north. Truly I am this whole universe.

'Next the teaching concerning the Self.

'The Self is below, the Self is above, the Self is to the west, to the east, to the south, to the north. Truly the Self is this whole universe.

'The man who sees and thinks and understands in this way has pleasure in the Self, plays with the Self, copulates with the Self, and has his joy with the Self: he becomes an independent sovereign. In every state of being freedom of movement is his.'

This is the other God: he is your true Self and at the same time the lover of yourself. This, as the same Upanishad says, is 'what you should seek out and really want to understand', for this is the 'Kingdom of God within you'.

7. *Chāndogya* Upanishad, 7.25.

3

MYSTICISM AND LSD

The quotation with which the last chapter concluded is from the *Chāndogya* Upanishad, among the most sacred of the Hindu scriptures. It is particularly relevant since it seems to describe more accurately than any similar Eastern text I know the experience (or rather some of the experiences) claimed by the apostles of the psychedelic cult, and particularly by Dr Timothy Leary in his recent book *The Politics of Ecstasy*. It represents pantheism at its widest and at the same time it makes room for sexual love, which is sublimated in Christian mysticism but used by the Tantric Hindus and Buddhists as a sacramental enactment of that love which they believe pervades the whole universe and unites the male and the female principles which together compose what the Hindu philosopher, Rāmānuja, describes as the 'body of God' and which harmonizes all conceivable opposites in a divine synthesis of interpenetration and harmony. Pantheism plus love: the way of the Upanishads and the *Bhagavad-Gītā* in Hinduism, the way of the Mahayana in general and of Zen in particular in Buddhism, the way of many Christian and Muslim mystics, the way of what some would call 'natural' as opposed to 'revealed' religion. Pantheism and sex: the way of the so-called left-hand Tantra among both Hindus and Buddhists, the way of Timothy Leary and the psychedelic cult.

We have already said enough about pantheism in the last chapter, we must now say a few words about love and sex in the mystical context. It has long been taken for granted in India that sexual union and mystical love in what appears to be a sexual form are the highest (because the most natural) manifestations of the ultimate reconciliation of all opposites in the One which is beyond all dualities – sexual union in the sphere of matter, mystical rapture in the sphere of spirit. Among the worshippers of Shiva in India it is represented by the love of the God Shiva for his Shakti, his 'power' by which and through which all things are made – the creative Logos in the Hindu scheme of things. In its purely philosophical form this love is entirely spiritual but none the less fruitful, for the union of the two aspects of deity results in the creation of the world. 'Shiva generates Shakti, and Shakti generates Shiva. Both in their happy union produce worlds and souls. Still Shiva is [ever] chaste and his sweet-speeched Shakti remains [ever] a virgin. Only sages can comprehend this mystery.'[8] In this view sexual union is the sacramental re-enactment of an eternal truth. Dr Leary and his associates take this literally since, for them, sex is an integral part of the psychedelic experience.

Until very recently the propagandists of psychedelic religion have not emphasized this aspect of the psychedelic 'trip'. In our present permissive society it is not easy to understand why. Dr Leary, however, has now destroyed this last remnant of prudery: LSD not only transports you into immensely expanded fields of consciousness, it is also a most powerful aphrodisiac. 'An enormous amount of energy from every fibre of your body is released under LSD – most especially including sexual energy. There is no question that LSD is the most powerful aphrodisiac ever discovered by man. ... Merging, yielding, flowing, union, communion. It's all love-making.... You're in pulsating harmony with all the energy around you.... The natural and obvious way to take LSD is with a member of the opposite sex, and an LSD session that does not involve an ultimate merging with a person of the opposite sex isn't really complete. One of the great purposes of an LSD session is sexual union. The more expanded your consciousness – the further out you can move beyond your mind – the deeper, the richer, the longer, and more meaningful your sexual communion.'[9] And, in case the reader should have missed the point, he gives us this additional information: 'In a carefully prepared, loving LSD session, a woman can have several hundred orgasms.' This is surely an exaggeration, but it is precisely the kind

---

8. Cf. R. C. Zaehner, *Hinduism* (Oxford University Press, Oxford, 1962), p. 117.
9. Timothy Leary, *The Politics of Ecstasy* (MacGibbon & Kee, London, and G. P. Putnam, New York, 1970), pp. 106–7.

of exaggeration you would expect from the 'expanded consciousness' that LSD produces.

Most other writers on psychedelic drugs are more reticent about the sexual potentialities of LSD; but to the student of mysticism they are of considerable interest, for there is scarcely a form of *religious* mysticism (except the more orthodox Buddhist varieties) in which sexual imagery does not turn up. In Christian mysticism, for instance, the mystical treatise often takes the form of a commentary on the Song of Songs, now generally recognized for what it is – a frankly sensuous and secular love poem. Divine love and human love at their highest are both, it would seem, sexual, for sexual love surpasses even parental love, the love of a mother for her child. 'This is why a man leaves his father and mother and joins himself to his wife, and they become one body.' And this is why the Church made marriage a sacrament and regarded the marriage-tie as being indissoluble. The obverse of this sanctification of sexual union in marriage, however, is an almost pathological disgust at the essentially animal act, which enters Western Christianity with Augustine and culminates in the hypocritical Puritanism of the Victorians, the inevitable result of which is the present so-called 'sexual revolution'. Puritanism at its best is an attempt to preserve the sexual act itself from vulgarization, trivialization, and ultimately blasphemy. At its worst, it is a Manichaean condemnation of the body and the body's activities as such. Even – and indeed particularly – the Christian mystics who go into ecstasy over their spiritual espousals with God or Christ cannot accept the rapture of sexual union as anything but a diabolical caricature of the raptures of the spirit in which the soul is ravished by God. Yet 'ravishing' and 'rapture' are, after all, only a polite way of saying 'rape'. Even St François de Sales, the eminently civilized and urbane saint of seventeenth-century France, conscious though he was of the strong resemblance that exists between the 'raptures' of Christian saints and sexual union, cannot by any means admit that the two are facets of the same unifying and creative love manifesting themselves on a different plane. Of the first he says:

'Ecstasy is called rapture, for it is by means of ecstasy that God attracts us up to himself; and rapture is called ecstasy, for it is by means of rapture that we take leave of ourselves and remain outside and above ourselves in order to be united with God. ... If we think of the sheer power that God's beauty and goodness have to attract the soul's attention and diligence towards him, then it will seem that it does not only lift us up but ravishes us and carries us away. If, on the other hand, we think of the free consent of our will and the fervid movement by which the ravished soul flows in the wake of God's power of attraction, then it will seem that not only does it rise and ascend, but that it hurls itself out of itself, rushing into the Godhead itself.'

So much for God's 'rape' of the soul. 'Wonderfully sweet, gentle and delightful are the attractions by which we are drawn towards God.' But turn to the darker side – the raptures of fleshly love – so similar yet so violently contrasted. The good saint can see nothing good in this. For he goes on to say:

'The very same thing happens in that basest of ecstasies, that abominable rapture, which the soul experiences when it is drawn out of the spiritual dignity proper to it, enticed away by carnal pleasures and dragged below its natural state; for in so far as it follows this ill-omened sensory bliss of its own free will and rushes out of itself ... it can be said that it is in a state of sensual ecstasy, but in so far as sensual enticements draw it on with power and, so to speak, carry it off by force into this low and miserable condition, it can be said that it is ravished and carried out of itself because these gross, sensory joys deprive it of the use of reason and intelligence with so furious a violence ... that a man in this condition seems to have been overcome by epilepsy, so absorbed is his mind and as it were lost.'[1]

The resemblance is clear enough, for both in mystical rapture and in sexual union reason and intelligence are momentarily set at naught. The soul 'flows' and 'hurls itself out of itself'. It is 'as it were lost' because all consciousness of the ego has disappeared. As the Buddhists would say, there is no longer any 'I' or 'mine', the ego has been swallowed up into a greater whole.

The transcendence of reason and intelligence is precisely what

1. St François de Sales, *Traité de l'amour de Dieu*, 7.4.

Zen Buddhism is about, and what happens once reason has been transcended is described by the passage from the *Chāndogya* Upanishad I quoted at the end of the last chapter. In this state of 'transcendence' you realize your identity with all things beyond space and time, you *are* 'this whole universe', and so you are somehow also the self of the whole universe, and yet you must in some sense be distinct from it since 'you have pleasure with the Self' and 'copulate with the Self'. And so Dr Leary, as the good Hindu he claims to be,[2] can say that 'the three inevitable goals of the LSD session are to discover and make love with God, to discover and make love with yourself, and to discover and make love with a woman. You can't make it with yourself unless you've made it with the timeless energy process around you, and you can't make it with a woman until you've made it with yourself.'[3]

All this is in perfect agreement with the Upanishadic passage. You cannot discover your true self until you have discovered the Infinite first; for once you have done this you will have discovered the Infinite within yourself. Having discovered the Infinite without (what Leary here calls God) you can make love with him, and through this 'timeless energy process around you' you will be able to enjoy sexual intercourse with a woman, but, it would appear in an infinite dimension; for, as Leary is quick to point out, 'if a man and his mate take LSD together, . . . their sexual energies will be unimaginably intensified'.[4]

Herein Dr Leary would appear to part company with the nature mystics with the notable exception of Walt Whitman for whom, too, sex had a cosmic significance, as we saw in the last chapter. Leary does not deify sex, but he almost does so. For him 'God' and the 'timeless energy process around you' are synonymous terms. To the words 'around you' he should have added 'within you': then the parallelism with the Upanishadic passage would have been complete. For Spinoza, as for the nature mystics, God and Nature were interchangeable terms. Since Spinoza's day, however, science has taken enormous strides, and so Dr Leary can speak more clearly of '*God* or *evolution*',[5] or, more precisely still, he can say that

2. T. Leary, op. cit., pp. 130, 239.   3. Ibid., p. 107.
4. Ibid., pp. 108–9.   5. Ibid., p. 188.

'God is the DNA code because the DNA code, as biochemists describe it, is all the attributes that we have attributed to God: the all-powerful, ever-changing intelligence far greater than man's mind which is continually manifesting itself in different forms. . . . That's what the genetic code has been doing for 2 billion years.'[6]

Professor Monod would doubtless find all this a familiar and outmoded 'vitalist' fancy, the latest and craziest of the 'religions' that claim to be scientifically based and a fitting *reductio ad absurdum* of previous efforts, like dialectical materialism and the 'evolutionism' of Teilhard de Chardin which try to do much the same thing. But is it so absurd? For, after all, it all depends on what you understand by religion and what you mean by God. It is most emphatically not the God of the Old Testament or the Muslim Allah, nor is it the New Testament God, either the Father or the Son. Of course, there are the odd passages in the New Testament which are always being quoted at us by Hindu apologists or neo-Hindu enthusiasts like Dr Leary. Unfortunately we are now told by the biblical critics that the well-known phrase 'the Kingdom of God is within you'[7] is better translated as 'the Kingdom of God is among you', but there always remain the well-known texts, 'Father, may they be one in us, as you are in me and I am in you'[8] and St Paul's 'I live now not with my own life but with the life of Christ who lives in me',[9] but though this may and does imply an indwelling God, it can scarcely be a synonym for Nature or 'cosmic consciousness' (R. M. Bucke) or the genetic (DNA) code. Even the most extreme latitudinarians in the field of comparative mysticism might hesitate to make this last and most extreme identification.

Hinduism, however, is quite unlike the three religions of Semitic origin – Judaism, Christianity, and Islam – for which God is most emphatically *not* Nature or any of Nature's manifestations whether it be an *élan vital* (Bergson), the 'throes of matter' (Marx–Engels),[1] evolution, or the genetic code. It has room

---

6. Ibid., p. 164.   7. Luke 17:21.   8. John 17:21.
9. Galatians 2:20.
1. See R. C. Zaehner, *Dialectical Christianity and Christian Materialism* (Oxford University Press, London, 1971), p. 3 and *passim*.

enough for the pantheism of the Upanishads (which, as we have seen, *is* closely akin to nature mysticism and to psychedelic experiences, which often resemble it), for the theism of the *Bhagavad-Gītā*, the ecstatic cults rendered to both the great gods, Shiva and Vishnu, and for the atheistic (or 'transtheistic', as some people prefer to call it) dualism of the classical Sānkhya. All these are regarded by the Hindus as legitimate manifestations of the Supreme Being. When all is said and done what you believe about the Godhead is of little importance: it is the experience of it that matters and the manner in which you interpret that experience. As Dr Leary says:

'It depends on what you mean by religion. For almost everyone, the LSD experience is a confrontation with new forms of wisdom and energy that dwarf and humiliate man's mind. This experience of awe and revelation is often described as religious. I consider my work basically religious, because it has as its goal the systematic expansion of consciousness and the discovery of energies within, which men call "divine". From the psychedelic point of view, almost all religions are attempts ... to discover the inner potential. Well, LSD is Western yoga. The aim of all Eastern religion, like the aim of LSD, is basically to get high: that is, to expand your consciousness and find ecstasy and revelation within.'[2]

This is the kind of irritating generalization that amateurs of Eastern religions all too frequently indulge in. Dr Leary himself knows that the early Buddhists, so far from wanting to expand their consciousness into cosmic consciousness, wanted to be done with the ever-changing cosmos for ever: they were interested solely in bringing the whole dreary process of birth and death, re-birth and re-death, once and for all to a close. In his own inimitable way he says: 'There are two ways out of the basic philosophic isolation of man: you can ball your way out – by having children, which is immortality of a sort. Or you can step off the wheel. Buddhism ... says essentially that.' That is not, however, the Leary way. 'My choice', he says, 'is to keep the life game going. I'm Hindu, not Buddhist.'[3] He is, in fact, a typical vitalist so deeply deplored by Professor Monod. For him 'religion is ecstasy.

2. T. Leary, op. cit., pp. 112–13.   3. Ibid., p. 130.

It is freedom and harmony.'[4] Among the Eastern religions, then, he is drawn principally to the pantheism developed in ancient India by the authors of the Upanishads and to Taoism in China. In neither is God as a person relevant. Why, then, does Leary persist in talking about God, which for the average Christian and post-Christian means a personal God who has a will and makes his will known? Again his approach is purely empirical. LSD, he thinks, lays bare layer after layer of consciousness normally unsuspected by our ordinary everyday ego. Hence he can say without absurdity: 'The real trip is the God trip.' God in his sense is very real to him since he regards himself as being priest and prophet of a religious movement: he claims to have experienced God and, like any other prophet, thinks it his duty to proclaim him. 'I can teach you to find God', he says. 'I can teach you methods; that's my profession. To talk to God yourself, you are going to have to throw away all your definitions and just surrender to this process, and then you can come back and try to tune in and develop an art form which will communicate your vision. God does exist and is to me this energy process; the language of God is the DNA code. Beyond that, the language of God is the atom. Above that, the language of God is the exquisite, carefully worked out dialogue of the planets and the galaxies, etc. And it does exist and there is an intelligence and there is a planfulness and a wisdom and power that you can tune in to. Men have called this process, for lack of a better word, "God".'

The 'language of God': would not this be in Greek *logos theou*, the 'Word of God' with which we are all familiar from the prologue to the Gospel according to St John? Oddly enough Leary seems to be talking about what St Paul was talking about in his Epistle to the Colossians (1:15–17):

> He is the image of the unseen God
> and the first-born of all creation,
> for in him were created
> all things in heaven and on earth:
> everything visible and everything invisible,
> Thrones, Dominations, Sovereignties, Powers –
> all things were created through him and for him.

4. Ibid., p. 223.

> Before anything was created, he existed,
> and he holds all things in unity.

So too in the Epistle to the Hebrews (1:2-3) we read that it was through his 'Son' that God 'made everything there is', and that 'he is the radiant light of God's glory and the perfect copy of his nature, sustaining the universe by his powerful command'. This is surely what Leary means when he says that 'there is an intelligence and there is a planfulness and a wisdom and power that you can tune in to'. This is religious language by any standard, whether Eastern or Western.

No doubt many Christian eyebrows will be raised at this point. St Paul and Dr Leary: Christ and the DNA code! Well, you have to discount a lot of what Dr Leary says. All this talk about the genetic code, the nucleus of the atom, the galaxies, and so on, may seem a little far-fetched and – after Professor Monod – old-fashioned, but sometimes Leary reads almost like Teilhard de Chardin whom he describes as 'the great Jesuit philosopher [who] has spelled out the psychedelic vision in which the world will become unified in one field of consciousness'.[5] Teilhard, no doubt, is a good deal more precise since he makes a clear distinction between two types of mystical 'unity' – 'a unity at the base, by dissolution' and 'a unity at the top, by ultra-differentiation' to which we shall have to return. And, of course, Teilhard had never, so far as is known, taken psychedelic drugs; but there *is* a kinship between much of Teilhard's writings and some recorded psychedelic experiences. In both, as also in the nature mystics, God is seen as the principle of the interconnectedness of all things, the timeless manifesting itself in time, the spaceless in space, and, for Leary as for Whitman, the sexless, beyond sex and all sexuality, made known in sexuality itself.

All this is a far cry from orthodox Christianity, whether Protestant or Catholic, but Dr Leary is right when he adds that when he was at Harvard 'God' was a dirty word. This is true in the sense that to the dechristianized young the word 'God' has so little meaning that they simply stop listening once the word is uttered. Call him Omega Point, as Teilhard did, or even 'evolution'

5. Ibid., p. 217.

or the DNA code, and it is conceivable that boredom may turn into a mild interest. This obvious fact of modern life seems still largely to have escaped the notice of our priests, pastors, and theologians. It did not escape Bonhoeffer who wrote from prison what I suspect most Christians (if they are not completely submerged and congealed in an 'imbecile' conformism) must, if and when they are honest with themselves, feel in their heart of hearts:

'I often ask myself why a "Christian instinct" often draws me more to the religionless people than to the religious, by which I don't in the least mean with any evangelizing intention, but I might almost say, in "brotherhood". While I'm often reluctant to mention God by name to religious people – because that name somehow seems to me here not to ring true, and I feel myself to be slightly dishonest (it's particularly bad when others start to talk in religious jargon; I then dry up almost completely and feel awkward and uncomfortable) – to people with no religion I can on occasion mention him by name quite calmly and as a matter of course.'[6]

Notice the qualification 'on occasion'. Bonhoeffer, like Pope John XXIII, could make contact with the religionless majority because he was transparently good. Because he became increasingly estranged from the religious scribes and Pharisees of his day, he found all discourse with them nauseatingly irrelevant and inept.

'Religious people', he wrote, 'speak of God when human knowledge (perhaps simply because they are too lazy to think) has come to an end, or when human resources fail – in fact it is always the *deus ex machina* they bring on to the scene, either for the apparent solution of insoluble problems, or as strength in human failure – always, that is to say, exploiting human weakness or human boundaries. Of necessity, that can go on only till people can by their own strength push these boundaries somewhat further out, so that God becomes superfluous [even] as a *deus ex machina*.'[7]

Unfortunately, the God of German theology has become wholly superfluous to anyone but the theologians themselves. The younger generation, in America at least, is looking for another God – the God within – and some of them have found him in what they have

6. D. Bonhoeffer, *Letters and Papers from Prison*, p. 281.
7. Ibid., pp. 281–2.

experienced under psychedelic drugs and Eastern mysticism at third hand. Is it, then, entirely Leary's fault that it took him five years of taking LSD before he could say the word 'God' out loud? This, he says, is 'because you have to feel right to say it, and I feel very comfortable now in saying that I do talk to God and I listen to him'. And the God he talks to 'is a hipster, he is a musician, and he's got a great beat going. You'll never find him in an institution or in an American television stage set. He's never legal! [Rome, please note.] And he's got a great sense of humour.'[8]

Dr Leary can be irritating, but his denunciation of the bankruptcy of the 'Protestant work culture'[9] is echoed by so staunch a Protestant as Bonhoeffer himself, who also aspired after 'wholeness'.[1] Since the Lord God of Israel, who has for so long darkened the American scene, has proved superfluous, the 'other God' must be found. Whether the 'doors of perception' are opened by more traditional means or by LSD and other psychedelic drugs, the result is the same, and the result is, according to Leary, direct *religious* experience of the eternal being that pervades all that is ephemeral and transient. Where there is no lived experience, there is no living religion, let alone a *living* God whom the Christian scribes are forever preaching to amusedly incredulous ears. Without evidence of the experience of this supposedly living God which LSD can supply if appropriately administered, nobody is going to believe them. That apparently rules out Billy Graham[2] and all Evangelicals, but not the Catholic Mass, which he thinks is at least a symbol of LSD experience though few Catholics may be aware that this is so.

As we have seen, what Dr Leary understands by religion is basically the same as nature mysticism with a strong dose of sex added. On to this basically pantheistic experience he superimposes a good deal of semi-digested Hinduism and biological science. He has strayed very far from the postulate of objectivity so dear to Professor Monod and is quite as subjectively biased as any religious fundamentalist. This is a pity since it bedevils yet further the already rather hysterical controversy about the religious poten-

8. T. Leary, op. cit., pp. 223-4. 9. Ibid., p. 241.
1. D. Bonhoeffer, op. cit., p. 200. 2. T. Leary, op. cit., p. 249.

tialities of the psychedelic drugs. In an admirably well-balanced book, *The Varieties of Psychedelic Experience*, the authors, R. E. L. Masters and Jean Houston, after some mild and probably deserved criticism of the present author, draw attention to this danger which they sum up in these words: 'The leap out of the "games" and everyday "roles" of Western reality is usually into a nebulous chaos seen as Eastern "truth".'[3] Without mentioning Leary by name, since until he defied the laws against the use of psychedelic drugs promulgated in the United States in 1966, he was a respected member of a group of objective researchers into this vexed psychedelic problem, Masters and Houston go on to say:

'To at least some extent the responsibility for this seduction of the innocent must lie with such authors as Huxley, Alan Watts, and others who in their various writings imposed upon the psychedelic experience essentially Eastern ideas and terminology which a great many persons then assumed to be the sole and accurate way of approaching and interpreting such experience. Armed with such terminology and ideation, depersonalization is mistranslated into the Body of Bliss, empathy or pseudo-empathy becomes a Mystic Union, and spectacular visual effects are hailed as the Clear Light of the Void.'

This criticism is eminently sane and true. Mystical experiences are notoriously hard to put into words, and it is only natural that the mystic will interpret his experience in accordance with the religion or ideology in which he has been brought up. St Teresa, for instance, had 'intellectual' visions of the Trinity. This is not surprising since this was a doctrine with which she had been familiar all her life. It would be surprising indeed if such 'intellectual' visions were recorded by Muslim mystics: to the best of my knowledge they are not. Ibn 'Arabī, the great Andalusian Muslim mystic of the twelfth century, had a vision of Muhammad, but this was an 'ocular' vision rather than an 'intellectual' one and does not then come strictly within the category of the 'mystical' since visions, though they are attested in all religious mystical

---

3. R. E. L. Masters and Jean Houston, *The Varieties of Psychedelic Experience* (Anthony Blond, London, and Holt, Rinehart and Winston, New York, 1966), p. 260.

traditions, do not form part of the mystical experience itself and are indeed regarded by all the traditions as being snares on the way. An 'intellectual' vision, on the other hand, is rather a contemplative insight into what is taken to be Reality beyond space and time and causation, often referred to by the Christian mystics as 'infused contemplation'.

The 'conditioning' of religious mystics by their dogmatic beliefs, however, is a more complicated problem than is usually supposed, since the dogmas of any given religion are, from the exoteric point of view, already distorted by the mystic. The mainstream of Christian mysticism, for instance, is probably more influenced by Neo-Platonism and Pseudo-Dionysius (himself a Neo-Platonist whose writings only gained authority through his identification with the Dionysius the Areopagite converted by St Paul) than it is by anything in the New Testament; and Muslim mysticism in its early stages owed more to the Christian mysticism that preceded it in the Near East than it did to anything in the Koran. Indian and Neo-Platonist ideas were to invade it later to such an extent that, though the framework remained Islamic, the content retained almost nothing of orthodox Islam.

Moreover, the religious mystics are not usually describing individual personal experiences. These, no doubt, will influence what they have to say, but their works, with very rare exceptions, are not 'stories of my heart' (the obvious exceptions are Augustine, Heinrich Suso, and Teresa herself), rather they take the form of sermons, treatises, or commentaries on scripture – very often on the Song of Songs or in the case of the Hindus on the *Brahmasūtras* or the *Bhagavad-Gītā*. Moreover, for them mysticism is a way of life – a 'path' leading from this world to the eternal world – to God or an impersonal Absolute. The nature mystics, on the other hand, and the users of psychedelic drugs, rely for the most part on experiences of short duration – what the Muslims call *hālāt* – sudden flashes of illumination as opposed to the *maqāmāt*, the stages on the way of love and knowledge towards union (*tawhīd*). Any comparison between drug-induced mystical experience and the religious mystical traditions is therefore bound to be extremely

Mysticism and LSD

hazardous; for just as there are 'varieties of religious experience' and 'varieties of psychedelic experience', so there are 'varieties of mystical experience' as any attentive reader of my earlier book, *Mysticism Sacred and Profane*,[4] and my more recent *Concordant Discord*[5] will necessarily recognize unless he is prepared to equate the sexual pantheism of Whitman with the world-rejecting dualism of spirit and matter of the early Buddhists. It is, then, deplorable that a reputed authority on comparative religion and the history of religions, Professor Huston Smith of M.I.T., should be able to write with evident satisfaction that 'when the current philosophical authority on mysticism, W. T. Stace, was asked whether *the*[6] drug experience is similar to *the*[7] mystical experience, he answered, "It's not a matter of its being *similar*[8] to mystical experience; it *is*[9] mystical experience." '[1]

The only conclusion one can draw from this statement of Professor Stace is that neither he nor Professor Huston Smith have any conception of the *interreligious* dimension of the problem. 'Why do people reject evidence?' asks Huston Smith. To which one can only reply: 'Why do people *select* evidence?' The reply in both cases is given by Charles Péguy: 'A learned fool is a worse fool than an ignorant one.'[2] The worst fool of all, one might add, is the learned fool who is also ignorant.

It should, however, be noted with relief that whereas these two learned American professors adhere to the dictum of yet another professor (A. J. Arberry) that 'it has become a platitude to observe that mysticism is essentially one and the same, whatever may be the religion professed by the individual mystic',[3] those admirable and balanced investigators into the whole phenomenon of psychedelic drugs, R. E. L. Masters and Jean Houston, recognize that just as there are varieties of psychedelic experience, so there are varieties of mystical experience. To his credit Dr Leary realized this too,

4. Clarendon Press, Oxford, 1957.   5. Clarendon Press, Oxford, 1970.
6. My italics.   7. My italics.
8. Huston Smith's (or Stace's) italics.   9. Huston Smith's (or Stace's) italics.
1. Huston Smith, 'Do Drugs have religious import?', in *The Journal of Philosophy*, Vol. lxi, No. 18, 1964, pp. 523-4.
2. Charles Péguy, *Oeuvres en prose, 1909-1914* (Bibliothèque de la Pléiade, Gallimard, Paris, 1957), p. 394.
3. A. J. Arberry, *Sufism* (Allen & Unwin, London, 1950), p. 11.

otherwise he would not have described himself as a Hindu, not a Buddhist.

Of course Hinduism itself is not by any means free from dogmas and ideology; but the dogmas and ideologies are broadly based on sacred writings that are still in a state of ideological flux. The dominant 'flavour' of the Upanishads is pantheistic ('All is One', 'I am Brahman', etc.), but even within the Upanishads themselves there is a trend towards theism which exalts 'God' above both the sum-total of the universe and the individual soul seen as timeless, and also a trend towards pure monism which denies all reality except to the One, the Absolute. Both trends derive from the same pantheistic vision which is essentially the vision of the nature mystics of whom both Richard Jefferies and Walt Whitman are typical. Hence the importance of the Upanishads as raw material for 'spontaneous' mysticism. Perhaps the 'charter' of all pantheisms (and this includes the psychedelic variety too) is to be found in the *Ishā* Upanishad, 6-7:

> Those who see all beings in the Self,
> And the Self in all beings
> Will never shrink from it.
>
> When once one understands that in oneself
> The Self's become all beings,
> When once one's seen the unity,
> What room is there for sorrow? What room for perplexity?

To somebody who has never had even an intimation of what a mystical experience might be these words will be meaningless, but anyone who has had a spontaneous experience of nature mysticism will immediately understand their import. Unfortunately in the normal course of events these experiences which are almost invariably accompanied by a sense of exultant joy are impossible to recapture: they are what the Muslims call *hālāt*, not *maqāmāt*. In India, however, techniques were developed called Yoga the purpose of which was to enable anyone who was prepared to make the effort to reach this pantheistic vision of his own accord – and, in the classical Yoga, to pass beyond it into an isolation of pure spirit from all that conditions the phenomenal world. But this involves a great deal of time, a great deal of concentration, and unremitting effort; and this is quite as true of Zen as it is of the Hindu Yoga. This the *Bhagavad-Gītā* (7.3) makes quite clear when it says: 'Among thousands of men but one, maybe, will strive for self-perfection; and even among those who have won perfection, but one, maybe, will know Me as I really am.' ('Me' in the context refers to Krishna, the incarnate God, who is the teacher in this wonderful dialogue.) So too a modern Zen master, Abbot Zenkei Shibayama, speaks in a similar vein: 'It may not be difficult to *talk about* this experience of awakening to "Self-nature" or "True Self" which we have deep at the bottom of our personalities, but to come to this realization experientially as the fact of one's own actual experience, is not easy at all. It is so very difficult that it cannot be easily attained by ordinary people.'[4]

Huxley, Leary, and Masters and Houston have all claimed that LSD and similar drugs cause chemical changes in the body closely akin to those produced by ascetic practices. 'For the sake of achieving this integral knowledge', Masters and Houston write, 'men have willingly submitted themselves to elaborate ascetic procedures and have trained for years to laboriously master Yoga and meditation techniques. They have practised fasting, flagellation, and sensory deprivation, and, in so doing, may have attained to states of heightened mystical consciousness, but also have succeeded in altering their body chemistry. Recent physiological investigations of these practices in a laboratory setting tend to confirm the notion that provoked alterations in body chemistry and body rhythm are in no small way responsible for the dramatic changes in consciousness attendant upon these practices. The askesis or ascetic discipline of fasting, for example, makes for vitamin and sugar deficiencies which act to lower the efficiency of what Huxley calls the cerebral reducing valve.'[5]

So be it. But it is perhaps worth making two points here. First, the greatest masters of the spiritual life in India, the Buddha and the author or authors of the *Bhagavad-Gītā*, were strongly opposed to ascetic excesses which, in India, have always been associated

---

4. Abbot Zenkei Shibayama, *A Flower Does Not Talk* (Charles E. Tuttle, Tokyo, 1970), p. 105.
5. R. E. L. Masters and Jean Houston, op. cit., p. 248.

with the attainment of magical powers. According to the Buddhist legend Siddhartha, the Buddha-to-be, after he had wandered forth from his princely palace to adopt a homeless life in search of enlightenment submitted himself to relentless deprivation and self-torture – but to no avail, and it was only after he had come to terms with his body again and begun to eat normally though frugally that he finally attained enlightenment. Similarly the *Gītā* warns against ascetical excess: 'Yoga is not for him who eats too much nor yet for him who does not eat at all, nor for him who is all too prone to sleep, nor yet for him who always stays awake. Rather Yoga is for him who is moderate in food and recreation, controlled in his deeds and gestures, moderate in sleeping as in waking.'[6]

Of course in all religions you will find mystical enthusiasts who think that by torturing the body you can liberate the spirit. In Christianity (the religion of the Word made flesh!) there is a whole galaxy of them, but the most notorious were not the most successful mystics. The hallucinations of St Anthony are of course famous but we know little of his mystical insights, while St Simeon Stylites, perched on his idiotic pillar, was probably far more interested in spiritual status than anything else. Similar extremists are to be found among the Sufis, notably Abu Sa'īd ibn Abi'l-Khayr whose recorded self-mortifications would have satisfied even the most extreme of the Hindu ascetics; and the Sufi path is strewn not only with ascetic experts but with a whole galaxy of spiritual snobs. This, however, is not the 'middle way' of the Buddha, the *Gītā*, the Sufi path of 'sobriety', or the mainstream of Christian mysticism from St Augustine to St François de Sales.

In this connection it should be remarked *secondly* that the mortification – the 'making dead' – of the body must be seen as a preparation for the liberation or 'second birth' of the soul, the extinction of life (Nirvana, 'blowing out') being the necessary condition of eternal Being. '*Mūtū qabl an tamūtū*', 'Die before you die', as a (certainly spurious) Muhammadan tradition tells us.

It would, however, be foolish to deny that ascetic excess *has* been practised in the mystical traditions of all religions, but it is a

6. *Bhagavad-Gītā*, 6. 16–17.

fringe activity. It aims at making contact with the eternal experienced either as an impersonal Absolute or as the highly personal ravisher of the soul, but it may result in nothing more than either 'holy' or devilish apparitions, both of which, according to both Zen and St Teresa, should be rejected with contempt. Seeing visions of Christ or the Virgin or Muhammad or the Buddha or Shiva or Krishna have nothing to do with what Christians call the 'spiritual marriage' or what Muslims call union, and it is saddening to think that two so perceptive and balanced authors as Masters and Houston should accuse the present author of 'suppressing the evidence of drug-induced theistic mysticism'.[7] This misses the point entirely. Visions of Christ reported of members of the Native American Church are presumably visions of Jesus of Nazareth, rather like Ibn 'Arabī's vision of Muhammad: they have nothing to do with the spiritual marriage of the soul with Christ as God.

It would be pointless at this stage to discuss in detail the varieties of mystical experience, since I have recently done so at great length in my book *Concordant Discord* (pp. 40–171, 194–322), to which the reader is referred should he have the time to spare and the inclination to wander further in this labyrinth. Let us assume, for the moment, that psychedelic drugs can produce every and any kind of mystical experience from the fleshly pantheism of Whitman to the still, silent timelessness of the Buddhist Nirvana and the intellectual rapture of St Augustine and his mother at their window in Ostia in which they rose not only above all sensory things but even above their own souls in their hushed contemplation of eternal Wisdom.

Psychedelic experience, Dr Leary insists, is essentially religious, and it *can* be induced by LSD, given the right 'set and setting', that is, a friendly environment, sympathetic company, and a qualified and experienced 'guide' to see you through the psychedelic game of snakes and ladders. In the past such experiences were reserved for the spiritual athletes of this world alone: now they are available for the ordinary man and particularly for the ordinary teenager. If this is indeed true, then why all this opposi-

7. Masters and Houston, op. cit., p. 257.

tion from worthy people, both Christian and Zen, who claim to be religious?

It would seem, however, that opposition to the use of drugs to produce ecstatic experiences has deeper roots than are to be found in any specific religious denomination. Its roots are in man himself who is instinctively, if irrationally, scared that science and technology, of which the use of synthetic psychedelic drugs forms part, threaten not only his body but also – and far more important as Professor Monod has pointed out – his very soul. It is the reaction of anyone who still has some roots, however attenuated, in nature against a 'civilization' becoming every day more dehumanized, of which the United States of (North) America is not only the symbol but the reality. It is the instinctive reaction of the youth of America itself which now seems to be turning its back on 'synthetic' religion in favour of the more deeply-rooted American tradition of revivalism. It is the reaction of the man who is both spiritually and physically unhappy in a 'canned' society, who prefers fresh food to the canned and tasteless horrors in which the American bourgeoisie rejoices, who prefers not to be roasted in over-heated rooms in winter and frozen in air-conditioned ones in summer. For such a man the American way of life is, as Richard Jefferies would say, 'anti- or ultra-human, outside, and has no concern with man'.[8] For such a man the psychedelic trip, however well conducted, however cosy the 'set and setting', can only appear as an extension of soulless technology to the soul itself. Canned food, canned houses, canned music, and now canned mysticism stimulated by canned music (usually Bach for some totally inscrutable reason). Of course, this reaction is irrational, but it is deep-seated. There are still men left – not all of them teenagers – who would prefer to be men rather than ecstatic angels in a machine. They are probably at one with Dr Leary in his condemnation of American culture as 'an insane asylum'[9] and an 'air-conditioned anthill',[1] at one with him and Masters and Houston in their suspicion of much that goes by the name of psychology and psychiatry, but they remain convinced that psychedelic drugs are themselves part and

---

8. R. Jefferies, *The Story of my Heart*, p. 48.
9. T. Leary, op. cit., p. 241.   1. Ibid., p. 198.

parcel of the machine society from which Dr Leary and his friends pretend to be delivering them.

There is no need to waste time on the psychiatrists who oppose the wonder-drug, since its sometimes successful use in the treatment of mental illness threatens to price them out of the market. Let us turn to the more strictly religious establishment.

The Christian attitude and particularly the Protestant one is readily understood since the apostles of LSD dismiss them as not being religious at all: they *preach* the living God but quite obviously experience nothing even remotely alive. Nor can Protestants be particularly pleased to have their money-based 'work culture' dismissed by Dr Leary along with the professional bureaucracy as an essential ingredient in the 'insane asylum' which is modern America. 'Orthodox' Protestantism, moreover, whether Lutheran, Calvinist, or Episcopalian, is traditionally suspicious of mysticism of any kind, and the late Hendrik Kraemer, who had spent many years of his life spreading the 'Good News' in the mystical East, was not untypical of 'biblical realism' when he said: 'The mystic who triumphantly realizes his essential oneness with God, or the World-Order, or the Divine, knowing himself in serene equanimity the supreme master of the universe and of his own destiny, and who by marvellous feats of moral self-restraint offers a fascinating example of splendid humanity . . ., nevertheless, in the light of Biblical revelation, commits in this sublime way the root-sin of mankind – "to be like God". In other words: *he repeats the Fall.*'[2]

It is doubtful whether Dr Kraemer ever knew of the advance of the psychedelic cult. Had he done so, he would no doubt have welcomed it, if for no other reason than that, from the point of view of 'biblical realism', it was the *reductio ad absurdum* of *all* mysticism. It not only commits the root-sin of mankind – 'to be like God' – and thereby repeats the Fall, but it does so on the cheap.

Between this kind of Protestantism and mysticism of any kind there is a gulf fixed. Persons with a mystical temperament on the other hand simply do not understand what is meant by 'biblical

2. Hendrik Kraemer, *Religion and Christian Faith* (Lutterworth, London, 1956), p. 335.

faith' unless it be a terror of any direct experience of the divine which might short-cut all 'biblical' revelations – Old Testament, New Testament, *and the Koran*, which Islam, the most 'biblical' of all religions, regards as the Word of God made Book (*biblos*). Christians, however, do not greatly relish discussion on the Muslim 'Book', since it claims both to fulfil and abrogate their own. Faith in the one is pitted against faith in the other. Here there is no room for argument. As the Koran itself says: '[Only] God shall decide between them on the Day of Resurrection touching their differences.'[3] Mysticism, it is true, tends to blur differences, and no Western religious establishment likes that.

From the Christian side, both Protestant and Catholic, there is another reason for suspecting non-Christian mysticism – and also some forms of heretical Christian mysticism like that of the Brethren of the Free Spirit in the late Middle Ages – and that is that they are for ever speaking of a state which is beyond good and evil, right and wrong, and this concept is sometimes taken up by their psychedelic would-be imitators. There is no doubt at all that they *do* do this and anyone who cares to inspect the evidence can easily do so by looking up the entries on 'good and evil' and 'right and wrong' in my book, *Concordant Discord*. But here we are on singularly tricky ground for the Semitic God, both in the Old Testament and the Koran, is plainly responsible for evil as well as good. This very awkward fact we shall have to discuss in a later chapter.

For the Catholics Leary, like Jung, has a soft spot. His reasons, like Jung's, will seem bizarre to many, but as usual it all boils down to experience. The Catholics at least have their Mass which should be 'an incredibly powerful psychedelic trip, involving transubstantiation of energy, involving a birth-death sequence, and using all sorts of sensory techniques', but 'these early sacramental methods get worn out and routinized'.[4] And this, Dr Leary thinks, is where LSD can help us out. Hence one of his psychedelic celebrations 'was based on the life of Christ, and we used the Catholic missal as the manual for that'.[5] This should be unneces-

3. Koran, 2.107 (Arberry's translation).   4. T. Leary, op. cit., p. 211.
5. Ibid., p. 239.

sary since the Catholic host should give you a direct *experience* of God made man. As he says: 'The Catholic host should indeed give you a kick. LSD will give you a kick.' And to lessen the shock he adds: 'The kick means to me an ecstatic revelation ... A kick to me means flirtation – confrontation – with God.'[6] This is a perfectly fair account of Christian mysticism: it is the soul's love-affair with God and its spiritual marriage to him. It is not a merging into the All as so often in the Upanishads or with the nature mystics, nor is it the isolation of one's own eternal essence from all that is other than itself as in the Sānkhya-Yoga in India. Nor does it seem to have anything to do with the DNA code, or evolution in general. After all there are 'kicks' and 'kicks', and the Catholic's 'kick' is his participating in the Eternal breaking into time in the form of the flesh and blood of the God-man miraculously transformed into bread and wine. Unfortunately the reception of Holy Communion only rarely produces 'kicks' of this kind, whereas LSD can – if it doesn't give you a taste of hell. But as Dr Leary rightly says: 'At the present time, man is so sick that there are very few people who can use these ancient methods' – of breath-control, fasting, flagellation, solitude, diet, and so on – 'so that today it is safe to say that drugs are the specific, and almost the only, way that the American is ever going to have a religious experience.'[7]

What Dr Leary is in fact saying is that American Protestantism with its formal preaching and censorious ethic never was a religion, at least as he understands the word, since it is not even interested in experience of the divine, whereas the Catholic Mass, although it ideally should be the place of meeting between man and God, the temporal and the eternal, no longer has the intended effect. The salt has lost its savour. Both branches of institutional Christianity, therefore, stand condemned, not so much because they are not true as because they do not work. The Protestants never had the mystical goods to deliver which Dr Leary expects religion to supply: the Catholics have them but they are now so stale as to be of little or no use.

And now, for fear of once again being accused of suppressing

6. Ibid., p. 242.   7. Ibid., p. 241.

evidence, I cannot refrain from discussing what appears to be known in psychedelic circles as 'The Miracle of Marsh Chapel'.[8] This was conducted by a Dr Walter N. Pahnke on Good Friday in 1962 and has been described by him both in a symposium edited by Richard C. DeBold and Russell C. Leaf, entitled, *LSD, Man & Society*,[9] and in a similar symposium edited by Bernard Aaronson and Humphrey Osmond entitled *Psychedelics*.[1] The experiment was carried out in order to test the hypothesis that persons who were given psilocybin would have experiences resembling those reported by 'spontaneous' mystics. It is odd that Dr Pahnke should have confined himself to 'spontaneous' mystics, that is to say, mystics like R. M. Bucke and those quoted by William James in his *The Varieties of Religious Experience* on whom he heavily relies, and should have disregarded the specifically *religious* mystical traditions. This, however, was not his fault but that of his religious advisers. However, before we return to them, let us first give the 'set and setting' of the experiment.

Twenty theological students from middle-class Protestant backgrounds 'were carefully prepared in groups of four with two leaders for each group. All thirty participants listened over loudspeakers to a meditative Good Friday service in a private basement chapel, while the actual service was in progress in the church above. The experiment was so designed that half of the subjects received 30 mg of psilocybin' (the effects of which are similar to LSD) 'and the rest, who became the control group, got as an active placebo 200 mg of nicotinic acid, which causes no psychic effects, only warmth and tingling of the skin. From our preparation all the subjects knew that psilocybin caused autonomic changes. Those who got nicotinic acid thought that they had received psilocybin, and suggestion was thus maximized for the control group. The drugs were administered double-blind, so that neither the experimenter nor the participants knew the specific contents of any capsule.'[2] The students had been carefully prepared beforehand,

8. Masters and Houston, op. cit., p. 253.
9. Faber & Faber, London, 1969, and Wesleyan University Press, Middletown, 1967.
1. Hogarth Press, London, and Doubleday, New York, 1971.
2. DeBold and Leaf, op. cit., pp. 66–7.

and this 'preparation was meant to maximize positive expectation, trust, confidence, and reduction of fear. The setting was planned to utilize this preparation through group support and rapport; through friendship and an open, trusting atmosphere; and through prior knowledge of the procedure of the experiment in order to eliminate, if possible, feelings of manipulation that might arise.'[3]

A typology of spontaneous mysticism had been compiled based largely on the work of W. T. Stace. According to this typology spontaneous mystical experience is characterized by nine main features. These are:

1. *Unity*: which may be either external or internal.

(a) *External*: a sense of cosmic oneness in which all distinction between subject and object seems to fade away. 'The subject feels a sense of oneness with [external] objects because he "sees" that at the most basic level all are a part of the same undifferentiated unity.' 'All is One.' This is what Bucke called 'cosmic consciousness' and Freud the 'oceanic feeling'.

(b) *Internal*: 'Although the usual sense of identity or ego fades away, consciousness and memory are not lost.' 'In the most complete experience, this consciousness is a pure awareness beyond empirical content, with no external or internal distinctions.' This is the experience of undifferentiated unity which may be interpreted as identity with the Absolute: the 'I am Brahman' of the Upanishads, the 'I am the Truth (*al-haqq*) or God' of Al-Hallāj, the famous Muslim mystic who was crucified in 922 A.D. for what were considered his blasphemous utterances. Alternatively it may be interpreted as the realization of the undifferentiated unity of one's own soul beyond space and time as is the case in the Indian Sānkhya system in which the mystic's goal is the 'isolation' of the individual soul from matter (which includes mind, intellect and will) and from all other souls. This is a timeless condition. In the Yoga system of philosophy which admits the existence of a personal God who keeps the universe in being as well as of an infinite number of distinct and individual timeless souls, this state of 'isolation' means also isolation from God. The Sufis (Muslim mystics) refer to this as *ifrād*, 'isolation' again; and the patron

3. Aaronson and Osmond, op. cit., pp. 152–3.

saint of all subsequent 'orthodox' and 'sober' Sufis, the tenth-century Al-Junayd of Baghdad, calls this 'the ground of one's finite roots'.[4] On this subject Martin Buber is perhaps more revealing than anyone. This is what he says:

'Now from my own unforgettable experience I know well that there is a state in which the bonds of the personal nature of life seem to have fallen away from us and we experience an undivided unity. But I do not know – what the soul willingly imagines and indeed is bound to imagine (mine too once did it) – that in this I had attained to a union with the primal being or the godhead. This is an exaggeration no longer permitted to the responsible understanding. Responsibly – that is, as a man holding his ground before reality – I can elicit from those experiences only that in them I reached an indifferentiable unity of myself without form or content. I may call this an original pre-biographical unity and suppose that it is hidden unchanged beneath all biographical change, all development and complication of the soul. Nevertheless, in the honest and sober account of the responsible understanding this unity is nothing but the unity of this soul of mine, whose "ground" I have reached, so much so that, beneath all formations and contents, my spirit has no choice but to understand it as the groundless. But the basic unity of my own soul is certainly beyond the reach of all the multiplicity it has hitherto received from life, though not in the least beyond individuation, or the multiplicity of all the souls of the world of which it is one – existing but once, single, unique, irreducible, this creaturely one: one of the human souls and not the "Soul of the All"; a defined and particular being and not "Being".'[5]

This passage from Buber is of extreme importance for any study of mysticism since it shows that this experience of absolute oneness must at first sight appear like the realization of one's own identity with absolute Being, so overwhelming is the sense of absolute unity. That Buber should have come to see that it was false cannot be explained by the fact that he was a Jew (since nobody in Israel

4. See R. C. Zaehner, *Hindu and Muslim Mysticism* (Athlone Press, London, 1960), p. 122.
5. Martin Buber, *Between Man and Man* (Routledge & Kegan Paul, London, 1947), p. 24–5.

was likely to persecute him for heresy!) but by the fact that he had long pondered on the experience and decided in favour of what in India would be a Sānkhya position, not one of absolute monism or non-dualism (*advaita*) as the Hindus prefer to call it. Stace prefers to dismiss Buber's later interpretation of his experience in these words: 'There can be, I surmise, little doubt that the environmental pressure of the culture to which he belongs was basic cause of a change of mind which quite obviously went against the grain of his own more spontaneous feelings.'[6] This merely means that Stace thinks himself better qualified to interpret Buber's experience than Buber himself. It would be neither more nor less silly to say: 'There can be, I surmise, little doubt that the environmental pressure of the culture to which Stace belongs impels him to a monistic rather than a pluralistic or theistic interpretation.' We shall have more to say about Stace. Meanwhile let us pass on to Pahnke's second category.

2. *Transcendence of time and space*: the subject passes into 'a realm of eternity or infinity'. This is very common and is rarely dissociated from the category of unity in some shape or form.

3. *Deeply felt positive mood*: this 'contains the elements of joy, blessedness, peace and love to an overwhelming degree of intensity'. The epitome of this is surely Pascal's: '*Joie, joie, joie, pleurs de joie*' – 'Joy, joy, joy, tears of joy.'

This category might well have been further subdivided. Joy, blessedness, peace, and love are very far from being interchangeable terms: any of them may be present without the other.

4. *Sense of sacredness*: 'a non-rational, intuitive, hushed, palpitant response of awe and wonder in the presence of inspiring realities.' It is not quite clear how this sense of sacredness (which Rudolf Otto called the 'numinous') is to be distinguished from the equally vague term 'blessedness' which is lumped together with joy, peace, and love in the last category.

5. *The noetic quality*[7] or *Objectivity and Reality*.[8] What this means is that anyone who has had a mystical experience of any

6. W. T. Stace, *Mysticism and Philosophy* (J. B. Lippincote, Philadelphia and New York, 1960), p. 157.
7. So in DeBold and Leaf, op. cit., p. 64.
8. So in Aaronson and Osmond, op. cit., p. 150.

kind – 'natural', psychedelic, or 'religious' – is convinced that the experience is infinitely more real than anything that everyday experience has to offer. The subject *knows* or *sees* that it is and must be true. Like Bucke 'he sees and knows that the Cosmos is not dead matter but a living Presence, that the soul of man is immortal, that the universe is so built and ordered that *without any peradventure*[9] all things work together for the good of each and all, that the foundation principle of the world is what we call love and that the happiness of every one is in the long run absolutely certain.' One *sees* and *knows* all this. Unfortunately, Bucke's seeing and knowing do not agree with those of Richard Jefferies or Proust. The mystical 'certainties' do not always coincide. Pascal was content to say no more than *'Certitude. Certitude'* – 'certainty, certainty.'

6. *Paradoxicality*: what appear to be mutually contradictory propositions do not in this mystical state appear to contradict each other. The classic example of this is perhaps *Ishā* Upanishad, 5:

> It moves. It does not move.
> It is far, yet it is near:
> It is within this whole universe,
> And yet it is without it.

7. *Alleged ineffability*: this means that the mystic cannot put his experience into words that will make any kind of sense to the non-mystic. What at the time seems to him an accurate description of his experience (e.g. 'I am this whole universe') will look very much like madness to someone who has never had a similar experience. This category is obviously practically the same as the foregoing category of paradoxicality.

8. *Transiency*: 'means that the psychedelic peak does not last in its full intensity, but instead passes into an afterglow and remains as a memory.' This is true of what the Muslim mystics call *hālāt*, 'sudden inspirations', but not true of their *maqāmāt*, 'stages' on the mystic path which, once mastered, should remain with one permanently. In Zen this 'peak' experience is called *satori* in Japanese. It is claimed, however, that it can be retained provided one con-

9. My italics.

tinues the spiritual exercises (*zāzen* or 'sitting meditation') one has practised beforehand.

9. *Persisting positive changes in attitudes and behaviour*: 'toward self, others, life and the experience itself.'[1]

In my own analysis of mystical experience, relying mainly on the Indian tradition, I concluded that there were four main types of experience corresponding roughly to Pahnke's categories 1 to 3 (his 4, 'sacredness', adds nothing to the equally vague 'blessedness' of 3). I concluded[2] that in Hinduism four types of mysticism can be distinguished:

1. The transcending of spacial limitations and the consequent feeling that one is the All.

2. The transcending of temporal limitations and the consequent realization that one cannot die.

3. The intuition of oneness outside both space and time in a realm in which there is no becoming, only Being. This state is normally achieved by a process of Yoga – of introspection and integration of all the faculties into a timeless inner core. This is a 'contraction' into the One rather than an 'expansion' into the All. All three experiences invariably bring peace and joy: sometimes they are considered to transcend good and evil. Of love there has hitherto been no hint.

4. The love of God in the context of pure spirituality beyond space and time and beyond the 'One'. In the Hindu tradition this first appears in the *Bhagavad-Gītā*.

My category 4 is totally lacking in Stace's analysis for reasons I have already considered. Significantly it is only very rarely present in LSD experiences, and when it occurs it seems to be a kind of diffused feeling of general benevolence quite unlike the exclusive love that the theistic mystic has for God whose presence and exacting demands are felt with the same or an even greater certainty than some 'spontaneous' mystics feel about the timelessness and placelessness of their experiences. That the two are quite distinct

---

1. All quotations from this section on Pahnke's nine categories are from either DeBold and Leaf, op. cit., or from Aaronson and Osmond, op. cit.
2. *Concordant Discord*, p. 204.

seems too obvious to need stressing. On this subject Masters and Houston are particularly good.

'The psychedelic subject', they stress, 'while rarely a philosopher, psychologist or even a good student of those arts, is nonetheless affected by the *Zeitgeist* and gropes towards a solution of problems dimly or clearly sensed. And a good many subjects seem strongly affected by one of the most influential and popular notions of our time: that "love" is the means whereby man will find himself able to transcend his own singularity and also be able to break through the wall of separateness that encloses the other and makes the other inscrutable and inaccessible to him. . . . Not bothering to define "love" too closely [this idea] exerts its most powerful impact on the young. . . . An easy shortcut to authentic lovingness is strenuously desired. . . . The authors are not . . . opposed to anyone's becoming genuinely imbued with love and tolerance and brotherhood. But experience has taught us the need for assessing the extent to which universal love proclamations are hypocritical, based on neurotic need and wishful thinking, or involve self-deceit and self-delusion with consequent damage to the individual. The delusion that one loves when one does not, but only wishes to, can lead as it sometimes does among those in the Drug Movement to mere indiscriminate associations offered up as proof of loving everyone.'[3]

On the genuineness of LSD love-experiences Masters and Houston are refreshingly more sceptical than most of their colleagues including Pahnke. Their account of an LSD session with a fifty-year-old widow is highly diverting and, though an extreme case, must put the unbiased observer on his guard against these claims to universal love which, it should be stressed again, never even remotely resemble the theistic mystics' descriptions of the outpouring of *God*'s love which, so far from being an experience of general benevolence, can be very painful indeed. Well, here is Masters and Houston's account of this particular session:

'Several hours into the session S fell into a kind of solipsistic reverie in which it seemed to her that nothing existed but herself. She reported that, at the start of this experience, the room became

3. Masters and Houston, op. cit., pp. 122–4.

Mysticism and LSD

misty and persons and objects in the room were seen merely as "thicknesses of mist" – that is, she got rid of them. She then extended her arms in Christ-like imitation and performed a reverent genuflection to herself. After that, she murmured, "I am the universe. I am Love. Love. Love. Love. Love."' Asked to expand a little upon her rapture, she spoke at some length, cataloguing the range and various beneficiaries of her cornucopic feelings. While lamentably this lady's exact words were not preserved, the oration went pretty much like this: ' "Negroes and little fishes, lampshades and vinegar. These I love. Coats and hats and three-ring pretzels. Radios and Russians, bobolinks and tree sap, medicine chests and Freud and the green line down the center of the street on St Patrick's Day, these I love. These I cherish.... Hair spray and Buddha and Krishna Menon. My love overfloweth to all. My nephew – and mushrooms. Red cars, red caps, porters, Martin Luther King, Armenians, Jews, Incas, and John O'Hara. Love. Love. Love. Love. Big yellow Chrysanthemums and the sun and pancakes and Disneyland and Vermont and cinnamon and Alexander the Great. The UN and aluminium foil and apple cider and cigars. Clark Gable, Tony Curtis and salamanders, crochet, the aurora borealis and dimples, mustard plasters and even Mayor Wagner. I am just bursting with joy, with love. I want to give ... Give to all ... Give ... My Love ... To ... All ..."

'And so on. And on. And on. And on.

'No joke or leg pull here, rather – "An effluvium of joy, an efflux of love/wisdom effulgent, effused from Above".'[4]

No doubt even the most extravagant advocate of psychedelic mysticism will find this effusion slightly embarrassing, but on the Stace–Pahnke rating (and even on my own) the good widow scores pretty high. There is plenty of 'unity': 'I am the universe. I am Love.' A rather bad failure, it seems, on transcendence of time and space. Plenty of joy and love, but not much about blessedness or peace. Sense of sacredness? Well, yes: she 'performed a reverent genuflection to herself'. Objectivity and Reality: this does not come through. Paradoxicality and ineffability: very high score, you

4. Ibid., pp. 126–7.

cannot understand a word she says. 'Transiency': in LSD experiences this may be assumed. 'Persisting positive changes': 'There was no subsequent observable change in her behaviour.'

This example shows that no amount of analysis of the mystical experience suffices to determine what is a 'genuine' experience and what is not. In terms of Jung's psychology there is all the difference in the world between what he calls integration of the personality or 'individuation' and what he called 'positive inflation', in which 'the personality becomes so vastly enlarged that the normal ego-personality is almost extinguished. In other words, if the individual identifies himself with the contents awaiting integration, a positive or negative inflation results. Positive inflation comes very near to a more or less conscious megalomania; negative inflation is felt as an annihilation of the ego.'[5] In the present case it is fair to assume that what was experienced was positive inflation since no kind of integration took place afterwards. 'By their fruits shall ye know them', seems to be applicable to religious, spontaneous, and psychedelic mystics alike. Hence the claims the Yogis not infrequently make to omnipotence and omniscience must be treated as cases of positive inflation rather than of Pahnke's category No. 1 ('a sense of cosmic oneness', that is, 'cosmic consciousness'). So too the passage from the *Chāndogya* Upanishad quoted at the end of chapter 2 must be seen not only as an extreme case of cosmic consciousness and a transcendence of space (the ego, the universal Self, and the Infinite are all identified), but also as an example of the most thoroughgoing 'positive inflation'.

The distinction is not easy to make, and even among theistic mystics 'cosmic consciousness' is always liable to break in. Yet, when all is said and done, it would appear that the hall-mark of the 'real thing', whether it is Buddhist enlightenment, Hindu liberation, or Christian-Muslim union with the divine, is a profound sense of humility and gratitude that such marvels can happen to *me*. Even the profoundly cautious Masters and Houston admit that in a very small number of drug cases 'authentic' religious and mys-

5. C. G. Jung, *Collected Works*, Vol. xvi, (Routledge & Kegan Paul, London, and Princeton University Press, Princeton, 1954), p. 262.

tical experiences can occur, but they have no doubt at all that the vast majority of mystical experiences claimed are simply cases of positive or negative inflation caused in all probability by reading the works of such authors as Aldous Huxley, Alan Watts, and, of course, Timothy Leary interpreted in accordance with their syncretistic views. The Zen Buddhists had the same trouble, and the most stringent note of warning was issued by the eleventh-century Muslim mystic Al-Qushayrī. Their combined testimony is impressive. Let us take Masters and Houston first.

'Given this type of misunderstanding', they say, 'it is no wonder that the psychedelic drugs have resulted in a proliferation of "fun" mystics and armchair pilgrims who loudly claim mystical mandates for experiences that are basically nothing more than routine instances of consciousness alteration. The mandate being falsely and shallowly derived, the subsequent spiritual hubris can be horrendous, the subject announcing to whoever will listen that all mystic themes, all religious concepts, all meanings, and all mysteries now are accessible and explainable by virtue of his "cosmic revelation". It is frequent and funny, if also unfortunate, to encounter young members of the Drug Movement who claim to have achieved a personal apotheosis when, in fact, their experience appears to have consisted mainly of depersonalization, dissociation, and similar phenomena. Such individuals seek their beatitude in regular drug-taking, continuing to avoid the fact that their psychedelic "illumination" is not the sign of divine or cosmic approval they suppose it to be, but rather a flight from reality. Euphoria then may ensue as a result of the loss of all sense of responsibility; and this can and often does lead to orgies of spiritual pride and self-indulgence by those who now see themselves as the inheritors of *It*! . . .

'The situation is complicated by the fact that many such persons are caught up in a quasi-Eastern mystique through which they express their disenchantment with the declining Western values and with the proliferating technology, the fear of becoming a machine-man, and the yearning for some vision of wholeness to turn the tide of rampant fragmentation. This vision they pursue by means of a wholesale leap to the East without, however, having gained the stability, maturity, and elasticity needed to assimilate the Eastern values.'⁶

This needed saying, and it is well said. We now turn to a similar verdict from Zen. The 'subject' in this case is a twenty-five-year-old Japanese girl, Yaeko Iwasaki, who achieved enlightenment after some five years of Zen exercises (*zāzen*). A week later she died, but in the course of that week she wrote some remarkable letters to her Zen master, Harada Roshi. The seventh of these ends with the following words:

'In the whole universe I am supreme, and it is perfectly natural. I am astonished that I am that One. How wonderful, how marvellous! I am in good spirits, so please don't worry about me. I look forward with the greatest pleasure to seeing you again. Yaeko.

'P.S. Tears of gratitude and joy well up in me when I think that I have accomplished the practice of Zen from first to last without strain . . .'

Here are the Zen master's comments:

'An ancient Zen saying has it that to become attached to one's own enlightenment is as much a sickness as to exhibit a maddeningly active ego. Indeed, the profounder the enlightenment, the worse the illness. In her case I think it would have taken two or three months for the most obvious symptoms to disappear, two or three years for the less obvious, and seven or eight for the most insidious. Such symptoms are less pronounced in one as gentle as she, but in some they are positively nauseating. Those who practise Zen must guard against them. My own sickness lasted almost ten years.'⁷

But perhaps the most telling indictment of 'positive inflation' or 'expansion' as the Muslims appropriately call it is that of Al-Qushayrī:

'Expansion', he says, 'comes suddenly and strikes the subject unexpectedly so that he can find no reason for it. It makes him quiver with joy, yet scares him. The way to deal with it is to keep quiet and to observe conventional good manners. There is the

---

6. Masters and Houston, op. cit., pp. 259–60.
7. Philip Kapleau, *The Three Pillars of Zen* (Harper and Row, New York, 1966), pp. 288–9.

greatest danger in this mood, and those who are open to it should be on their guard against an insidious deception. ... The Sūfīs therefore say, "Be chary of expansion and beware of it." ... Expansion has been considered by those who have investigated the truth of these matters to be something in the face of which one should take refuge in God, for both [expansion and "contraction"] must be considered a poor thing and a harmful one if compared with the spiritual states which are above them, such as the (apparent) annihilation of the mystic and his integration (*indirāj*) in the Truth. ...

'The expanded man [indeed] experiences an expansion great enough to contain [all] creation; and there is practically nothing that will cause him fear. Nothing affects him in whatever state he may be.'[8]

From the available evidence it would appear that the state which LSD produces in the vast majority of those who take it is what the Muslims call expansion and contraction, what Jung calls positive and negative inflation, which appear to resemble the manic and depressive stages of manic-depressive psychosis. There are exceptions, the most impressive of which appears to be that supplied by Dr Pahnke in DeBold and Leaf's symposium.[9] One thing, however, does seem worth pointing out in connection with LSD experiences. By now it has become a commonplace to observe that no beneficial effect can be expected from psychedelic drugs unless the 'set and setting' are right, the atmosphere relaxed and friendly, and the session directed by an experienced 'guide'. Throughout the average LSD session the greatest use is made of sensory aids – visual, auditory and tactile. Almost invariably music is played. This is in sharp contrast to the practice of religious contemplatives for whom the suppression of all sensory impressions is the first step on the mystic path. St John of the Cross most appropriately calls this the 'dark night of the *senses*' which must precede the total denudation of the soul he calls the 'dark night of the *soul*' which is that state of utter spiritual desolation which

8. *Al-Risālat al-Qushayriyya*, ed. Dr 'Abdu'l-Halīm Mahmūd and Mahmūd bin al-Sharīf, Vol. i (Cairo, 1966), pp. 197–8.
9. See below, pp. 103 ff.

for him must precede the state of union with God. For the early Sufis too silence and solitude were considered essential for contemplation, since it is the senses that distract one from the act of contemplation itself. This they call the 'cutting out of all that is creaturely in order to concentrate exclusively on God' (*inqitā' 'an al-khalq ilā'l-haqq*). It was only later that sensory aids were introduced in order to promote ecstasy. *Mutatis mutandis* these aids correspond fairly exactly to the aids used by LSD adepts. In place of the inevitable record-player you have love poems accompanied by musical instruments. A friendly atmosphere was supplied by the members of the fraternity whose togetherness was enhanced by a ritual dance under the direction of the Shaykh ('elder') who corresponds to the psychedelic 'guide', while the standard visual aid was the presence of handsome youths whose created beauty was supposed to call to the mind of the devotee the uncreated beauty of God. By the eleventh century all this had become standard Sufi practice though it had been strenuously opposed by earlier generations as being unwarrantable innovation and a most suspect deviation from the norm of conduct set by the Prophet. Those deviations, however, received the stamp of approval from the great mystical theologian, Al-Ghazālī, towards the end of the eleventh century, the only proviso he insisted on being that the contemplation of youthful beauty should not be enhanced by physical contact. Bolder spirits, needless to say, disregarded this advice and, as in the case of Dr Leary and his friends, (homo)sexual activity was also brought in to heighten the ecstatic experience. This would sometimes lead to much unseemly extravagance.[1] All this left its mark on Sufi literature, and the purely mystical aphorisms of the earlier generations gave way to ecstatic love poetry ostensibly addressed to God (the Beloved) but seemingly more applicable to a human beloved. Finally recourse was had to hashish (pot) and *ma'jūn* (a confection made of hemp leaves, datura seeds, poppy-seeds, honey, and ghee).[2]

The parallelism between later Sufism and the LSD cult is ob-

1. Details are supplied by the Persian poet Sanā'ī, *Hadīqat al-haqīqa*, ed. M. Razavī (Tehran, A.H. (solar) 1329), pp. 662–70.
2. Ibn al-Jauzī, *Talbīs Iblīs* (Cairo, A.H. 1368), p. 374.

vious. It should, however, be pointed out in addition that with the development of new techniques in Sufism the goal too shifted. Solitary meditation had originally been used as being the method most appropriate to finding the eternal God either within you or, more personally, as the lover of your soul. 'God only' to the exclusion of all created things had been the slogan of these early adepts. There was no question of achieving ecstasy for its own sake. This was known as the way of sobriety. With the introduction of music and dance and visual aids, usually in the form of handsome young men, the atmosphere became charged with emotion and in the hagiographies of the thirteenth century and later scene after scene of wild excitement is depicted in which, at the height of the 'session', mystical 'states' (*hālāt*) were reached in which the mystic would involuntarily shriek aloud, throw himself on the ground, rend his clothes, and, in some cases, die out of the sheer excess of his emotion. At the same time those who followed the path of 'sobriety' developed a counter-technique. Music, dance, and the contemplation of youthful beauty had come to stay. So the hallmark of 'sobriety' now came to be a rigid control of the emotions in emotionally charged situations, that is to say, the acceptance of such situations as a challenge to be withstood. Tempted by phenomena designed to excite 'expansion' (Jung's 'positive inflation') the saint would demonstrate his sanctity by preserving a 'holy indifference' as St François de Sales calls it. With regard to expansion itself it is not at all clear whether there is any valid distinction between it – what Jung calls 'positive inflation' – on the one hand and what Bucke and Freud call 'cosmic consciousness' or the 'oceanic feeling' on the other. There is a difference of mood, but is there a difference of content? It is difficult to say, but I rather doubt it.

It will be remembered that the Hindus dispute among themselves on the nature of the experience of absolute Oneness 'without a second'. Does it mean that one has reached the 'ground of Being', what Meister Eckhart sometimes calls the Godhead beyond the three Persons of the Trinity, or does it mean what Buber calls 'the basic unity of my own soul beyond the reach of all multiplicity it has hitherto received from life'?

In this connection it should be noted too that within the Hindu tradition itself – and most clearly of all in the *Bhagavad-Gītā* – the transcendence of time and space (what it calls 'becoming Brahman') *precedes* the timeless soul's union with God. And it will be remembered that Richard Jefferies had an intense experience of the eternal Now but none of communion, let alone union, with what he calls the 'higher than deity' and other people call God. The point I am making is in fact made with absolute clarity in the last chapter of the *Bhagavad-Gītā* itself, and I can scarcely do better than quote it: Krishna, the incarnate God is speaking:

'Let a man be integrated by his soul [now] cleansed, let him restrain himself with constancy, abandon objects of sense – sound and all the rest – let him cast out passion and hate. Let him live apart, eat lightly, restrain speech, body and mind; let him practise meditation constantly, let him cultivate dispassion; let him give up all thought of "I", fear, pride, desire, anger, and possessiveness; let him think of nothing as mine – at peace: if he does this, he is conformed to becoming Brahman (that is, to participating in a timeless and spaceless form of existence).

'Once he has become Brahman, with self serene, he does not grieve nor does he desire; the same to all contingent things he gains the highest love and loyalty to me. By love and loyalty he comes to know me as I really am, how great I am and who. And once he knows me as I am, he enters me forthwith. . . .

'And now again listen to this, my highest word, of all the most mysterious: "I love you well." Therefore will I tell you your salvation.

'Bear me in mind, love me and worship me, sacrifice, prostrate yourself to me. So will you come to me, I promise you truly, for you are dear to me. Give up all things of the law, turn to me, your only refuge, for I will deliver you from all evils; have no care.'[3]

It is to be hoped that the reader will have come to understand that just as there are varieties of psychedelic experience so there are

---

3. For a detailed account of the theology of the *Gītā* see my edition of that work, *The Bhagavad-Gītā* (Clarendon Press, Oxford, 1968), and *Concordant Discord*, pp. 117–49.

varieties of mystical experience which we can trace not only in Hinduism, but also in Islam, Christianity, and Buddhism. The digression, however, seemed necessary since there are plenty of people who, happily disregarding the evidence, can say with Stace: 'It's not a matter of [psychedelic experience] being *similar* to mystical experience: it *is* mystical experience.' Clearly this sententious aphorism is as misleading as it is provocative.

This digression on the varieties of mystical experience will, it is hoped, have helped to clear the ground to enable us to consider the Good Friday 'miracle' of Marsh Chapel already referred to (p. 88). There the 'set and setting' were described and the typology of mysticism which had been devised by Dr Pahnke relying mainly on the ideas of Professor Stace outlined. After the experiment each subject wrote an account of it as soon as was convenient. These, so far as I know, have not yet been published, but will, it is hoped, form part of Dr Pahnke's Harvard thesis when it appears. It will be remembered that the twenty subjects were graduate-student volunteers, all of whom were from middle-class Protestant backgrounds. During the session they listened to a two-and-a-half-hour religious service and, being Good Friday, one would have expected them to be meditating on the Passion of Christ as is the habit of Christians even in these decadent post-Christian days. Unfortunately in the hitherto published material there is no direct evidence of this. All we are given is a summary of percentage scores according to the Pahnke–Stace typology. This was the result:

	Category	*Percentage*
1	Unity	62
	A Internal	70
	B External	38
2	Transcendence of time and space	84
3	Deeply felt positive mood	57
	A Joy, blessedness and peace	51
	B Love	57
4	Sacredness	53
5	Objectivity and Reality	63
6	Paradoxicality	61
7	Alleged Ineffability	66
8	Transiency	79

9	Persistent positive changes in attitude and behaviour	51
	A Toward self	57
	B Toward others	40
	C Toward life	54
	D Toward the experience	57[4]

The 'scores' of the control group which had not been administered the drug were sensationally lower, as might have been expected. The statistics are impressive but tell us very little of the *religious* experience of these young Protestants, since they were never even asked how the drug affected their understanding of the meaning of the events of Good Friday – the meaning of the crucifixion of the God-man, Jesus, who was after all the founder of their religion and, as God made man, presumably in the forefront of the thoughts of these pious youths on the anniversary day of their redemption and salvation. One might have supposed that texts like Galatians 2:19-20 were uppermost in their minds where St Paul says: 'I have been crucified with Christ, and I live now not with my own life but with the life of Christ who lives in me. The life I now live in this body I live in faith: faith in the Son of God who loved me and sacrificed himself for my sake.'

Admittedly the typology presented them offered no category in which this 'death-rebirth sequence' as Dr Leary calls it could naturally express itself, and responsibility for the inadequacy of the typology must rest with those who devised it. 'Love' without qualification is almost meaningless in the context of religious mysticism. In the *Bhagavad-Gītā*, the earlier Muslim mystics, and practically all Christian mystics 'love' means a one-pointed love of God to the exclusion of all creatures. With the Christians this is somewhat tempered by Christ's second commandment to love your neighbour as yourself, but this is a concession to the Christian religion which in this instance seems to be at variance with a mysticism based on the exclusive love of God. It could mean almost anything to the LSD user as is shown by the dithyrambs of the fifty-year-old widow quoted from Masters and Houston above (pp. 94-5). Indeed, since on this particular day one might

4. Walter N. Pahnke, in Aaronson and Osmond, op. cit., pp. 155-6.

have supposed that these young men's thoughts would have been drenched in feelings of love and awe, it is surprising that their score, despite the apparently ideal setting and the undeniably powerful effect of the drug, was so low when it came to the categories of 'love' and 'sacredness'.

In fairness to Dr Pahnke it should be noted that in his contribution to DeBold and Leaf's symposium published in 1969 he contrasts the experience of these young theological students with that of a 'Christian ministerial student (Lutheran?) who took a compound from the psilocybin series in a carefully controlled experiment that was conducted in a German research institute under the supervision of an experimenter who was not particularly interested in mystical experiences'.[5] This student could scarcely have scored higher marks according to the Pahnke–Stace typology, and Dr Pahnke claims that he actually did have an 'experimental' mystical experience although he states most emphatically that the subjects of the Good Friday 'miracle' did *not*.[6]

Dr Pahnke's standards are not so rigorous as those of Masters and Houston, but they are fairly rigorous all the same, and the example of the German ministerial student he quotes would indeed seem to rank as a mystical experience, but rather of the 'Hindu' type than of the 'Christian–Muslim'. His description of the experience was probably influenced by his 'acquaintance of mystic literature of both east and west', just as was Huxley's description of what he experienced under mescalin. The essential part of his description runs as follows:

'Relatively soon after receiving the drug, I transcended my usual level of consciousness and became aware of fantastic dimensions of being, all of which possessed a profound sense of reality.

'... It would seem more accurate to say that I existed "in" these dimensions of being as I had not only transcended my ego, but also the dichotomy between subject and object.

'It is meaningful to say that I ceased to exist, becoming immersed in the ground of Being, in Brahman, in God, in "Nothing-

5. DeBold and Leaf, *LSD, Man & Society*, p. 69.
6. Ibid., p. 71 (Pahnke's italics).

ness", in Ultimate Reality or in some similar religious symbol for Oneness. . . .

'The feelings I experienced could best be described as cosmic tenderness, infinite love, penetrating peace, eternal blessing and unconditional acceptance on one hand, and on the other, as unspeakable awe, overflowing joy, primeval humility, inexpressible gratitude and boundless devotion . . . .

'It is misleading even to use the words "I experienced", since during the peak of the experience (which must have lasted at least an hour) there was no duality between myself and what I experienced. Rather, I *was* these feelings, or ceased to be in them and felt no loss at the cessation. . . . At this time it seemed as though I was not M.R. listening to a recording, but paradoxically *was* the music itself. . . . The "love" I was experiencing became so overwhelming as to become unbearable or even painful. The tears I shed at this moment were in no sense those of fear, but ones of uncontainable joy.

'. . . During the height of the experience, I had no consciousness of time or space in the ordinary sense. I felt as though I was beyond seconds, minutes, hours, and also beyond past, present, and future. In religious language, I was in "eternity".'[7]

Well, it is all there except God – and by God I mean the God that was the primary and overwhelming subject of Pascal's unique experience on that memorable evening of 23 November 1654: 'God of Abraham, God of Isaac, God of Jacob, not the God of the philosophers and scientists.'[8] It is strange that a Christian who claims to be acquainted with mystical literature of both East and West should not have associated his experience, if not with the God of Pascal, then at least with the God of St Augustine as he is described in the mystical parts of the *Confessions*. The words he uses to describe his experience are not drawn from the central Christian mystical tradition, but are easily identified: the 'ground of Being' (Tillich), 'Brahman' (Hinduism in general), 'Nothingness' (Mahayana Buddhism, Pseudo-Dionysius, and Meister Eckhart – Christians certainly, but not typical ones), 'Ultimate Reality' (Tillich again). It is also interesting that the word 'love'

---

7. Ibid., pp. 70–1.   8. Pascal, *Oeuvres complètes*, p. 554.

is put in inverted commas and seems to be qualified as '*cosmic* tenderness' and '*infinite* love', not apparently in any way related to the God of whom Augustine says: 'Thou hast made us for thyself and our hearts are restless till they rest in thee.'[9] Further, in assessing these LSD experiences there is an imponderable element that can only be called 'qualitative': each of them has a distinctive flavour. Masters and Houston had no difficulty in dismissing the pretensions of their fifty-year-old widow to 'being the universe' and 'being love' as 'a psychological and semantic mask behind which [she took] her narcissistic, egoistic holiday'.[1] Similarly, in the case of the German ministerial student there seems to be more than a hint of *Schwärmerei* ('gush') that accounts for the tone of the description if not for its content which is after all a classic instance of 'cosmic consciousness' for which Richard Jefferies has been our model.

In fairness, however, it should be added that in the opinion of the subject himself his drug experience did have a beneficial effect on his inner and outer life (as was also true of Pahnke's young theological students). 'The spasmodic nature of my prayer life has ceased', he wrote, 'and I have yielded to a need to spend time each day in meditation which, though essentially open and wordless, is impregnated by feelings of thanksgiving and trust. This increased need to be alone is balanced by what I believe to be a greater sensitivity to the authentic problems of others and a corresponding willingness to enter freely into genuine friendships. I possess a renewed and increased sense of personal integration and am more content simply to "be myself" than previously.'[2] Unfortunately we have no independent account of his self-integration, although such cases *are* attested in the literature.

What Masters and Houston regard as an undoubted case of a religious experience brought about by LSD sessions, however, seems to be so far removed from anything the present author has come across in his quite extensive reading of the mystical writings of most of the religious traditions that he cannot possibly class it

9. *Confessions*, 1.1.
1. Masters and Houston, *The Varieties of Psychedelic Experience*, p. 127.
2. DeBold and Leaf, op. cit., p. 70.

as specifically mystical. It seems to be a fascinating case involving what Jung called 'individuation' in which psychedelic visions – not mystical experiences – take the place of dreams in what seems to be a classical Jungian analysis.[3] In this particular case God does appear – as a lion! – while the subject himself is transformed into a tiger. Now, with all respect to the authors, in the literature of religious mysticism God simply does not appear as a lion of however 'awesome [a] stature and beauty', nor is the mystic himself turned into a tiger and then again into a lion which 'rubs against a great hand (God's hand) with his cheek and nuzzles'.[4] This is typical of a Jungian analysis and *has* religious significance both to the subject and his 'guides'; but to call it religious *mysticism* is to stretch the words unbearably.

In modern times it was Aldous Huxley more than anyone else who claimed that psychedelic drugs could produce religious mystical states. 'The Beatific Vision, *Sat Chit Ananda*, Being-Awareness-Bliss', he wrote, 'for the first time I understood, not on the verbal level, not by inchoate hints or at a distance, but precisely and completely what those prodigious syllables referred to' (above p. 41). A week before his death, however, at a time when he had reached a stage in which he thought that under the influence of LSD he could remain indefinitely in a state of timeless bliss which the Tibetan Buddhists call the 'Clear Light of the Void', he realized that this was probably a gross misrepresentation of what was actually happening. While he was under the influence of dilaulid (a sedative, not a psychedelic drug), his wife made a tape-recording of their conversation. He had had the impression that he was privileged to make 'an absolute ... *cosmic* gift to the world ... [in a] *vast* act of benevolence ... in which *I* should have the sort of star role'. 'This whole thing', he said, 'has been very strange because in a way it was very good – but in a way it was absolutely terrifying, showing that when *one thinks one's got beyond oneself, one hasn't*. ... I began with this marvellous sense of this cosmic gift, and then ended up with a rueful sense that one can be

---

3. This fascinating case is told in great detail in Masters and Houston, op. cit., pp. 267–301.
4. Ibid., pp. 293–4.

deceived. ... It was an insight, but at the same time the most *dangerous* of errors ... inasmuch as one was worshipping oneself.'[5]

It seems that in his dying days Huxley realized that what he had taken to be transcendent wisdom – the 'Clear Light of the Void' – was far more akin to the Muslim idea of 'expansion', Jung's 'positive inflation', in which he finally understood that he was doing no more than worshipping himself. Taking a less severe attitude towards his psychedelic experiences he said a little while later:

'We must not attempt to live outside the world, which is given us, but we must somehow learn how to transform it and transfigure it. Too much "wisdom" is as bad as too little wisdom, and there must be no magic tricks. We must learn to come to reality without the enchanter's wand and his book of the words. One must find a way of being in this world while not being of it. A way of living in time without being completely swallowed up by time.'[6]

Huxley's last words belie practically everything he had said before: they are his recantation and his last will and testament, a warning indeed to all who would foolishly maintain that psychedelic experience is not merely similar to mystical experience but is identical with it.

Of course, no one will probably deny that there are parallels between *some* aspects of religious mysticism (particularly some Hindu varieties) and *some* LSD experiences – notably cosmic consciousness and an experience of an eternal Now and an omnipresent Here beyond time and space. But the experience of Pascal's God and the God of the *Bhagavad-Gītā* who transcends eternal Being itself has not, to my knowledge, come to light in purely psychedelic experience. Typical of such experience is probably that enjoyed by St Augustine and his mother at their window in Ostia. This was the climax of Augustine's (very intellectual) mystical quest, but for him, as for the 'orthodox'

---

5. Laura Archera Huxley, *This Timeless Moment* (Chatto & Windus, London, and Farrar, Straus & Giroux, New York, 1968), pp. 268–9 (Mrs Huxley's italics).
6. Ibid., pp. 289–90.

mystical traditions in all the major religions that have mystical traditions at all, 'knowledge' or 'wisdom' is balanced by an intense love for a God personally experienced and adored. The 'flavour' of the passage is quite unlike the case of the German ministerial student, and the perceptive reader should not find it difficult to detect and feel the difference. These are Augustine's words in F. J. Sheed's translation:

'Our conversation had brought us to this point that any pleasure whatsoever of the bodily senses, in any brightness whatsoever of corporeal light, seemed to us not worthy of comparison with the pleasure of that eternal Light, not worthy even of mention. Rising as our love flamed upward to that Selfsame, we passed in review the various levels of bodily things, up to the heavens themselves, whence sun and moon and stars shine upon this earth. And higher still we soared, thinking in our minds and speaking and marvelling at Your works: *and so we came to our own souls, and went beyond them*[7] to come at last to that region of richness unending, where You feed Israel forever with the food of Truth: and there life is that Wisdom by which all things are made, both the things that have been and the things that are yet to be. But this Wisdom itself is not made: it is as it has ever been, and so it shall be forever: indeed "has ever been" and "shall be forever" have no place in it, but it simply is, for it is eternal: whereas "to have been" and "to be going to be" are not eternal. And while we were thus talking of His Wisdom and panting for it, with all the effort of our heart we did for one instant attain to touch it; then sighing, and leaving the first fruits of our spirit bound to it, we returned to the sound of our own tongue, in which a word has both beginning and ending. For what is like to your Word, Our Lord, who abides in Himself forever, yet grows not old and makes all things new!'[8]

But should it be thought that Augustine strikes too intellectual a note, let us hear what the urbane St François de Sales has to say on the subject of 'knowledge' and love in the soul's love-affair with God. It is strangely reminiscent of Huxley's last words:

---

7. My italics.
8. St Augustine, *Confessions* (Sheed & Ward, London and New York, 1943), 9.10.

'The first mark of a truly *holy* ecstasy is that it never engages or attaches itself to the understanding as much as it does to the will, which it moves, warms, and fills with a powerful affection for God; so that if an ecstasy is more beautiful than good, more luminous than warm, more speculative than affective, it is highly dubious and much to be distrusted. I do not say that one cannot have raptures, or even prophetic visions, without charity; for I am well aware that just as one can have charity without being enraptured and without prophecy, so too can one be enraptured and prophesy without possessing charity. But I do say that when a man enraptured has more clarity in his understanding with which to wonder at God than he has warmth in his will with which to love him, then he had better be on his guard; for there is a danger that this ecstasy may be false, inflating rather than edifying his spirit, ranking him indeed among the prophets like Saul, Balaam, and Caiaphas, but leaving him none the less among the outcast.'[9]

9. *Traité de l'amour de Dieu*, 7.6.

4
LSD AND ZEN

From what we have said in the last chapter it would seem clear why the Christian establishment should disapprove of the use of psychedelic drugs. First there is an instinctive religious reaction that it is sacrilegious to suppose that the use of drugs can produce the same transports as have been recorded in the history of Christian mysticism. This reaction is instinctive, not rational. Secondly, in circles traditionally opposed to mysticism even in its Christian form, the habitual identification by the users of psychedelic drugs of their 'peak' experience with the experiences recorded in Hindu and Buddhist literature in which 'God' appears not as a person but as an eternal and unconditioned state of being – what Dr Leary calls the 'timeless energy process around you'[1] – must appear doubly suspicious; for the implication is that the personal God they claim to experience in faith does not really exist because many Hindus and most Buddhists do not experience him in this way at all but claim to experience him, or rather 'it', immediately in the innermost core of their being. The instinctive Christian reaction to this is one of panic, for when their 'blind' faith – the usual gibe levelled at them not only by the psychedelic extremists but also by neo-Zen Buddhists and neo-Vedantins – is contrasted with the certainty the latter feel about the absolute reality of the unity of the universe in an eternal Now and an omnipresent Here, they may well feel that, 'seeing through a glass darkly' as they do and not 'face to face', they may have to reconsider the very foundations of their faith. And this was precisely the predicament of Jung's father, a pious and conventional Protestant pastor, who had the misfortune to have a son who from his earliest boyhood had direct experiences of God and what he called 'God's world' that were quite beyond his comprehension. Finally, of course, he did lose his faith, became subject to intensely depressive moods, and

1. Above, p. 70.

died a soured and embittered man.² The combined challenge of Eastern mysticism and psychedelic drugs can indeed be profoundly disturbing to the Christian establishment, for they offer a far more attractive type of religion to the restless young in place of traditional Christianity which has nothing comparable to offer. Alternatively traditional Christians may simply become hardened in their attitude towards mysticism in general and Eastern mysticism in particular since these mystical states can apparently be artificially produced: they cannot, therefore, be of God. And that, for them, is that.

There remains a third class of Christian which is mildly irritated by the extravagant claims made by persons who ought to know better that *the* psychedelic experience is identical with *the* mystical experience. About these persons we have already said enough in the previous chapter. Perhaps we may be allowed to repeat the sagacious remarks that Masters and Houston have made on this subject: 'To at least some extent the responsibility of this seduction of the innocent must lie with such authors as Huxley,³ Alan Watts, and others⁴ who in their various writings imposed upon the psychedelic experience essentially Eastern ideas and terminology which a great many persons then assumed to be the sole and accurate way of approaching and interpreting such experience.'⁵

The Zen Buddhists, on their side, disapprove of the psychedelic cult on somewhat different grounds. Dr Leary and his friends claim that LSD demonstrates, among other things, the truth of the Mahayana and Zen contention that 'all men are the Buddha', that all men are, so to speak, pregnant with eternity, that all men are potentially, and can realize actually, that they are at one with all Nature. To anyone who has neither achieved Zen enlightenment nor a 'peak' experience with LSD or similar drugs, however, most descriptions of Zen enlightenment and some of LSD experience would appear to be almost identical. There is the same 'oceanic

2. C. G. Jung, *Memories, Dreams, Reflections*, pp. 98–100.
3. Huxley, however, made ample amends for his previous *naïveté* in the week before he died. Above, pp. 108-9.
4. Notably, among philosophers, W. T. Stace, and among psychedelic propagandists of course Timothy Leary.
5. Masters and Houston, *The Varieties of Psychedelic Experience*, p. 260.

feeling', the same transformation of *self*-consciousness into *cosmic* consciousness, the same 'becoming one with Nature and the universe and in this union [the same] experience [of] an immense joy'.[6] 'This joy', the author of these words adds, 'is so deep that it cannot be diminished but is, rather, strengthened through suffering and adversity.' This is, surely one of the main differences between Zen and the average LSD experience. True, many serious writers on psychedelic drugs have pointed to well-authenticated cases in which character changes for the better have taken place after one or more carefully supervised sessions, but, in the present stage of our knowledge, these would appear to be exceptional. It is also true, however, that not many who had undertaken courses of Zen meditation have stayed the extremely arduous course out and won through to enlightenment the hard way. But the resulting experience of seeing all things as One and One as all *does* seem to be the same. All that is lacking in Zen is Dr Leary's now loudly proclaimed experience of cosmic sex, the gate to which is individual sex heightened a thousand times by LSD; but then Dr Leary's sexual ecstasies seem on the whole to be foreign to the mainstream of psychedelic orthodoxy, and his religion includes not only Zen Buddhism but also the bolder experiments in sexuality practised by the Hindus of the left-hand Tantra. 'Our philosophy', he writes, 'about the spiritual meaning of LSD, comes closer to Hinduism than to any other. Hinduism ... recognizes the divinity of all manifestations of life, physical, physiological, chemical, biological, and so forth.'[7] And there are certainly many Hindus who would agree with him, but few of them would welcome the comparison of their religion to Dr Leary's 'religious philosophy' dependent as it is on the use of psychedelic drugs. In a recent book the distinguished Indian sage, Krishnamurti, once designated by the Theosophical Society to be the new Messiah, asks: 'What is the necessity of taking drugs at all – drugs that promise a psychedelic expansion of the mind, great visions and intensity? Apparently one takes them because one's own perceptions are dull. Clarity is

---

6. H. M. Enomiya-Lassalle, *Zen – Way to Enlightenment* (Burns & Oates, London, 1966), p. 80.
7. T. Leary, *The Politics of Ecstasy*, p. 239.

LSD and Zen

dimmed and one's life is rather shallow, mediocre and meaningless; one takes them to go beyond this mediocrity.'[8] And to stress the difference between meditation and psychedelic experience even more radically he writes in another context: 'Meditation is not the mere experiencing of something beyond everyday thought and feeling nor is it the pursuit of visions and delights. An immature and squalid little mind can and does have visions of expanding consciousness, and experiences which it recognizes according to its own conditioning. This immaturity may be greatly capable of making itself successful in this world and achieving fame and notoriety. The gurus whom it follows are of the same quality and state. Meditation does not belong to such as these.'[9]

Can Krishnamurti have had Dr Leary in mind when he wrote these words? Perhaps not Leary personally but surely the whole drug cult with its incessant emphasis on 'expansion of the Mind' as the be-all and end-all of *religious* experience. After all Krishnamurti is what the sociologists of religion, in their crude, unpleasing jargon, call a 'religionist', and a highly distinguished one at that; and he clearly knew the distinction between Al-Qushayrī's 'expansion' (Jung's 'positive inflation') and what he calls 'meditation' — the sinking of one's mind into the depths of one's being which he calls the 'flowering of love'.[1]

Similarly among the Zen Buddhists of Japan Abbot Zenkei Shibayama may well have had Dr Leary's League for Spiritual Discovery and similar psychedelic cults[2] in mind when he wrote: 'Recently there have been people who talk about instant enlightenment, or those who take drugs in an attempt to experience *satori* (= enlightenment in Japanese). Whatever claims they may make, I declare that such approaches are not authentic, true Zen at all.'[3]

That tell-tale word 'authentic' again![4] The Abbot speaks *ex cathedra* but the onus of proof rests squarely on him. He has

---

8. J. Krishnamurti, *The Only Revolution* (Gollancz, London, and Harper & Row, New York, 1970), pp. 173–4.
9. Ibid., p. 85.   1. Ibid., p. 50.
2. See W. N. Pahnke, in DeBold and Leaf, *LSD, Man & Society*, pp. 74–6, and John W. Aiken, in Aaronson and Osmond, *Psychedelics*, pp. 165–82.
3. Z. Shibayama, *A Flower Does Not Talk*, pp. 47–8, cf. pp. 116–17.
4. See above p. 29.

achieved *satori*, that is, in his own Zen Buddhist terminology, he has discovered his True Self or the Buddha-nature within him, the oneness that pervades all multiplicity which practically all the mystics of all religions and of none attest, whether or not they take the further step of seeing both oneness and multiplicity as rooted in a God who is in some sense personal; and he has achieved it in the hard, orthodox Zen Buddhist way. But, owing to his mistrust as a religious man of artificially produced ecstasies, he has taken no psychedelic drugs in order to make an unbiased comparison and to justify his wholesale condemnation. Moreover he weakens his own case by admitting that 'authentic' Zen must remain the privilege of the few. For, as he says, 'true as it may be that Zen is really a supreme way to the Truth, it is obvious that not everyone can be expected to have the training required for the attainment of the exquisite moment of *satori*'.[5] Dr Leary, on the other hand, claims that, given the right dispositions and expert guidance, you can, through LSD, find the Buddha-nature within you and, whatever religion you belong to, you will penetrate to the inner core of that religion through what he describes as a 'death-rebirth sequence'.[6] 'We hope that anyone that comes to all of our celebrations will discover the deep meaning that exists in each of these.'[7]

Dr Leary claims for LSD precisely what Abbot Shibayama claims for Zen, for by Zen the Abbot understands not just Zen ('meditation') *Buddhism* but the deepening, through the experience of guided and controlled meditation, of any positive religion. 'Zen', he says, 'is to be understood independent of the Zen School of Buddhism. Zen does not belong inclusively and exclusively to the Zen School of Buddhism. I believe Zen is the universal truth that brings true wisdom and peace to the lives of the people in the world. Any religion or culture should avail itself of whatever spiritual value Zen can offer. ... Dogen, [for instance,] the founder of Soto Zen in Japan, declared, "Anybody who would regard Zen as a school or sect of Buddhism, and call it *Zen-shu*, Zen School, is a devil." '[8] Zen, in this sense, which few Zen

5. Z. Shibayama, op. cit., p. 48.   6. T. Leary, op. cit., p. 239.
7. Ibid.   8. Z. Shibayama, op. cit., p. 81.

Buddhists would accept, does, then, not remain simply the core of Buddhism but works to deepen and revive any religion or philosophy. But, he insists, even after *satori* Zen meditation and Zen spiritual exercises must continue. So too, for Dr Leary, your first trip, if all goes well, will transport you into what Jung calls 'God's world', the same world of Oneness and interpenetration of which the Zen Buddhists speak, the same world which the nature mystics experience, but which, for most of them, remains only a memory of paradise lost; but once you take the drug again, the memory will once more become a blazing reality, and from that reality, it is alleged, you will be able to help others because you will have found your own true self. Leary sees that 'dropping out' into the 'true self' or 'Buddha-nature' is not enough because it would be selfish. This was the temptation of the Buddha himself, but he overcame it and taught his doctrine of salvation to a distracted world. The message of the Buddha, according to Leary, is: 'Drop out: turn on: tune in.'[9] He 'dropped out' of the secular world where he was the son of a king, preferring to lead the life of a religious mendicant. His experiments with the more extreme forms of self-mortification were, however, of no avail: only after relaxing did he win through to enlightenment. In Leary's terminology he had 'turned on'. Though 'turned on', he was tempted to leave matters there and keep the ineffable message to himself. In Leary's own racy words applied to the old story, 'the message of the Buddha is to tune in. . . . Tune back in, not the old game. You have to stay dropped out of that. You drop back in to life. You come back down and express your revelation in acts of glory and beauty and humour. Help someone else drop out and turn on.'[1] And, remembering that the Buddha's message was to drop out *and* turn on, he adds: 'You can't *do* good until you *feel* good. You can't free others until *you* are free.' There is much method in this madness; but should we not emend the text to: 'You can't *do* good until you *are* good'? Of the Zen monks Fr Enomiya-Lassalle, a German Jesuit who has identified his whole life with Japan even to the extent of taking out Japanese nationality and who is believed to have achieved enlightenment himself, has written: 'Truly en-

9. T. Leary, op. cit., p. 247.   1. Ibid., pp. 249-50.

lightened monks are not proud. On the contrary, they are very humble and congenial. Anyone who lives in a Zen monastery for a short time will confirm this. In a monastery there prevails an atmosphere of benevolence and charity which is not often found elsewhere.'[2] Can LSD really provide this assured peace from which alone charity can well up? And what is the secret of Zen which enables it (sometimes) to put forth such sweet fruits?

'You can't do good until you are good.' Clearly this is the 'goodness' – the tranquillity, benevolence, and charity – that Fr Enomiya-Lassalle found among the Zen monks with whom he had lived. The unanswered question, however, remains: How does one become good? For early Buddhism the supreme good was Nirvana – 'the blowing out' of the lamp or fire of existence when all sensation will have 'grown cold', peace, disgust at all transient existence, detachment from it, its total cessation, tranquillity, wisdom, liberation, and enlightenment, the total destruction of the three root evils – passion, hatred, and delusion – the destruction of craving and becoming. This means nothing less than the destruction of life, of the human condition as we know it. Indeed the man who has reached Nirvana and thereby brought all activity to a standstill will differ from a dead man only in so far as he retains physical life, heat, and the senses, though he will be totally detached from and unaffected by these: his only characteristics will be indifference and insight.

One of the key doctrines of Buddhism, however, is that of 'not-self', that is to say, all existence as we know it is transient, devoid of self, and compounded of suffering or 'unease' – what existentialists call *Angst*, 'anxiety and anguish'. If there is no self, then what is 'liberated' from the painful chain of existence? To obviate the idea that anything at all we normally identify with ourselves, including what Christians call the soul, continues to exist in Nirvana, one of the formulas habitually used to describe this state is *vimuttam vimuttasmim*, 'something is liberated in what is liberated and free'. Sometimes we are told more positively that what is liberated is 'transcendent reason' or 'wisdom', but existing on its own and detached from any subject. It is the exact reverse

2. H. M. Enomiya-Lassalle, op. cit., p. 46.

of cosmic consciousness. When the German ministerial student cited by Dr Pahnke says, under the influence of a psychedelic drug: 'There was no duality between myself and what I experienced. Rather, I *was* these feelings. ... At this time it seemed as though I was not M.R. listening to a recording, but paradoxically *was* the music itself',[3] he is not experiencing Nirvana but identifying himself with sense perceptions which, by definition, do not exist in Nirvana: he is immersed in cosmic consciousness with which Nirvana has nothing whatever to do since it is far beyond and above the cosmos. More positively Nirvana is 'transcendent reason' or 'wisdom' liberated from all trace of transience. Though it is certainly the extinction of life as we know it, it is also a state of liberation, of spiritual freedom uninhibited by space, time, and causation. It is also health, and the Buddha is the surgeon who makes health possible: it is health, but there is no healthy man. It is compared to a level and charming countryside and the scent of a flower. Once this freeing of transcendent reason and wisdom from the bondage of the root-evils of passion, hatred, and delusion is compared to a man observing oysters, shells, and fish in limpid water without any trace of attachment to them, let alone of any sense that he *is* them. It is seeing things as they really are from the point of view of eternity:

> Who sees contingent being as it really is
> And then transcends it,
> He is set free in existence as it really is
> By the destruction of the craving to become.
>
> If a mendicant has gained insight
> Into contingent being,
> All craving gone for what becomes and what does not become,
> By making contingent being cease to become,
> He will never be born again.[4]

It is clear, then, that the ineffable peace of Nirvana which is also pure wisdom and insight is something that has no connection with the world of space and time which is not only the locus of un-ease, discomfort, or suffering (*dukkha*), but the very stuff of

3. Above, p. 106.
4. For references to these descriptions of Nirvana see R. C. Zaehner, *The Bhagavad-Gītā*, pp. 159, 213-14.

suffering and anxiety and torture in all its forms. The whole world is on fire and is kept blazing by the root-evils of passion, hatred, and delusion. It is based on cosmic ignorance and craving, and it is Māra, the Devil, whose name literally means 'death', and who is the ruler of this world: all the senses and their objects are his, so are the mind, ideas, and the thought process itself. How, then, is it possible to escape him? His power lies in the fact that he creates the delusion of separate personalities who insist that the senses, the objects of the senses, and whatever it is that links the two are *their* senses, the objects of *their* senses, and *their* processes which link the two and seem to give them cohesion. The only possible way of escape is to awaken to the fact that the ego and all individuality and personality are illusory: there is no such thing as 'I' or 'mine': once you have realized this you will have passed out of the reach of Māra, the Devil, who is both death and *life*.[5]

The world is in a perpetual state of flux (*samsāra*) in which life and death are inextricably intertwined. For the individual, or rather the bundle of sensations, ideas, thoughts, impressions, feelings, conations, and consciousness which create the impression of an individual, no escape is possible from this process since death is followed by birth in another body, and this again by re-death and re-birth and so on *ad infinitum*. The builder of these transitory abodes we call bodies inhabited by minds and souls, is Māra, the Devil. Only by the total destruction of this transitory abode can salvation, or rather liberation, be achieved:

> Long have I sought for the builder of the house;
> Long have I hurried through the flux of many births!
> How dismal to be reborn again and again!
>
> Builder of the house, I've seen you!
> Never again will you build a house for me!
> Broken are all your rafters, your roof destroyed!
> Wisdom has passed beyond all things compounded
> And attained to the destruction of all desires.[6]

So did the Buddha proclaim his liberation from this world which is death-in-life and life-in-death. For him there could be no question of salvation of the world, there could only be salvation *from* the world. Drop out of the world, turn on the infinite, tune

5. *Samyutta Nikāya*, 1.114–17 (iv.2).   6. *Dhammapada*, 153–4.

in to the infinite, and let the world stew in its own juice. That was the temptation of the Buddha, but he resisted it. He had compassion on the world and decided to teach the one sure way of transcending phenomenal existence and of escaping from the world for ever. But he was sorely tempted.

'If', he thought, 'I were to teach this doctrine and others did not understand it, it would be so much trouble wasted, so much tiresomeness. ... How much trouble I took to win it! There is no point in proclaiming it. How should people wracked with lust and hatred understand this teaching? How should they see it? For it goes against the stream of life, is clever, deep, difficult to discern, and subtle – and they are wracked with lust and enveloped in darkness.'

The great god Brahmā Sahampati, however, read his thoughts and begged him to preach the doctrine out of compassion for suffering creatures. And so the Buddha made up his mind.

'Paying attention to Brahmā's request and because I had compassion on the people, I looked down upon the world with a Buddha's eye and I saw ... that some had little impurity, others much, some had keen faculties, others dull, some had good dispositions, others evil, some were easy to teach, others difficult. ... Just as among lotuses there are some that are born in water, grow up in it, but do not rise out of it and grow fat submerged in it, while others are born in it, grow up in it, remaining on a level with it, and others again are born in it, grow up in it, but grow beyond it and cannot be splashed by it, so I saw that some creatures had but little impurity, others much, some had keen faculties, others dull, some had good dispositions, others evil, some were easy to teach, others difficult.'[7] And so the Buddha resolved to teach the doctrine because he had compassion on the world. This seems a little incongruous since what his enlightenment had taught him was the utter insubstantiality or 'emptiness' of all contingent beings. This being so, what could be the point of teaching these essentially non-existent creatures-in-flux? This insight into the hollowness of all things accounts for the Buddha's initial reluctance to pass on the truth he had discovered. Strictly speaking to teach anyone

7. *Majjhima Nikāya*, i. 168–9.

anything was meaningless – and yet the Buddha was moved with compassion! Illogical maybe, but absolutely essential to every form of Buddhism including Zen.

With the early Buddhists of the so-called School of the Elders 'enlightenment', that is, the apprehension of Nirvana and keeping oneself unspotted by the world as the full-grown lotus is unspotted by the water and mud from which it had grown, became an obsession. The Buddha had laid down the doctrine – the path by which Nirvana could be reached – and he had founded the *Sangha* – the community of celibate monks who had but little impurity, keen faculties, good dispositions, and were easy to teach and who could therefore alone be expected to have some chance of achieving Nirvana in this life – but it was up to each to attain his own enlightenment though, of course, he might receive support from the example of other monks. In Dr Leary's terminology to 'drop out' of the world and to 'turn on' to the impassible peace of Nirvana meant an even more intensive 'tuning in' to that infinite peace – to the total exclusion of the world of space and time which, so far from being 'very good' as the Book of Genesis would have us believe, was a blazing fire of insatiable desire and invincible ignorance. Between time and eternity there was a gulf fixed which nothing could span.

With the advent of the Mahayana (the 'Great Vehicle') at about the beginning of the Christian era, Buddhism underwent two radical changes. The first was the emergence of the Bodhisattva ideal, the second the bridging of the gulf between Nirvana and *samsāra*, eternity and time, tranquillity and the never-ending, agitated flux of earthly existence, freedom of the spirit in transcendental wisdom and bondage to matter.

The word *Bodhisattva* (literally 'enlightenment-being') in the earlier texts meant a Buddha-to-be, that is to say, one who throughout many reincarnations was destined to be a *teaching* Buddha – a 'fully awakened one' who would renew the Buddhist doctrine or law (*dhamma/dharma*) for the welfare of all sentient creatures. Hitherto the ideal had been that of the *Arahat* (literally 'one who is worthy') who, though himself enlightened and thus liberated in the climate of Nirvana, was content to stay that way without troubling himself overmuch about his fellow-men (who were in any case 'not-selves' and therefore essentially non-existent). The Bodhisattva, on the other hand, was filled with the Buddha's compassion as well as with his wisdom, and he therefore put off his Nirvana, which meant a total break with this world, in order to assist his fellow-men. Each Bodhisattva (and theoretically all men are Bodhisattvas, for, one day, even if this means after millions of years, they are destined to become Buddhas) takes the following vow:

> However innumerable beings are, I vow to save them;
> However inexhaustible the passions are, I vow to extinguish them;
> However immeasurable the *dharmas* ('things, doctrines') are, I vow to master them;
> However incomparable the Buddha-truth is, I vow to attain it.[8]

Thus the notion of 'grace', that is, favour bestowed on ordinary mortals for no particular merit of their own, was introduced into Buddhism while the Buddha himself was transformed into a divine Trinity consisting of the *Dharmakāya*, 'the body of Truth (or the Law)', that is, the Absolute, the *Sambhogakāya*, 'the body of Enjoyment' which seems to be the link between the Absolute and the relative, and the *Nirmānakāya*, 'the construct body' which is an apparent incarnation of the Absolute and the last of which was Siddhārtha Shākyamuni, the historical Buddha. All this transformed the original atheistic or, if one prefers the term, 'transtheistic' character of Buddhism into a religion of divine grace. But none of this had any interest for the Zen school which relied neither on scripture nor on doctrine but only on meditation (Japanese *Zen* from Chinese *ch'an* from Sanskrit *dhyāna*) and its fruits which are perfect wisdom and perfect compassion.

Far more important from the Zen point of view was the transformation of the complete dichotomy between Nirvana and *samsāra* into an absolute identity of the two. As Nāgārjuna, the great Mahayana philosopher of the second century A.D., puts it: 'There is no distinction whatever between *samsāra* and Nirvana, nor is there any distinction whatever between Nirvana and *samsāra*. The extent of *samsāra* is the same as that of Nirvana;

8. Cf. D. T. Suzuki, *Manual of Zen Buddhism* (Rider, London, 1950), p. 14.

there is not the slightest difference between the two.'[9] And yet even this seeming identity is again negated in what is called 'Emptiness' or the 'Void': 'Since all factors of existence are empty, what is the finite, what the infinite, what both finite and infinite, what neither finite nor infinite? What is meant by "this" or "other", "permanent" or "impermanent", what is "both impermanent and permanent" or what is "neither the one nor the other"?' The aim of this 'negative dialectic' would seem to be a deliberate attempt to destroy logical, 'dualistic' thought, thereby forcing the discursive intellect to give up in despair so that it may be enlightened by a flash of intuition which enables you to 'see' and 'know' that Nirvana and *samsāra*, the Eternal and the world-in-flux are identical in what is totally unconditioned and beyond all categories, all opposites and all dualities, what, for lack of a better word, the Mahayana Buddhists called 'Emptiness', the 'Void', or simply 'Suchness'.

In China Buddhism met with a firm ally in Taoism which was equally illusive and very much more poetic. For the Taoists the indescribable Absolute was normally called the 'Tao', the 'Way'; but even that is saying too much. Better to say simply:

> The Way that can be told is not an Unvarying Way;
> The names that can be named are not unvarying names.
> It was from the Nameless that Heaven and Earth sprang;
> The named is but the mother that rears the ten thousand creatures, each after its kind.[1]

Like the Buddhist 'Emptiness' and 'Suchness' the Tao of the Taoists is also called the 'Void', 'Quietness', and the 'always-so':

> Endless the series of things without name
> On the way back to where there is nothing.[2]

'Where there is nothing' is the Buddhist 'Suchness'. There, there is neither Nirvana nor *samsāra*, neither Oneness nor multiplicity. Or, more positively, you could say that it is a Oneness

---

9. Nāgārjuna, *Mūlamadhyamakakārikā*, 25. 19–20, ed. Kenneth K. Inada (Hokuseido Press, Tokyo, 1970), p. 158; Frederick J. Streng, *Emptiness*, (Abingdon Press, New York, 1967), p. 217.
1. *Tao Tê Ching* 1, tr. Arthur Waley, as *The Way and its Power* (Allen & Unwin, London, 1934), p. 141.
2. Ibid., 14; Waley, p. 159.

beyond all number or a 'Goodness' beyond good and evil. 'Love, and do what you will', St Augustine is alleged to have said. A Zen master of the Tokugawa period said in a similar vein: 'Die while alive, and be completely dead: then do whatever you will, all is good.'[3] So too in modern times Abbot Zenkei Shibayama himself writes that 'True Thought' which is also ' "no-thought" is often likened to the "infant-like mind". The non-defiled mind of an infant has no traces of discrimination, between good-and-evil, you-and-I, and so it is as lucid as a mirror',[4] – and, one may add, as amoral as a newborn babe. And in a like vein the sixth Zen patriarch, Hui Nêng, when about to depart this world, gave these instructions to his disciples: 'Feel just as though I were still present. Sit still correctly for a while, so long as there is neither activity nor tranquillity, neither production nor annihilation, neither coming nor going, *neither right nor wrong*,[5] and neither remaining nor going away.'[6] This is the result of 'being identified with the universe and being one with all things'.[7] In such a state 'all is good', for everything is seen from an eternal point of view and everything fits into its proper place. This feeling of release from all the opposites, including right and wrong, good and evil, brings with it an effortless spontaneity beyond all definitions and man-made rules of conduct – and this is the Taoist paradise.

Much of the attraction of Zen Buddhism to the 'drop-out' youth of today lies in its alleged spontaneity. Nothing could be further from the truth. For the achievement of Zen enlightenment an apprenticeship of gruelling toil is the indispensable prerequisite. The late Professor D. T. Suzuki, whose main concern was to present Zen to the West as attractively as possible, was largely responsible for minimizing the hardness of the Zen way. Abbot Shibayama leaves us in no doubt about the 'crucifixion' the Zen aspirant must endure before he can hope to obtain enlightenment. 'He has to look deep into his inner self, go beyond the last extremity of himself, and despair of himself as a "self which can by no means

3. Z. Shibayama, *A Flower Does Not Talk*, p. 106.
4. Ibid., p. 121.   5. My italics.
6. *The Platform Scripture*, 53, tr. Wing-Tsit Chan (St John's University Press, New York, 1963), p. 147.
7. Z. Shibayama, op. cit., p. 182.

be saved". "Emptying oneself" comes from the bitterest experience, from the abyss of desperation and agony, of throwing oneself down, body and soul, before the Absolute.'[8] This, surely, is only to be expected, for the goal is to realize the Absolute – it doesn't matter whether you call it Self-nature or Buddha-nature – within you. What the Hindus call *samādhi*, 'deep concentration', usually meaning the integration of all the faculties and even the total loss of them in a timeless dimension as in Proust's case, can be deceptive; for it 'often tends to be just "a psychological state of being one with something",' and lacks the basic prajñā (true wisdom) to develop. The ultimate Zen experience is rather ' "testifying to the truth of Self-nature", which is deep enough to fundamentally change the personality.'[9] 'The word Self-nature ... means one's basic nature which he primarily has, deep at the bottom of his personality. It is the True Self, in contrast to the superficial self. It is the "Primary Buddha Nature" referred to' in the phrase ' "All beings are primarily Buddhas." "To testify to the truth of Self-nature" is to awaken to our primary Buddha Nature which we have deep in ourselves, and to become enlightened beings ourselves.'[1] 'The individual's training may differ from person to person', Abbot Shibayama continues, 'but I can still declare that there is not a single case where one is enlightened without going through the hard and difficult training process.'[2] This is because the ultimate Zen experience is not just a flash in the pan, a flash of lightning that lights up the whole universe revealing the truth of Nāgārjuna's paradox that 'there is no distinction whatever between Nirvana and *samsāra*, nor is there any distinction whatever between *samsāra* and Nirvana': rather it 'effects a fundamental change in oneself, philosophical and intellectual, as well as psychological. It is the total conversion of one's personality to where one is reborn with absolute freedom and creativity. I cannot assent, therefore, to the idea of attempting to taste Zen experience by means of drugs.'[3] Similarly Mr Philip Kapleau, a recent American convert to Zen Buddhism (not just Zen), rams the same point home. 'That an intense energy must be aroused for the tremendous effort of

8. Ibid., p. 172.   9. Ibid., p. 114.   1. Ibid., p. 105.
2. Ibid., p. 107.   3. Ibid., p. 117.

reaching enlightenment, whether it is instigated from outside by a stick or from the inside by sheer will power, has been taught by all great masters.'[4] This may be so, but if the essence of Zen is 'being identified with the universe and being one with all things',[5] then it is really no more than an experience of nature mysticism which the practice of Zen techniques can and does prolong for longer periods of time. There *is* a rebirth: all things are seen as new, but there is no trace of a 'spiritual marriage'. The stage is reached in which a man 'whose self is integrated by spiritual exercise sees the Self in all beings standing, all beings in the Self: the same in everything he sees', as the *Bhagavad-Gītā* puts it.[6] But the following stage is not reached, or at least is not thought to have been reached, of which the incarnate God, Krishna, says: 'Who sees *me* everywhere, who sees the All in *me*, for him I am not lost, nor is he lost to *me*. Who standing firm on unity communes in love with *me* as abiding in all beings ... that athlete of the spirit abides in *me*.'[7]

For the Zen people as for the nature mystics there is no sense of God as a Person who is both absolutely lovable and absolutely *terrible*; there is rather a sense of a fusion with all Nature, and Nature, as Richard Jefferies so rightly pointed out, knows nothing of good and evil. So, too, for the man at one with Nature good and evil are swallowed up into an indifferent and undifferentiated One. And this spells freedom and spontaneity in which moral commands and prohibitions have no place.

Spontaneity, indeed, is what the hippies are seeking above all things, a form of 'goodness' that wells up from a deeper level than the prescribed goodness of the religious orthodoxies. This they find both in Zen and in Taoism by which Chinese Zen was so deeply influenced.

Taoism was in many respects a sharp reaction against Confucian moralism, the cardinal virtues of which were human kindness, righteousness (or morality), propriety (or ritual), and wisdom. These, for the Taoists, were purely human inventions, departures from the spontaneous goodness, the 'always so', of the Tao:

4. Philip Kapleau, *The Three Pillars of Zen*, p. 89.   5. Above, p. 125.
6. *Bhagavad-Gītā*, 6.29.   7. Ibid., 6.30–1.

> After Tao was lost, then came the 'power'.
> After the 'power' was lost, then came human kindness.
> After human kindness was lost, then came morality.
> After morality was lost, then came ritual.
> Now ritual is the mere husk of loyalty and promise keeping
> And is indeed the first step towards brawling.[8]

Like the hippies and drop-outs of today the Taoists reacted against what seemed to them the regimentation of society in the name of civilization. Man had become 'abnormal' in a 'normal' universe, he had lost the sense of being at one with Nature and a part of Nature which spontaneously responded to the rhythm of the whole. The Tao had been lost and man had no resource but to try to reintegrate himself into it by unlearning all that civilization had taught him and returning to the simplicity, the 'Uncarved Block', of Nature. The Confucians agreed with them in thinking that a golden age of harmony and equilibrium had vanished in which all could be achieved without effort, simply by letting things go. They looked back to the purely mythical golden age of the three sage Kings who, by doing nothing in the right way, ensured that all things were rightly done. Take the case of the second sage King, Shun: 'Among those that ruled by inactivity surely Shun may be counted. For what action did he take? He merely placed himself gravely and reverently facing due south; that was all.'[9] The golden age, however, was over, for man had become fully self-conscious, and had to adjust himself and the knowledge he had acquired through becoming self-conscious to the natural order of things. The universe could no longer be described simply as 'heaven and earth' but as 'heaven, *man,* and earth', a triad in which man found himself to be the middle term. Heaven and earth continued to follow their natural Tao, but man by becoming self-conscious, having eaten, as it were, of 'the tree of the knowledge of good and evil', was left to find his own Tao which would be specifically human, yet in tune with the rhythm of the Tao of heaven and earth. This purely human Tao they found in the four

---

8. *Tao Tê Ching,* 38.
9. *Analects of Confucius,* 15.4, tr. Arthur Waley (Allen & Unwin, London, 1938, and reprints).

cardinal virtues of human kindness, righteousness, propriety, and wisdom. Human kindness (*jên*), as its name implies, meant not only to be human but also humane, not only kind but also good: righteousness meant not only doing the right thing but also justice and morality in general: propriety meant not only good manners, respect for one's parents, and the preservation of finely graded family relationships, but also the participation in elaborate rites and music designed to emphasize the solidarity of the community and its reintegration into the natural Tao out of which it had inadvertently slipped; while 'wisdom' was mainly exemplified in conscience, the unique privilege of the human animal which enabled him to choose between right and wrong.

All these virtues, admirable in themselves, were liable to degenerate into a caricature of themselves. Human kindness must inevitably reduce itself to being a 'do-gooder', righteousness degenerate into self-righteousness, propriety into conformism, and wisdom into prying into other peoples' consciences while remaining neglectful of one's own. Moreover, one tendency in Confucianism tended to exalt man over Nature, seeking not so much to harmonize with it as to dominate it and direct it. And so Hsün Tzŭ had asked himself:

> Is it better to exalt Heaven and think of it,
> Or to nourish its creatures and regulate them?
> Is it better to obey Heaven and sing hymns to it,
> Or to grasp the mandate of Heaven and make use of it?
> Is it better to long for the seasons and wait for them,
> Or to respond to the seasons and exploit them?
> Is it better to wait for things to increase of themselves,
> Or to apply your talents and transform them?
> Is it better to think of things but regard them as outside you,
> Or to control things and not let them slip your grasp?
> Is it better to long for the source from which things are born,
> Or to possess the means to bring them to completion?[1]

The answer to these questions is obviously intended to be 'Yes' to the second alternatives; for this is a Confucian document and it was the aim of the Confucian to regulate, improve, and exploit Nature, and to adapt Nature to the new situation created by the

---

1. Hsün Tzŭ, 17.19, in Burton Watson, *Hsün Tzŭ, Basic Writings* (Columbia University Press, New York, 1963), p. 86.

emergence of man as a rational and social animal. It has a curiously modern ring, for it seems to inaugurate an era of progress, organization, science, and technology. Against all this the Taoists reacted violently, for they were quite literally the drop-outs of their time – anti-intellectual, anti-organization, anti-status-seeking, anti-moralist. Indeed, the following lines from the *Tao Tê Ching* (19) might be taken as the hippies' charter:

> Banish wisdom, discard knowledge,
> And the people will be benefited a hundredfold.
> Banish human kindness, discard morality,
> And the people will be dutiful and compassionate.
> Banish skill, discard profit,
> And thieves and robbers will disappear.
> If when these three things are done they find life too plain and unadorned,
> Then let them have accessories;
> Give them Simplicity to look at, the Uncarved Block to hold,
> Give them selflessness and fewness of desires.

For the Taoist every advance in civilization, every technical achievement, is a cutting and hacking at the Uncarved Block, that primitive state of unity in which man felt himself to be at one with all Nature and with his fellow-men. Since individual consciousness was not yet born, there was no knowledge of death, for the life of the individual was still bound up with the group, and death was, then, as Tennyson was to say, an 'almost laughable impossibility'. This is how things used to be before men started to meddle with things they did not understand. For 'the True man of ancient times knew nothing of loving life, knew nothing of hating death. He emerged without delight; he went back in without a fuss. He came briskly, he went briskly, and that was all. He didn't forget where he began; he didn't try to find out where he would end. He received something and took pleasure in it; he forgot about it and handed it back again.'[2]

There is a freshness and elusiveness about the Taoist classics that give them a grace and charm quite lacking in the early Hindu and Buddhist texts. Their precepts too are alluring in that they

2. *Chuang Tzŭ*, 6.2, in Burton Watson, *The Complete Works of Chuang Tzŭ* (Columbia University Press, New York, 1968), p. 78.

LSD and Zen

bid us have done with all the irksome conventions of 'civilized' life and return to a pure state of nature in which 'men live the same as birds and beasts, group themselves side by side with the ten thousand things. Who then knows anything about "gentleman" or "petty man"? Simple and unwitting, men have no "wisdom"; thus their Virtue does not depart from them. Simple and unwitting, they have no desire; this is called uncarved simplicity. In uncarved simplicity the people attain their true nature.

'Then along comes the sage, huffing and puffing after human kindness, reaching on tiptoe for righteousness, and the world for the first time has doubts; mooning and mouthing over his music, snipping and stitching away at his rites, and the world for the first time is divided. Thus, if the plain unwrought substance had not been blighted, how would there be any sacrificial goblets? If the white jade had not been shattered, how would there be any sceptres and batons? If the Way and its Virtue had not been cast aside, how would there be any call for human kindness and righteousness? If the true form of the inborn nature had not been abandoned, how would there be any use for rites and music? ... That the unwrought substance was blighted in order to fashion implements – this was the crime of the artisan. That the Way and its Virtue were destroyed in order to create human kindness and righteousness – this was the fault of the sage.'[3]

Such was the paradise lost which the Taoists vainly hoped to regain against the rising tide of 'culture' and 'civilization', and such is the state of original innocence which the hippies today are pathetically trying to recapture. The Taoists made themselves ridiculous ('mine is indeed the mind of a very idiot'[4]) because they dropped out of the dominant civilization of their day: the hippies too make themselves ridiculous because they are trying to do what can only be done without trying. Try to be spontaneous and you only succeed in becoming conventionally unconventional, and that is perhaps the dreariest form of all conventionality. Jesus said, 'Unless you change and become like little children you will never enter the kingdom of heaven.'[5] He did not say, 'Try your

3. Ibid., 9.2; Burton Watson, pp. 105–6. 4. *Tao Tê Ching*, 20.
5. Matthew 18:3.

damnedest to become like little children', because he knew that the more you try the more certain you are to become a crashing bore.

To become like a little child means to be born again, and if you are to be born again, you must first die. 'Die while alive, and be completely dead',[6] Zen says. And again: ' "To die once the Great Death", we have to "empty" this vessel called self.'[7] This is what Buddhism is all about, and this is what Christianity is all about, but despite Dr Leary's talk about a 'death-rebirth sequence' I am not at all sure that this is what LSD is all about. He speaks of the risks that LSD involves – the risk that 'expanded consciousness' may lead not to the discovery of the true, eternal self but to madness, and this he would compare to the great leap into the dark that the Zen Buddhists know they may have to make before enlightenment dawns. But the 'dark' of Zen is not madness, though the risk of madness is always there. As for all the mystics the first commandment is: 'Detach yourself from all things.' But what if you become attached to detachment itself? There lies the greatest danger. And so Hui Nêng, the sixth Zen patriarch, warns us: 'I also know some who teach people to sit and look into the mind as well as to look at purity, so that the mind will not be perturbed and nothing will arise from it. Devoting their efforts to this, deluded people fail to become enlightened; consequently, they are so attached to this method as to become insane.'[8] This is not the 'dark' of Zen any more than it is the 'dark night of the soul' of St John of the Cross: it is not the dark night of death – the death of the ego and with it of all desire – and the awakening of the Buddha-nature within you just as the Buddha himself 'awoke' (for that is what the word 'Buddha' means) from death to immortality.

This is Zen, and it is sensible non-sense, but has it really very much to do with LSD? A little, a very little, perhaps, but people are always ready to deceive themselves, not least the nature mystics (Richard Jefferies is the exception) and the devotees of LSD. Let

6. Above, p. 125.
7. Z. Shibayama, *A Flower Does Not Talk*, p. 173.
8. *The Platform Scripture*, 14: Wing-Tsit Chan, p. 49.

LSD and Zen

them beware of their cherished expanded consciousness, for 'there is the greatest danger in this mood, and those who are open to it should be on their guard against an insidious deception'.[9]

Perhaps we have discussed the mystical pretensions of LSD enough. What are we to conclude? I do not question that LSD can produce an almost unlimited expansion of consciousness and that this may add a totally new, awesome, and numinous aspect to life; nor do I question that LSD can deepen religious experience if it is already there, or even arouse a religious experience, if the desire to have done with self and all selfishness is there; nor does it seem wrong to me to use LSD or other psychedelic drugs as aids to meditation or even as substitutes for meditation. But 'there *is* the greatest danger in this mood', since the drug can induce psychosis, attempted homicide or suicide, in some cases actual suicide.[1] For as Al-Qushayrī says: 'The expanded man experiences an expansion great enough to contain [all] creation; and there is practically nothing that will cause him fear.'[2] He will have illusions of omnipotence and may throw himself out of a window thinking that he can fly! Since this is so, I would most emphatically say that LSD experiments (and they still are experiments and involve physical and psychical risks as all responsible experimenters, including Dr Leary, seem to agree) should never be indulged in for kicks but only under the guidance of one who is both holy and sane and has experience of both religious contemplation and the religious experience LSD is alleged to provide. Of course practically no one has these four qualifications since 'holy' men like Abbot Shibayama and Krishnamurti will have no part in such goings on. And people who have the other three must be exceedingly few and far between – perhaps one in a thousand psychoanalysts, of whom Jung was certainly one; maybe a saintly priest or two who, like Pope John, are good not because they try to be good but because they don't need to try since they have lost their ego and therefore all egoism, and are thus open to that spontaneity which is the Holy Spirit. This is, I suspect, what the Zen Buddhists mean by the Buddha-

---

9. Above, pp. 98–9.
1. See Donald B. Louria, in DeBold and Leaf, *LSD, Man & Society*, pp. 37–41.
2. Above, p. 99.

nature which is potentially present in all men and came to life in Pope John.

As to Leary, LSD and sex – well, Dr Leary's experiences in this matter seem to be highly exceptional, and in the opinion of one qualified investigator,[3] 'perhaps the most reprehensible and misleading statement regarding LSD is the claim that it is a potent aphrodisiac.... This claim is made by the avowed proselytizers, and more than any other single statement is effective in recruiting new converts to the LSD cult.... They, of course, neglect to mention that the overwhelming majority of those taking LSD have no interest in sex, preferring their solipsistic trance, and that others who have taken LSD and attempted intercourse have found it impossible to consummate.'[4] Dr Leary's claims in this respect are clearly designed to attract the increasingly large proportion among the young who have refused to bow down and worship the machine and have deified instead the creative urge that compels the whole animal world to reproduce itself, while taking care more often than not that reproduction does not in fact take place.

Of course it is true that the puritanical attitude to sex, which we so largely owe to the fleshly peccadilloes of the young Augustine and his intellectual Manichaeanism which so strongly condemned them, was wrong and has been responsible for much needless unhappiness, but I cannot see that the opposite swing of the pendulum culminating in 'several hundred orgasms' during 'a carefully prepared, loving LSD session'[5] is any solution to this problem, which is both serious and religious. Even in the left-hand Tantra in Hinduism sex is regarded as a sacrament representing the indissoluble union of God with his Shakti, his creative power mythologically represented as his wife. Thus the religious argument against promiscuity is that it is the desecration of a sacrament and a vulgarization of the holy. For in mystical writing, whether Christian, Muslim, or Hindu, sexual imagery of the most passionate kind is used to represent the union of God, the male,

3. Dr Donald B. Louria (B.S., M.D. Harvard University), Assistant Professor of Medicine at Cornell Medical College and head of the Infectious Disease Laboratory of Bellevue Hospital, New York.
4. DeBold and Leaf, op. cit., p. 42.
5. T. Leary, *The Politics of Ecstasy*, p. 107.

with the soul, the female. This is no doubt why Pope Paul VI so vigorously upholds the celibacy of the clergy in the Latin Church, for the priest is by his very vocation a spiritual 'bride' of Christ. This, and not the changing fashions of that ephemeral world for which Christ refused to pray, marks him out as one who has renounced the strongest tie that attaches him to this world. Such acts of renunciation are understood and respected in India, for renunciation has always been the hall-mark of the genuinely religious man in that country. Maybe, in modern Europe and the USA, the standard set is an impossible one for the average man, but a priest, one had hoped, was more than an average man – more even than an average *Dutch* man. But the world is all awry and perhaps there is nothing we can do but abandon it to the silent, gloating malice of Satan in whom we do not believe, and seek solace in the 'solipsistic trance' and the 'expanded consciousness' which we are told we will find in LSD.

5

BEYOND GOOD AND EVIL

There was a man called John: Pope John XXIII, Supreme Pontiff of the Roman Catholic Church. The word 'pontiff' derives from the Latin 'pontifex', a 'builder of bridges'. Pope John was just that: he sought to build bridges that would restore communication between the 'prisoner of the Vatican' and the outside world, to Christians independent of Rome, to the non-Christian religions, to the humanists and Marxists, indeed to all the non-Catholic ideologies; but above all he must have been thinking, like his master, Jesus, of an opening out to the disinherited and alienated who had no ideological or spiritual home. He made his breakthrough and for his all too short pontificate he became what Marx had said about religion itself, 'the heart of a heartless world' and 'the spirit of a spiritless situation'.[6] Pope John was that too; and though his heart was extinguished all too soon, his spirit remains nostalgically with us, although the minds of clever men and the inflated self-importance of those who cannot or will not renounce seem intent on stifling it once again. 'Renounce', one of the Upanishads says, 'and then enjoy'.[7] Once again India teaches us the truths of our own religion, for we have forgotten how to renounce and only want to enjoy. This may be the way of much of the modern world, but it is not the way of Christ. For it was he, not the Buddha, who said: 'I tell you, most solemnly, unless a wheat grain falls on the ground and dies, it remains only a single grain; but if it dies, it yields a rich harvest.'[8]

John died, and the harvest, I suppose, has been rich enough, but, as usual, the tares have grown up with the wheat because these tares are rich and fat and bourgeois and self-righteous, and it is not *in* them to renounce. This is our modern world, and two

---

6. Marx and Engels, *On Religion* (Moscow, 1957), p. 42.
7. *Īśā* Upanishad, 1.   8. John 12:24.

world wars and their grisly aftermath have taught us nothing. No doubt we would have had a third one long ago had it not been for the fact that the balance of terror is so evenly maintained by the two superpowers, the USSR and the USA – powers which, symbolically enough, haven't even got a name, only anonymous initials. This is typical of this 'world come of age' in which we live.

But why should Bonhoeffer have thought that the world has come of age? Every single civilization before our own has probably thought exactly that about itself. It might make some sense to say that Christianity has come of age, but there is an equally good case to be made that Christianity has reached the age of puberty with all its confusions and uncertainties, or that it is growing old, or that it is already in senile decay, or that it is already dead and rotting in the grave though we haven't even noticed it. If Christianity was once the 'heart of a heartless world', no one can believe that now, unless it is a heart already wrenched from the body, beating alone, drawing in not blood but empty air.[9] But then a heart transplant is always possible: psychiatry maybe? humanism? or why not LSD?

But do not the prophets of doom make altogether too much fuss about the so-called 'anguish' and 'anxiety' (*Angst*) of the modern age? *Angst*, after all, is a very bourgeois disease, and Bonhoeffer, serene as ever in those last months in prison before they hanged him, could write with quiet equanimity about the disappearance of God from the world but with an almost savage bitterness against those who, he thought, sought to fill the empty throne:

'Efforts are made to prove to a world thus come of age that it cannot live without the tutelage of "God". Even though there has been surrender on all secular problems, there still remain the so-called "ultimate questions" – death, guilt – to which only "God" can give an answer, and because of which we need God and the church and the pastor. So we live, in some degree, on these so-called ultimate questions of humanity. But what if one day they no longer exist as such, if they too can be answered "without God"? Of course, we now have the secularized offshoots of

9. Cf. Georges Bernanos, *Monsieur Ouine*, in *Oeuvres romanesques*, p. 1485.

Christian theology, namely existentialist philosophy and the psychotherapists, who demonstrate to secure, contented, and happy mankind that it is really unhappy and desperate and simply unwilling to admit that it is in a predicament about which it knows nothing, and from which only they can rescue it. Wherever there is health, strength, security, simplicity, they scent luscious fruit to gnaw at or to lay their pernicious eggs in. They set themselves to drive people to inward despair, and then the game is in their hands. ... And whom does it touch? A small number of intellectuals, of degenerates, of people who regard themselves as the most important thing in the world, and who therefore like to busy themselves with themselves. The ordinary man, who spends his everyday life at work and with his family, and of course with all kinds of diversions, is not affected. He has neither the time nor the inclination to concern himself with his existential despair, or to regard his perhaps modest share of happiness as a trial, a trouble, or a calamity.'[1]

This was written twenty-eight years ago; and much of what Bonhoeffer said is still true today. Probably there still is a reasonably contented majority with families and hobbies and interests which keep them perfectly happy, the people whom William James called the 'healthy-minded' and Teilhard, less flatteringly, 'the dull, inert mass of those who believe in nothing at all'.[2] But, with ever-increasing urbanization and the progressive mechanization and dehumanization of urban life, how long can it last? The vast majority of urban jobs are mechanical and dull; and so man is more and more dependent on distractions which the mass media are all too ready to supply in superabundance. It would be stupid to cavil at this since so far the Churches, whose demise as institutions Bonhoeffer seemed to view almost with satisfaction, have not been able to make the Gospel message seem in any way relevant to the modern world. In the centuries before our mechanized age work and distraction (*divertissement* in Pascal's sense of the word) were much the same thing. Work *was* the 'distraction' of all but

1. D. Bonhoeffer, *Letters and Papers from Prison*, pp. 326–7.
2. P. Teilhard de Chardin, *L'avenir de l'homme* (Éditions du Seuil, Paris, 1959), p. 101; E.T. *The Future of Man* (Collins, London, and Harper & Row, New York, 1964), p. 76.

the most privileged: leisure was the privilege of the upper social crust, and, according to Pascal, there is nothing more dangerous than leisure. Give the people leisure and take away their distractions, and what happens? 'They would see themselves, they would think about what they are, from whence they came and where they are going; and so you cannot keep them busy enough and turn them away from such thoughts as these. And that is why, after providing them with so much to keep them busy and they still have time to relax, we advise them to seek distraction, to play, and be constantly and completely occupied.'[3] And what is the result of this perpetual distraction, this refusal to face life and what, if anything, it means. Boredom (since that seems to be the only possible translation of the French *ennui*), and that has always been the worm that does not die nagging at the heart of the well-to-do. For indeed 'there is nothing so intolerable to a man as to be completely at rest, without passions or occupation, without distractions or hobbies (*application*). For then he feels his nothingness, his dereliction, his inadequacy, his dependence, his impotence, his emptiness. Then from the depths of his soul there will immediately spring forth boredom, a black mood, listlessness, worries, rancour, and despair.[4] ... How hollow is the heart of man, how full of filth!'[5]

Thanks to science and technology leisure is no longer the privilege of the few, but we have not even begun to teach the new leisured classes how to use their leisure. How could we, since we do not know how to use it ourselves? We intellectuals, we professors, we scribes and Pharisees, berate the mass media for the trivial distractions they provide, unless, of course, we are asked to provide them ourselves; but why should you expect them to do otherwise since nobody in our modern society is going to handle unsaleable goods? Ideologically we are bankrupt. God has been dethroned, and so far as the younger generation can see, nothing has been put in his place but Mammon, that is, in good English, 'money'. How true it is then, as Professor Monod, speaking in the name of science, says: 'It is at this point that modern man turns

3. Pascal, *Pensées*, in *Oeuvres complètes*, p. 1145.
4. Ibid., p. 1138.   5. Ibid., p. 1145.

towards science, or rather against it, now seeing its terrible capacity to destroy not only bodies but the soul itself.'[6] But why turn to science or to this or that scientist? It is their business to see how the universe of matter works, not to reason why. That hitherto was the department of religion. And so men turn to our new priests, the pseudo-scientists in all their wide variety, not only to the old religious surrogates like astrology, occultism, even witchcraft, all of which seem to flourish in their different ways, but also to the social 'scientists' and of course the psychologists and psychiatrists who agree just about as little as philosophers do and for the same reason – they are not dealing with matter, which is subject to mathematical measurement of one sort or another, but with the soul (or, if you prefer it in Greek, the psyche), which is not subject to measurement at all. They too are broken reeds – and usually very expensive ones: and so, once again we find ourselves 'in an indeterminate sphere, among the stones and the rafters, in the rain'.

Science, and technology which applies science for our benefit and comfort, has delivered the goods as never before; and we have become completely dependent on them. Meanwhile, with the old gods dethroned, we are left in a spiritual desert. Science has made leisure possible for all, but leisure means boredom, and rather than face *this* we have the extraordinary spectacle of the workers of the bankrupt Upper Clyde Company taking over the plant in order to make good their right – not to strike but to work! – to apply themselves to something in order not to be left face to face with themselves.

Teilhard de Chardin, whom Professor Monod so cordially dislikes, has indeed written a great deal of nonsense about all kinds of things and never more so than when he launches into social affairs. Thus on the subject of unemployment he can write: 'Unemployment can be defined as the sudden appearance of a mass of human energy violently released by an internal adjustment of the noosphere[7].... But just as inevitably (and beneficially)

---

6. J. Monod, *Chance and Necessity*, p. 161.
7. This unlovely neologism means little more than that part of living matter which is capable of thought, in other words, the human race.

as the advance of the universe, it manifests with singular clarity, for anyone with eyes to see, the reality of that advance itself.'[8] Tell that to the unemployed!

But then Teilhard thinks in terms of evolutionary time – in millions rather than hundreds of years; and we must suppose that from this Olympian standpoint the fate of a few thousand men on the banks of an insignificant little river in an insignificant little island is of about as much interest as is the fate of his precious 'noosphere' (that is, us) to 'the eternal silence of these infinite spaces', which cares not a jot for this life-infected planet of ours.

Teilhard has his admirers – and for obvious reasons. Like Marx (and much more so Engels) he gives us hope based on what he (and they) advertise as being solid scientific and evolutionary grounds. When he is talking about mysticism he sometimes talks sense, but his glowing vision of a future in which a unified human race will converge upon itself and its God in union-in-diversity and joy is, in the present state of this unhappy planet, a pipe-dream and a mockery of human distress. When he emerges from the pipe-dream he occasionally has some wise things to say, but as these are mainly concerned with death, they are best left to a later chapter.

Teilhard was, of course, a Jesuit and, despite persecution and the suppression of his works by his superiors and the Curial authorities in Rome, his faith in and love for the Catholic Church was never severely shaken because, with his collectivist ideas, he could see no frame in which the collective destiny of mankind could work itself out except within a reformed and open Catholic Church. On the Protestant side there is no one of equal stature except Bonhoeffer, and he was cut off in his prime. There remain, in the religious sphere, only two men of comparable stature. Neither is a theologian, as might have been expected. One is the Swiss psychologist, C. G. Jung, whom nobody with an interest in religion can afford to neglect: the other is the French novelist, Georges Bernanos, a Roman Catholic in every fibre of his being, who, like Teilhard, saw far more clearly the appalling scandal of

---

8. P. Teilhard de Chardin, *L'énergie humaine* (Éditions du Seuil, Paris, 1962), p. 155: E.T. *Human Energy* (Collins, London, 1969), pp 123–4.

compromise and fence-sitting and cowardice that the pre-war Church represented than do our latter-day rebels so vociferous today.

Bernanos was a prophet and, like Jeremiah, he was a prophet of doom. The fact that in France at least his greatness is at last acknowledged (he died in 1948) is some sign that his harsh message is finally beginning to strike home.

We are a sick society: and however much we may paper over our wounds, we can no longer fool ourselves all the time. And we are a very vulnerable society because we have taken for granted all the superfluities of life which science and technology have showered on us so that we can no longer do without them: this was proved only too conclusively during the electricity work-to-rule at the end of 1970. We, following the USA, are the real materialists much more than the Communist bloc, for, though some of us may still pay lip-service to spiritual values, basically we care for nothing but material welfare and material comfort. We have grown flabby and rotten inside. 'All that is solid melts into air, all that is holy is profaned, and man is at last compelled to face with sober senses his real conditions of life and his relations with his kind.'[9] Unfortunately he does not face them: he prefers to shut himself off in a hermetically sealed, centrally heated or air-conditioned room in which he need not think about the horrors that are taking place in less privileged parts of the world, in Bangla Desh and Vietnam or wherever it may be. He may talk about compassion, but he has no compassion. Oh, yes: 'sympathy, compassion, συμπαθεῖν, to "suffer together". Better to say "*rot* together".'[1] This is the vision that Bernanos had of the modern world – a world in full suppuration and decay, a kind of spiritual entropy,[2] the symptom of which is boredom, the reality despair.

'My parish is eaten up by boredom,' says the country priest who is the hero of his most famous novel and whose diary the novel purports to be, 'that's the right word. Like so many other parishes. Boredom is eating them up under our eyes and there is

---

9. See above, p. 21.   1. G. Bernanos, *Monsieur Ouine*, p. 1464.
2. Hans Urs von Balthasar, *Le chrétien Bernanos* (French translation, Éditions du Seuil, Paris, 1956), p. 496.

nothing we can do about it. One day, maybe, the contagion will catch up with us too; we will discover this cancer within ourselves. You can live a long time like that. ... Perhaps someone will say that the world has long got used to boredom, that boredom is man's real condition ... But I wonder whether men have ever really known this contagion which is boredom – this leprosy: an aborted despair, a disgraceful form of despair which is, I suppose, like the fermentation of a Christianity in a state of decomposition.'[3]

The 'parish', as in all Bernanos's major novels, is a microcosm of the modern world. The world is not on fire as it was for the Buddha but just slowly rotting away, rotting through the fault and the default of the old.[4] It has reached the stage when even evil bores it:[5] it desires neither good nor evil.[6]

Bernanos had entitled his first novel *Sous le soleil de Satan*, 'Beneath the sun of Satan' – and rightly so, since at no stage are we allowed to forget that 'it is not against human enemies that we have to struggle, but against the Sovereignties and the Powers who originate the darkness in this world, the spiritual army of evil in the heavens'.[7] Maybe we do not see it in quite this way, but never, I think, has evil been so palpable a fact as it is in this twentieth century. The old virtues like honour and being true to one's word, which were both fundamental and axiomatic for Bernanos, appear slightly ridiculous in the atmosphere of moral decay in which we live. Of course he is right when he says: 'The world needs honour. What the world lacks is honour. ... The world has lost its self-respect.'[8] But it is not the fact that it has lost its self-respect that illuminates its rottenness but the fact that it no longer seems to want to regain it. What is the point of talking about the dignity of man to people for whom the word 'dignity', like honour, has lost all meaning?

We have become so used to dishonour on the international scale that it is hardly surprising that it has ceased to have any meaning on the individual level. When the Kaiser invaded Belgium without

3. G. Bernanos, *Journal d'un curé de campagne*, in *Oeuvres romanesques*, pp. 1031–2.
4. *Monsieur Ouine*, p. 1511.   5. Ibid., p. 1469.
6. Ibid., p. 1537.   7. Ephesians 6:12.
8. Quoted in Urs von Balthasar, op. cit., p. 518.

a declaration of war in 1914, the world was genuinely shocked. Unfortunately the precedent had been set – and set by the Prussian ruling class which, with all its defects, had always prided itself on its honour. How should one be surprised, then, that the example of 'honourable' men should thereafter be followed by other 'honourable' men? It was after all 'honourable' men who connived at Mussolini's invasion of Ethiopia and Albania and who handed over Czechoslovakia to Hitler. When 'honourable' men behave like this and put their faith, as they did in 1938, in a dishonourable thug, it was hardly surprising that the thug himself should invade Poland, Denmark, Norway, Holland, Belgium, and finally the USSR (which had aided and abetted him in the partition of Poland), without any declaration of war. This had now become common international practice: the Japanese followed suit and the British were little better when they invaded Iran in 1941. As to the invasion of Czechoslovakia by its own allies, with the USSR at their head, in 1968, even our radical young did not find this worth demonstrating about very much. What did they care about 'Communism with a human face'? Honour, justice, fair play – well, maybe we have seen them parodied often enough, but this does not mean that they are not values intrinsic to the human race: deep down even in this rotting world of ours there is a hankering for a return to decency. But no one nowadays seems interested in 'Communism with a human face' or anything else for that matter 'with a human face'; and the Curé of Fenouille in Bernanos's masterpiece, *Monsieur Ouine*, is quite right when he says that, with the progressive dehumanization of man, 'you will see all manner of beasts emerge whose names men have long since forgotten, assuming that they had ever been given one'.[9]

Pope John XXIII and Dietrich Bonhoeffer had both hoped to bring Christ out of the tabernacle into the world 'come of age'. Bonhoeffer indeed spent his last months in trying to find a 'worldly' interpretation of Christianity. He had read some Bernanos and admired him, and on fundamentals he agreed with him, but his vision of the modern world was less starkly prophetic, or, if you prefer it, less jaundiced. Sometimes Bonhoeffer seems

9. G. Bernanos, op. cit., p. 1508.

perfectly happy to jettison the Church in favour of the world. Bernanos saw in the modern world that world *for which Christ would not pray*.¹ 'The hour is at hand', he had said, 'when, on the ruins of what is still left of the old Christian order, the new order will be born which will really be the order of the world, the order of the Prince of this world, of the prince whose kingdom is of this world. Then, under the hard law of a necessity stronger than any illusion, the pride of the churchman, so long maintained by simple conventions surviving all beliefs, will have lost its very object.'² Bernanos had no illusions: the modern world is ruled not by God, nor by science, but by Satan, the Prince of this world.

Evil is the theme of two of Bernanos's great novels – *Sous le soleil de Satan* and *Monsieur Ouine*. But there is a considerable difference between the two: in the first the title is absolutely fitting, there can be no doubt at all against whom the hero (again a country priest) is pitted. From the very beginning the novel is heavy with evil; but at the very moment when the priest's courage seems to fail him he meets with a horse-dealer – a jolly lad 'whose voice has a certain secret gaiety, absolutely irresistible'.³ For a while, in his exhaustion, the priest relaxes in the presence of his new-found friend, but very soon it turns out that his friend is no less a person than Satan himself. The priest looks into his eyes and groans for he sees in a flash just what damnation means:

'Imagine a man with both his hands tied to the top of the mast – imagine him suddenly losing his balance. He sees, yawning and swelling out beneath him, no longer the sea but the whole starry abyss and the foam of all the galaxies in the process of formation seething trillions and trillions of miles away across the void which nothing can measure and which he must cross in his eternal fall. Such a man would not feel a more absolute giddiness in the pit of his stomach [than the Abbé felt in looking into those eyes]. His heart beat twice as furiously against his ribs and stopped. His guts were turned upside-down with nausea. His fingers, clutching desperately, the only thing left alive in a body petrified with horror, scratched at the soil like claws. Sweat streamed between his

---

1. John 17:9.   2. G. Bernanos, op. cit., pp. 1494–5.
3. *Sous le soleil de Satan*, in *Oeuvres romanesques*, p. 168.

shoulders. This dauntless man, bent double and wrenched from the earth by the immeasurable attraction of nothingness, this time saw himself lost beyond recall.'[4]

This is the foretaste of damnation, and the early Bernanos has this fearful vision of it in the eyes of the Devil: but beyond damnation there is 'perdition' – 'being lost', that is to say passing beyond not only salvation but damnation too: 'lost, gone astray, out of reach, no longer in question',[5] beyond the reach of both God and his eternal enemy, Satan – alone and unnoticed – in the void.

There are two ways of passing beyond good and evil: one is to pass into what the Tibetan Book of the Dead calls the 'Clear Light of the Void' which is the pure peace and joy that knows neither space nor time. The other is what Bernanos saw; this too is a pure vacuity and emptiness, but from here all joy is forever excluded: it can only be likened to absolute cold.[6] It is true that in Bernanos there are traces of nature mysticism, but his Christianity was basically dualistic, with the dualism of the Zoroastrians, not of the Manichees. For him Satan is a terrifying reality, 'all evil, full of death, a liar and a deceiver',[7] as the Zoroastrian confession of faith puts it. In *Sous le soleil de Satan* he is no doubt not co-equal with God, but it still might be said of him what Zoroaster said of the Evil Spirit in his *Gāthās* ('Songs'):

'I will speak out concerning the two Spirits of whom, at the beginning of existence, the Holier thus spoke to him who is Evil: "Neither our thoughts, nor our teachings, nor our wills, nor our choices, nor our words, nor our deeds, nor our consciences, nor yet our souls agree."'[8]

Like the Zoroastrian Devil, Bernanos's Satan can imitate the ways of God. Even the mystic is not free from his insidious deception, for 'he is in the prayer of the hermit, in his fasts and penances, at the heart of the deepest ecstasy, and in the silence of the heart. He poisons holy water, burns in the consecrated wax, breathes in

---

4. Ibid., p. 177.   5. *Monsieur Ouine*, p. 1557.   6. Ibid., p. 1490.
7. See R. C. Zaehner, *The Teachings of the Magi* (Allen & Unwin, London, 1956), p. 23.
8. *Yasna*, 45.2.

the breath of virgins . . . corrupts every religious way. He has been caught lying on the lips half opened to spread the word of truth: in the midst of the thunder and lightning of the beatific rapture he pursues the just right into the arms of God. What need has he to struggle for the souls of so many men on this earth where they crawl about like animals, waiting for it to cover them up again tomorrow? This dark and medley flock meets its destiny of its own accord. . . . His hatred is reserved for the saints.'[9]

What do the Buddhists say of their Nirvana? Silence – peace – solitude – the Void. Well, Satan can counterfeit this too: for 'he comes suddenly, in a flash, without warning, horribly peaceful and assured. But however much he may stress this likeness to God, no joy can ever proceed from him, but, far higher than the pleasures that only stir your entrails, his masterpiece is a silent peace, solitary, icy, comparable only to the enjoyment of nothingness. When this gift is offered and accepted, our guardian angel turns his face away, amazed.'[1]

Sous le soleil de Satan was Bernanos's first major novel: *Monsieur Ouine* was his last. It is also the most difficult because nothing is certain. Like the Buddhist *samsāra*, it is a flux which flows through your hands without your being able to catch hold of anything tangible. Yet, from the very first line you feel that evil surrounds you – oh, nothing so obvious as Satan masquerading as a horse-dealer, but an indefinable sense of corruption which envelops everything, stifles everything, yet never allows itself to be seized at its source. Even pity is powerless here, it has about as much chance as a surgeon operating on a mass of pus,[2] for the world 'come of age', from which the spirit of childhood has been banished, is already turning into 'rottenness and gangrene',[3] beyond the range of Satan himself.[4]

The action takes place in a village in Artois in northern France; and the village stands for what Bonhoeffer described as a 'world come of age', but which Bernanos saw as a world from which not only God but the spirit of man had been banished. The hero, like

---

9. G. Bernanos, *Sous le soleil de Satan*, p. 154.
1. Ibid., p. 213.   2. *Monsieur Ouine*, p. 1464.
3. Ibid., p. 1492.   4. Ibid., p. 1490.

the title, of the book is Monsieur Ouine – Ouine standing for *oui-non*, 'yes-no', the eternal enigma, or the 'union of opposites' so dear to Heraclitus, the Hindus and the Mahayana Buddhists. But if *this* is the union of opposites, then it would seem to be a diabolical caricature of what is usually understood by that term. The Zen Buddhists speak of a state which they call 'emptiness' or the 'void' which transcends right and wrong, good and evil,[5] and the Neo-Confucians were to explain this as a 'Good' – a *summum bonum* – which transcends what is normally called good and evil.[6] The Zen Buddhists too had said: 'Die while alive, and be completely dead: then do whatever you will, all is good.'[7] For what is beyond good and evil is an Absolute which makes room for compassion as well as wisdom. In *Monsieur Ouine* you will find the same terminology but here the Void which transcends good and evil, 'yes' and 'no', is the absolute desolation of a soul which has lost all interest in itself and is slowly rotting away. Here words mean nothing, for there is nothing to *prove* that the 'emptiness' in which Monsieur Ouine is engulfed is not the same as the 'Emptiness' of the Mahayana Buddhists. Indeed it is identical in the sense that it is 'beyond good and evil', but it is obviously not the Neo-Confucian 'Good' but a monstrous 'Evil' beyond any name – the entropy of the soul.

I do not know how often I have read this amazing book, but it is certainly more than ten times. To say that I fully understand it even now would be a senseless boast since good and evil are so inextricably mixed up in the book that it is impossible to separate them out with any conviction. The setting indeed is clear enough: an impalpable sense of evil hovers over the village and the local château which houses a moribund châtelain and his crazy wife who drives senselessly round the countryside in a trap behind her enormous mare. There is, however, a third inmate of the château, Monsieur Ouine himself, a 'professor of living languages', obviously an intellectual, but how or why he came to live in such improbable surroundings or what, if anything, he is doing there is never

---

5. Above, p. 125.
6. See R. C. Zaehner, *Concordant Discord*, pp. 274–5.
7. Z. Shibayama, *A Flower Does Not Talk*, p. 46.

explained; nor are we ever told his Christian name. The young hero, Philippe, whom his mother insists on calling by the ridiculous English name of Steeny, lives with his mother, Michelle (we are never told their surname), and her English companion, Daisy (again no surname), with whom she appears to have a cloying Lesbian relationship. There is an insufferable and suffocating sweetness about the house which Philippe cannot abide: it has the sickly-sweet smell that is the harbinger of death. To escape it he runs off from time to time to his only friend – a cripple – who holds mysterious communion with the souls of the dead and suffers anguish for Philippe's sake, for the boy is already dangerously poised on the tight-rope from which he may fall either into the unfathomable goodness of God or – and this seems much more likely – into a yawning abyss of pure ambiguity where everything is relative and evil wears the mask of good and good itself is hidden beneath an ever-shifting mire of evil.

The village is dying of boredom: and the village is the symbol of the modern world. Against boredom such as this there is no defence, for it 'will finish off everything, it will soften up the [whole] world':[8] and 'even pity would not know how to operate in it, just as a surgeon would not know how to operate in a lake of pus'. But the 'lake of pus' is even so pregnant with monstrous evil that it only needs the slightest touch to make the whole putrid thing boil over into senseless violence.

A wretched little cowherd's apprentice is murdered. Nobody knows why, for nobody in the village has the slightest motive for doing away with so insignificant a life. But it is enough: the pus begins to stir: the village is no longer bored. For the village is a quagmire of indeterminate filth. No doubt 'there are some quagmires which lie still as if they were asleep', as Monsieur Ouine remarks, 'but the slime of this one seems to have become devilishly active for some time. You can almost hear it boil and hiss.'[9] You can indeed: for everyone seems to have been wrenched out of their habitual torpor, and a spirit of insane violence now seems to hold the village in its grip. The châtelaine, careering over the plains behind her enormous mare, twice tries to run Philippe down –

---

8. G. Bernanos, op. cit., p. 1465.   9. Ibid.

Philippe whom she calls her 'angel': neither he nor she nor anyone else can understand why. But the crisis comes at the funeral of the murdered boy. The Curé, inspired by some power he does not himself understand, delivers a funeral oration of merciless power in which he refuses even to bless the innocent victim whose murder had started it all off. Why should he? How can he, a parish priest, bless a parish that no longer exists? 'What good could it do you if I blessed this wretched little corpse today? He has turned out to be the innocent instrument of your perdition. This is the sin of all of you, and I will not bless your sin.'[1]

By now the village is on the boil. Things are made no better by the mayor – already half mad with an obsessional hatred of his own body and an impurity he feels is eating it up. Representing the civil power, he too must have his say, but the words will not come out in any sort of coherent order. The crowd is already in a state of intense exasperation; but, to crown everything, the mad châtelaine must needs appear at this precise moment, dragged along behind her enormous mare, now madder than herself, which plunges into the crowd, kicking out at whoever happens to be in its way. By now the blood-lust of the mob is thoroughly aroused: it surges forward, and the châtelaine is lynched.

Who or what was responsible for this insane eruption of mob violence? Nobody knows: but the reader is left with the suspicion that somehow – he does not know how – Monsieur Ouine, the inexplicable guest at the château, is behind it all.

Who is he? Monsieur Ouine: *Oui-Non* – 'Yes' – 'No': the eternal enigma whose oppressive and all-prevailing presence no one can understand.

In the other novels of Bernanos the sons of light can be clearly distinguished from the sons of darkness. In *Monsieur Ouine* everything is ambiguous. There is no ground on which you can take your stand: there is no ground to stand on – only a filthy quagmire in which you can only sink. Even the mad châtelaine, aimlessly careering around the plains behind her murderous mare, has her 'moments of truth'. Abject herself, and wallowing in her own degradation, despised even by the village lads who boast of having

1. Ibid., p. 1490.

tumbled her on the grass, she can yet on occasion reveal a 'profile of unbelievable purity';[2] and, of her martyrdom (if that is the right word) it is said that 'she vanished, ... she soared beyond the reach of anyone: ... she soared aloft like a flame or like a cry'.[3] Does this mean that at the last moment she escaped from the abyss of self-hatred and self-degradation to which she had doomed herself? Probably. We are not told: for this is a world ruled by half-truths and lies – a world in which all distinctions are blurred and all precision is blunted.

And then there is Monsieur Ouine. Old, flabby, flaccid, and fat, he yet has 'an extraordinary self-control and an incalculable psychic force'.[4] A little nondescript perhaps, 'for you might have taken him for some sort of foreman', but even this cannot be true, for his face had an 'extraordinary nobility, the lines of which were so simple, so pure, that neither old age nor suffering nor even a certain clammy, unhealthy fattiness could alter its profound benevolence or its expression of calm and lucid acceptance'.[5]

The young hero, Philippe, immediately falls for his fascinating charm, marvelling at the sheer serenity in which this obese old man whose forehead is ashen pale seems to bathe. 'Could this be what people call a saint?'[6] he wonders, for Monsieur Ouine is quite unlike anyone he has met. He is completely under the old man's spell, for he obscurely feels that beneath the 'benevolence' and 'purity' the former 'professor of living languages' exudes, there is something uncanny he does not understand. ' "You frighten me," said Steeny, "I would follow you to the ends of the world." '[7]

The love of an old man for a boy and a boy's fascination with an older man? Well, there is nothing new in this. But Monsieur Ouine does *not* love Philippe as a person, nor is he vulgar enough simply to desire his fresh young body. There is nothing vulgar about Monsieur Ouine. What he sees in Philippe is his own lost childhood, 'the child I once was',[8] and which he can never be again. But Philippe is no longer a child: he has reached the threshold that separates the innocence of childhood from the passionate am-

2. Ibid., p. 1425. 3. Ibid., p. 1559. 4. Ibid., p. 1359.
5. Ibid., p. 1362. 6. Ibid., p. 1366. 7. Ibid., p. 1370.
8. Ibid., p. 1546.

biguities of adolescence, the exact moment when purity first comes face to face with corruption which has been the object of Monsieur Ouine's lifelong curiosity. For long he has been watching the boy from the window of his dilapidated room in the decaying manor-house. 'Oh yes,' he confesses to the spellbound boy, 'this was indeed the image I cherished for so many years – a life, a young human life, all ignorance and all daring, that part of the universe which is bound to pass away, the only promise that will never be kept – unique and marvellous. For you mustn't kid yourself, Philippe, real youth is as rare as genius, or perhaps it really is genius, a challenge to the order of the world and its laws, a blasphemy. A blasphemy!'[9]

Once again we meet man's nostalgia for paradise lost, for a childhood that will never return, for the ancient Tao in which death is swallowed up in life and old things are ever made new. 'Can you maintain an entire simplicity?' the Taoist sage Chuang Tzŭ had asked long ago. 'Can you become a little child [which] . . . moves without knowing where it is going and sits at home without knowing what it is doing?'[1] But Monsieur Ouine has no illusions about a benevolent Tao, a kindly Nature that rears and blesses her children. Oh no! 'Nature, which takes advantage of everything like some ghastly housewife, broods over youth with an alert hatred and lovingly opens her charnel-houses. But youth leaps over them and flies away . . . When all else degenerates, corrupts, and returns to its original slime, only youth can die, only youth knows death.'[2] Mysterious words, but Philippe will discover soon enough what they mean.[2a] For the moment he is only too happy to bask in the cool light of this 'saintly' man.

'Dear Monsieur Ouine', he muses. 'Ever since this simple man first looked at him, all revolt died down in his savage heart. Ever since he first looked at him . . . for of all those words he had since spoken the child scarcely retained anything except the monotonous tone of voice so poignantly sweet yet so absolutely firm and im-

---

9. Ibid., p. 1369.
1. *Chuang Tzŭ*, 23.5: pp. 80–1 in James Legge's translation (*Sacred Books of the East*, vol. XL): p. 253 in Burton Watson's translation (*The Complete Works of Chuang Tzŭ*).
2. G. Bernanos, loc. cit.   2a. See below, pp. 190-1.

perious. "If I had to be hanged," he thought, "I should want it to be he who read my sentence." '³

What in Monsieur Ouine attracted him? Philippe, who had never known the love of anyone except the touching devotion of his crippled friend, thought (or thought he thought) that he had at last found someone to whom he could devote himself, someone who could understand him and make him understand himself. And so 'it occurred to him in a flash that [Monsieur Ouine] corresponded in the most marvellous way to that part of himself which he knew least well, a part of himself so secret that he couldn't yet say whether it was strength or weakness, the principle of life or the principle of death'.⁴ He was soon to find out.

On leaving Monsieur Ouine he runs into the mad châtelaine (it is still early in the book and she is still alive). What does *she* think of Monsieur Ouine, for after all he lives in her house? She hates him like death. Though apparently so unassuming, he always gets his own way so that he is served 'like a God'. Yet he has no willpower: 'he has no more will than a child' – only whims, but, for no reason anyone can understand, his whim is law. The boy is not impressed: the woman is half mad anyhow and probably talks like this because she is really in love with him though she does not know it.

' "That's just a lot of talk", he sighed contemptuously. "If you hate him, why serve him? You're in love with him – in your own way. That's all."

' "In love with him!"

'She rose to her knees, stunned.

' "In love with him! He's fat, greasy, and clammy all over. His hands slide around all over the place. Don't you know that he is ill? His old voice vibrates as if he were speaking inside a kettle-drum. God! Love him! Why, my angel, you have only to go near him and you won't even *need* to love – what peace, what silence! Love him? Let me tell you, dear heart. Just as some people give out light and warmth, so does our friend absorb all light and all warmth. You see, the genius of Monsieur Ouine is the cold. In the cold the soul finds rest." '⁵

3. Ibid., p. 1419.   4. Ibid., p. 1420.   5. Ibid., p. 1423.

The châtelaine may be mad, but she has her moments of inspired lucidity, and this is one of them. Monsieur Ouine is the incarnation of the Cold, and it is absolute Cold that is hell,[6] the fixed, still Cold of eternal, loveless solitude, beyond the reach of good and evil.

But Monsieur Ouine is a moral man. Courteous, he has 'never said a word for or against religion, he seems only to be interested in the moral problem';[7] indeed 'he never speaks ill of anyone, and he is very kind, very indulgent'.[8] As he himself tells the village priest, of all the people in the village, only he and the priest himself are interested in souls[9] – and perhaps for reasons that are not so very different. The priest knows that it is his job to save souls but, since the murder of the cowherd boy, evil has so monstrously erupted throughout the parish that he finds that there is no parish left to save. Monsieur Ouine, on the other hand, is not quite so pessimistic: for him there is at least one soul left who is still relatively untouched by evil – Philippe, the image of his childhood whose eyes he longs to open so that he too may taste of the 'fruit of the tree of the knowledge of good and evil'. He loves Philippe with the tender love of a gourmet for that supreme moment of sensuous relish when he savours to the full the exquisite taste of a fruit that has reached that point of perfection which immediately precedes decay.[1]

The Hindus and Buddhists are eternally speaking of 'liberation', by which they mean liberation from the bondage of time and space which imprisons them in this ephemeral world. Monsieur Ouine too longs for liberation, but it is not from the bondage of time and space but from the one constraint he has always hated – conscience, 'the principle of which was within him, the consciousness of good and evil, like another being within Being – that worm'.[2] Monsieur Ouine is an intellectual – an erstwhile professor of living languages: and like most intellectuals he is corrupt: 'he had no appetite for truth in any shape or form.'[3]

Since the lynching in the churchyard the châtelaine has died:

6. Ibid., p. 1490.   7. Ibid., p. 1359.   8. Ibid., p. 1534.
9. Ibid., p. 1466.   1. Below, p. 156.   2. *Monsieur Ouine*, p. 1471.
3. Ibid., p. 1472.

there have been three suicides and there is another to follow. Monsieur Ouine's turn has come. This is the climax of the book, and it took Bernanos years to settle its final form. And rightly so, for what he is depicting is not just damnation, but the disintegration, the liquefaction, the spiritual entropy, of a soul already divided against itself but not yet wholly annihilated. The beloved disciple, Philippe, is there: but the spell has evaporated, and what he witnesses is not the death of a saint, but the slow putrefaction of a soul that no longer *is*. The old man rambles on, but his words no longer have any coherence, 'words which he can no longer articulate and which Steeny thinks he can hear hissing and writhing somewhere – in the shadows – like a knot of reptiles intertwined'.[4]

He is like a snake hacked in two. 'I am wearing myself out', he says, 'in trying – not to find myself again but to join myself together. Yes, to join myself together like two parts of a snake cut in two by a spade. Too late, I'm afraid, the bits of my life, of my being, will never come together again.' This is hell – the 'perpetual alienation from our true being, our true self, which is in God'.[5]

Monsieur Ouine is dying: and it seems that he is trying to make a last bequest to Philippe. But even this is uncertain, for during the old man's agony the boy has managed to get through a bottle of port, and when the doctor finally arrives, he finds that the patient has already been dead for two hours though Philippe swears that when the doctor opened the door he had only just finished talking. However, it cannot matter very much, for Monsieur Ouine had no secrets to tell, nothing to impart, since he himself was empty, absorbed and dissipated into his own 'peace' and 'silence', his own diabolical caricature of Nirvana.

'Young man', he calls to the already befuddled boy: 'Is it possible? Now I *see* myself to the very bottom, nothing stops my vision ... no obstacle. There is nothing. Remember that word: nothing.'[6]

He is empty – and more than empty. He is like a bottle floating

---

4. Ibid., p. 1548.
5. Thomas Merton, *New Seeds of Contemplation* (Burns & Oates, London, 1961), p. 6.
6. *Monsieur Ouine*, p. 1550.

on the sea which some sailors saw and were convinced contained a message of vital importance. They took to the lifeboat, came level with the bottle, but the bottle broke, and nobody ever knew whether there was anything inside it or not. Monsieur Ouine is not only an empty bottle but an empty bottle smashed to smithereens. Needless to say the sailors who had risked their lives to find this nonexistent treasure were swallowed up in the angry sea and never heard of again.

Christ had said on the Cross: 'I thirst.' So too Monsieur Ouine, like the Devil who shows marvellous ingenuity in aping the things of God, murmurs: 'I am hungry – mad with hunger – dying of hunger.'

By the words, 'I thirst', commentators on the New Testament have thought that the dying God-man meant not only that he felt physical thirst but also that he thirsted for the salvation of souls. Monsieur Ouine too was maddened by hunger and thirst – not for righteousness indeed but for living souls to savour and absorb into his own substance which was 'nothing'. For after all he had a secret – the secret of how he had found a way to destroy human beings by depriving them of all sense of dignity, all self-respect, leaving them face to face with their souls, broken and empty like that bottle on the sea.

' "I will never be filled up again", the professor observed gravely. "It would take a lot of work to fill me up, and that work hasn't even begun. What was the point of opening myself up, swelling myself up? There was nothing to me but a mouth, breathing in, swallowing down, body and soul, gaping on every side. Like an ox wallowing in its provender, how careful I was to pick out from among the pastures offered me those most rich in sap, the most nourishing ones which only *looked* poor, sometimes repulsive no doubt and generally despised by fools. I was in no hurry, I flattered myself that I knew how to wait. Quietly I sized up my pleasure and profit, calculating the exact point at which the most perfect succulence would be reached, the ultimate ripeness which immediately precedes the beginnings of decay – always alone so that I should not have to share either my pleasure or my pain. But what, after all, would I have had to share? I desired, I swelled up with desire without satisfying my hunger. I didn't absorb any substance, *whether good or evil*.[7] My soul is nothing but a waterskin full of wind. And now, young man, it is my soul which is breathing *me* in in my turn. I can feel myself melting and disappearing into that voracious maw: it is softening me up right up to my bones." '[8]

In Hindu terms what Monsieur Ouine is experiencing is the disappearance of the ego into the eternal self beyond time and space, but this, so far from being a beatific experience, is a horrific one, a void that really *is* the Void, and not the Buddhist Void, the poles of which are wisdom and compassion. And so Philippe has an almost overpowering impression of 'duration without change or end, of eternity, an eternal equilibrium', and for the first time he feels a kind of pity for the wreck of this strange man he had once thought might be a saint. This is untypical of him: his normal reaction would have been an angry disgust. 'He didn't feel any fear, but a vague, undefined pity, a sort of painful serenity like that which sometimes follows the great crises in an illness when the long awaited dawn of convalescence is still below the horizon.'[9] This is perhaps the beginning of his salvation, for what Monsieur Ouine could never do was to have pity on himself: he had neither pity nor love for his victims, they gave him no satisfaction, so he could find no satisfaction in himself; like all Bernanos's anti-heroes he could only hate himself. But even this icy hatred which, according to Bernanos, is typical of the Devil, he lost as he lay dying: it dissolved into a complete detachment from all things, not unlike the detachment preached and practised by all the religious mystics, a 'detachment from detachment itself' which, in the case of Monsieur Ouine, is a foretaste not of heaven but of an icy 'nothing' which is hell.

Had Monsieur Ouine been able to share his 'secrets' with someone else, he might have been saved, but he had no secrets to share and did not in any case want to be saved. Only ' "that would save me", said Monsieur Ouine in a voice that was almost indifferent and in fact expressed not the faintest desire to be saved but rather a malevolent detachment from his own fate, an icy conviction'. Even the poisons within him which he had once so fondly

7. My italics.   8. *Monsieur Ouine*, pp. 1551–2.   9. Ibid., pp. 1554–5.

cherished had melted into thin air. 'One would have to concentrate them for centuries to get enough back to kill just one mouse.'

'Can you really still be thinking of poisons?' asks Philippe, for whom the spell that Monsieur Ouine had cast on him is now at last broken. 'Poisons! Come off it! Everything is a poison – or nectar – or even pure water. It all depends on who is drinking it.'[1] For as all things are pure to the pure, so is 'everything impure to the impure'.[2] The boy Philippe had spoken with a wisdom beyond his years, and the idea of pure water struck a chord in the disintegrating brain of the dying professor.

' "Water – pure water", repeated Monsieur Ouine in a voice that could scarcely be heard. "No, not pure – insipid, colourless, without freshness or heat. No coldness could ever dim it, it couldn't put out any fire. Whoever would want to drink this water with me? Steel is less hard, lead less compact, no metal could ever bite into it. It isn't pure – in the strict sense of that word – but intact, unalterable, polished like a diamond mirror. And my thirst is like it, my thirst and that water are one." '

It is very doubtful whether Bernanos knew anything about Buddhism, but this passage bears an uncanny resemblance to what the Zen Buddhists were to call the Buddha-nature of the Self-nature which is in all of us. It is like the 'limpid water' of the Nirvana of the early Buddhists, it is like the diamond 'mirror' of the Zen *Platform Scripture*:

> The mind is the tree of perfect wisdom.
> The body is the stand of a bright mirror.
> The bright mirror is originally clear and pure.
> Where has it been defiled by any dust?[3]

Buddhists tend to compare the peace of Nirvana to pure water rather than to a living flame as Christian mystics so often do. How this difference is to be explained need not detain us now. Whether it is the pure water of eternal rest or the living fire of love, it all depends on who experiences it, for all things are pure to the pure, everything impure to the impure. So too in the *Bhagavad-Gītā*[4]

---

1. Ibid., p. 1556.   2. Ibid., p. 1492.
3. *The Platform Scripture*, 9: Wing-Tsit Chan, p. 41.
4. II.21, 27, 29.

when God reveals himself as an all-devouring maw, the same
'voracious maw' perhaps of which Monsieur Ouine speaks; the
wicked are sucked into it in terror while the just rejoice in what,
for them is a blessed reunion with their source:

> Lo, the hosts of gods are entering thee:
> Some, terror-struck, extol thee, hands together pressed!
> Great seers and men perfected in serried ranks
> Cry out, 'All hail', and praise thee with copious hymns of praise.

But the wicked 'who will not serve'

> Rush blindly into thy gaping mouths
> That with their horrid tusks strike them with terror.
> Some stick in the gaps between thy teeth,
> See them! their heads to powder ground!
>
> As moths, in bursting, hurtling haste
> Rush into a lighted blaze to their destruction,
> So do the worlds, well-trained in hasty violence,
> Pour into thy mouths to their own undoing.

So too the pure water of the original Buddha-nature is 'homogenized' and 'entropized' in Monsieur Ouine into what seems to be identical with itself but is in fact its own decomposition, a suppurating caricature of itself, beyond thought or feeling, cold and dumb.

Monsieur Ouine reaches his own 'diabolical' Nirvana. So too is he sucked into his own 'inmost self', as the Hindus call the eternal essence of man: or is it the Hindu Absolute itself? It doesn't really matter, for Monsieur Ouine never really knew and may in any case have been physically as well as spiritually dead already, for Philippe, the sole witness of the ghostly monologue, was drunk, and the fate of the damned, or rather the 'lost', is as darkly mysterious as the 'wickedness of evil' itself. But let us leave the last word to this most deeply disquieting man:

' "My child", he continued with his old emphasis, "both during my university career and afterwards, I have never thought of denying the existence of the soul, and even today I could not question it, but I have lost all consciousness of mine although only an hour ago I experienced something like a Void, an expectation, an inner aspiration. Can it be that my soul has at last swallowed me up? I have fallen into it, young man, just as the elect fall into God. Nobody bothers to ask me for an account of it; and it cannot give an account of me, it doesn't know me, it doesn't even know my name. I could escape from any other gaol if only by desire. I have fallen precisely there where no judgment can reach me. I am going back into myself for ever, my child." [5]

This is not quite what Thomas Merton means by a 'perpetual alienation from our true being, our true self, which is in God', rather it is a case of being swallowed up in one's true self without the true self being conscious that anything at all has happened: it simply doesn't know, doesn't even know his name. The true self has devoured him and he has been fully entropized, reduced to nothing or evacuated like unusable dung.

You might think that we have now seen the last of Monsieur Ouine for ever: the *non* has finally triumphed over the *oui*, the 'no' over the 'yes'. But you would be wrong, for some faint trace of his lost childhood and innocence still remains. And so, 'to Steeny's stupefaction, Monsieur Ouine's frantic gasping turned into a laugh, smothered at first, then frank and limpid, something he would never have expected from that austere mouth. At the same time the shadow of his broad shoulders stopped hovering oppressively over him and he [Philippe/Steeny] found that he was standing up again, free.'

What does this 'frank and limpid' laughter mean? It was apparently enough to liberate his once faithful disciple, Philippe, from the oppressive shadow of his once powerful personality. Can it be that Monsieur Ouine too has found that 'liberation' of which both Hindus and Buddhists speak and which, among the Zen Buddhists at least, so often finds physical expression in laughter? Can it be that Monsieur Ouine has found the salvation he no longer so much as desires? The last words he ever uttered or did not utter – for the only witness of the macabre scene was already drunk – were these:

' "I am going through a ghastly time", he said with an enormous sigh. "To go back into oneself is not a joke, my boy. It would not have cost me more to return to the womb that made me, I have

5. *Monsieur Ouine*, p. 1560.

turned myself inside out . . . turned myself inside out like a glove."

'The faint noise of his laughter scarcely made itself heard above the silence, it was now like the hiccuping of water in a clay culvert or the pattering of a shower of rain on pebbles – like any unintelligible muttering of things, it no longer had any human meaning.'

But surely this too is what all the mystics teach us. However they may describe the final state, they all agree that the 'ego' must die if the 'self' is to be realized, if Nirvana is to be achieved; the 'old man' must die if the 'new man' is to rise again, the merely human must be set aside if there is to be room for the divine. Once again, as any assiduous reader of this amazing book must realize, the depersonalization and dehumanization of Monsieur Ouine are the exact opposite of what these words mean to the mystic. Should there be any doubt about it the laughter which a moment ago had seemed 'frank and limpid' is now indistinguishable from any old noise made by *things*. In the works of Bernanos we have met that laughter before, it is 'the laugh, the incomprehensible joy of Satan',[6] the laugh that shook the Abbé Cénabre the anti-hero of one of Bernanos's other novels, *L'imposture*, when he realized not only that he had lost his faith but 'that there was no longer any place for him on earth and that he would dissolve in the supernatural hatred from which he had been born'.[7]

The final dissolution of Monsieur Ouine bears all the outward signs of the mystic's melting away in the divine ocean, but it is at the antipodes of this. In its way it too transcends good and evil, but whereas the Neo-Confucians spoke of an ultimate 'Good' that is beyond good and evil as it is normally understood, Bernanos speaks of an evil that may masquerade as good (for, after all, Philippe at first thought that Monsieur Ouine might be a saint) but is in fact so evil that, compared with it, what we call evil gives no real indication of this absolute zero which stands over against the absolute infinity that so many mystics claim to experience. There is a mortal danger in playing at mysticism as there is mortal danger in playing with psychedelic drugs, for if it is true that, as Pascal says, 'Man is neither angel nor beast, it is his mis-

---

6. *Sous le soleil de Satan*, p. 255.
7. *L'imposture*, in *Oeuvres romanesques*, p. 365.

fortune that whoever would play the angel plays the beast',[8] of the mystics we might also say: 'Whoever would play at being the Godhead might find himself in a Void that Satan himself cannot reach, beyond the reach of all evil and all good.' Perhaps this is what Teilhard de Chardin meant by 'unity by dissolution'.[9]

We have seen that both the Hindus and the Buddhists speak of a state beyond right and wrong, good and evil. What the practical effects of passing into this state are is rarely discussed by the Buddhists. The Hindus, however, are sometimes embarrassingly frank in describing the consequences.

The Absolute (Brahman or the universal Self) is wholly indifferent to what goes on in the world: 'He does not speak and has no care.'[1] 'He neither increases by good works nor does he diminish by evil ones.'[2] Similarly in the case of the man who has realized that in the ground of his being he is identical with the Absolute 'these two thoughts do not occur to him, "So I have done evil", or "So I have done what is good and fair". He shrugs them off. What he has done and what he has left undone does not torment him: ... all evil he burns up.'[3] This is because, seeing the Self in himself and all things as the Self,[4] he will be indifferent to all actions, good or evil, which take place in the phenomenal world.

As the principle of eternity Brahman does not act, but as cause of everything he sustains the universe and controls it from within.[5] In the *Kaushītakī* Upanishad (3.1–2) the Vedic god, Indra, who personifies the universal Self or Brahman, goes so far as to boast of his evil deeds:

'Know me, then, as I am. This indeed is what I consider most beneficial for mankind – that they should know me. I killed the three-headed son of Tvashtri, I threw the Arunmukha ascetics to the hyenas. Transgressing many a compact, I impaled the people of Prahlāda to the sky, the Paulomas to the atmosphere and the Kālakānjas to the earth, and I did not lose a single hair in the process.

8. Pascal, *Pensées*, in *Oeuvres complètes*, p. 1170.
9. P. Teilhard de Chardin, *L'activation de l'énergie* (Éditions du Seuil, Paris, 1963), p. 231.
1. *Chāndogya* Upanishad, 3.14.3.   2. *Brihadāranyaka* Upanishad, 4.4.22.
3. Ibid., 4.4. 22–3.   4. Ibid.   5. Ibid., 3.8.9: 3.7. 3–23.

Beyond Good and Evil

'The man who knows me as I am loses nothing that is his, whatever he does, even though he should slay his mother or his father, even though he steal or procure an abortion. Whatever evil he does, he does not blanch.'

Similarly in the *Bhagavad-Gītā* (18.17) Krishna who is God incarnate says to his friend and pupil Arjuna: 'A man who has reached a state where there is no sense of "I", whose soul is undefiled – were to be to slaughter all these worlds, slays nothing. He is not bound.'

All this may sound very shocking, for though it may be understandable that the impersonal Absolute, the Brahman of the Hindus, the Godhead beyond God, may be beyond good and evil, it seems shocking to us that a personal God who is omnipotent and whose will rules the universe should not only be the author of what seems evil to man but should goad man on to commit evil deeds. But why should it seem so shocking, for when Jesus said, 'No one is good but God alone',[6] he was saying something that was not at all obvious from the Old Testament where God himself says: 'I make good fortune and create calamity',[7] and again, 'From where, if not from the mouth of the Most High, do evil and good come?'[8] For this is the God, after all, who advocated the genocide of the Canaanites[9] and who approved the treatment of Jericho in which men, women, young and old, even the oxen and sheep and donkeys were massacred by Israel, the chosen people of God.[1] It is, no accident that the Old Testament God is called the 'Lord God of hosts', that is, the Lord God of armies. It is not only Aldous Huxley and Jung, who had thrown off their different varieties of Protestantism, who protest against the savagery of the God of the Old Testament who seems to rejoice both in the destruction of Israel's enemies and in punishing Israel herself for her very natural desire to come to terms with them, but even Bonhoeffer protests against the immoralities committed by the chosen people to the greater glory of God. 'Why', he asks, 'is it that in the Old Testament men tell lies vigorously and often to the glory of God ... kill, deceive, rob, divorce, and even fornicate ... doubt,

6. Luke 18:19.   7. Isaiah 45:7.   8. Lamentations 3:38.
9. Cf. Joshua 8:2.   1. Ibid., 6:21.

blaspheme, and curse, whereas in the New Testament there is nothing of all this?'² He died before he could formulate a plausible answer.

Jung rejected his native Protestantism at a very early age for the simple and adequate reason that it did not work: it was a sad and meaningless convention which people went through with simply from the force of habit. ' "Why, that is not religion at all", I thought. "It is an absence of God; the church is a place I should not go to. It is not life which is there, but death." '³ This thought was impressed on him at his first Communion at which there was 'no sadness and no joy' because, as he suddenly realized, 'nothing at all had happened'.⁴ From the beginning his God had been the God within him, 'a mighty activity in my soul' who can and does become 'unpleasantly important'.⁵ It was only much later that he became interested in Yahweh, the Old Testament God. This, of course, did not mean a reconversion to the 'dead' biblical religion of his childhood, but because he had come to regard 'God' as the deepest content of the unconscious, containing within himself not only what he called his personality no. 2 which moved in 'God's world', but also the 'shadow' of that personality which was menacing, terrible, 'evil'. God is indeed beyond good and evil, and the author of both. This, for Jung, is a fact that has to be faced; and in this he differs greatly from the fashionable 'Eastern' mysticisms of today. To 'drop out' into a Nirvana, which, even if it is the real thing and not Monsieur Ouine's diabolical travesty of it, represents only an escape from this world and therefore the rejection of all responsibility for what goes on in it, is not enough. Somehow we have to come to terms with the evil that is inseparable from God and therefore from what is most fundamental in ourselves; but first of all, if we are Christians, we have to face the murderous 'wrath' of God as it manifests itself throughout the Old Testament. In his *Answer to Job* Jung challenges Christians to do just that and the very short introduction to that work ought to be compulsory reading for all Christians and particularly for the

2. D. Bonhoeffer, *Letters and Papers from Prison*, p. 157.
3. C. G. Jung, *Memories, Dreams, Reflections*, p. 64.
4. Ibid., p. 63.   5. *The Secret of the Golden Flower*, p. 129.

theologians who, though they may see in the divine savagery only outraged justice, never really face the awkward fact that, though God demands justice and mercy of man, he is himself unjust and amoral at least in the Book of Job. In his introduction to his *Answer to Job* Jung writes:

'The Book of Job is a landmark in the long historical development of the divine drama. At the time the book was written, there were already many testimonies which had given a contradictory picture of Yahweh – the picture of a God who knew no moderation in his emotions and suffered precisely from this lack of moderation. He himself admitted that he was eaten up with rage and jealousy and that this knowledge was painful to him. Insight existed along with obtuseness, loving-kindness along with cruelty, creative power along with destructiveness. Everything was there, and none of these qualities was an obstruction to the other. . . . A condition of this sort can only be described as *amoral* . . . .

'I am concerned with . . . the way in which a modern man with a Christian education and background comes to terms with the divine darkness which is unveiled in the Book of Job, and what effect it has on him. . . . In this way I hope to act as a voice for many who feel the same way as I do, and to give expression to the shattering emotion that the unvarnished spectacle of divine savagery and ruthlessness produces in us.'[6]

For Jung the God of the Book of Job is either amoral or immoral: he 'does not care a button for any moral opinion and does not recognize any form of ethics as binding'.[7]

It cannot be said that either Hinduism or Buddhism ignore the existence of evil. The early Buddhists identify it with matter, and salvation therefore consists in escaping from matter. Philosophic Hinduism regards Brahman as being totally beyond right and wrong since even *right* action binds you to the wheel of *saṃsāra* from which again you must escape. But in neither religion is there any idea of *spiritual* evil which becomes so prominent in Christianity. This is not native to Judaism, and it is not really prominent

---

6. *Answer to Job* (Routledge & Kegan Paul, London, 1954), pp. 3-4. Now also available in *Collected Works*, Vol. 11 (pp. 365-6).
7. Ibid., p. 10 (*Collected Works*, Vol. 11, p. 369).

in Islam, but in Christianity and particularly in the writings of St John it is central. The Devil is no longer God's instrument, as he is in the Book of Job, where God uses him to put a self-righteous man to the test. He is a formidable *spiritual* reality:

> He was a murderer from the start;
> he was never grounded in the truth;
> there is no truth in him at all:
> when he lies
> he is drawing on his own store,
> because he is a liar, and the father of lies.[8]

This is quite un-Jewish and must almost certainly be of Zoroastrian origin, for Zoroastrianism is unique in that it posits two *spiritual* principles, Ohrmazd and Ahriman, God and the Devil. But this complete dualism, which makes sense of Jesus's saying that 'no one is good but God alone', is a later development in Zoroastrianism itself, for in the *Gāthās* ('Songs'), which probably go back to Zoroaster himself, the Iranian Prophet says that the Good and Evil Spirits are *twins* who respectively *choose* to do good and evil:

'Of these two Spirits he who was of the Lie chose to do the worst things; but the most Holy Spirit, clothed in rugged heaven, chose Truth as did all who sought with zeal to do the pleasure of the Wise Lord by doing good works.'[9]

Since the two Spirits are twins and the supreme God, Ahura Mazdāh (the Wise Lord), is elsewhere said to be father of the 'Holy Spirit', it follows that he must be the father of the Evil Spirit too. This, however, was to become anathema to later Zoroastrian orthodoxy when the Wise Lord and the Holy Spirit were identified, and the Evil Spirit became an independent principle. The idea of two spirits created by God, however, passed into Judaism and in the Dead Sea scrolls the idea appears in the earlier Zoroastrian form not the later: God is still One and supreme, but he creates the spirits of truth and falsehood, light and darkness, from which good and wicked men are 'born', apparently through no fault of their own. This is almost exactly the position we find in St John. The relevant passage in the scrolls reads as follows:

8. John 8:45.   9. *Yasna*, 30.5.

'He has created man to govern the world, and has appointed for him two spirits in which to walk until the time of His visitation: the spirits of truth and falsehood. Those born of truth spring from a fountain of light, but those born of falsehood spring from a source of darkness. All the children of righteousness are ruled by the Prince of Light and walk in the ways of light, but all the children of falsehood are ruled by the Angel of Darkness and walk in the ways of darkness.

'The Angel of Darkness leads all the children of righteousness astray, and until his end, all their sin, iniquities, wickedness, and all their unlawful deeds are caused by his dominion in accordance with the mysteries of God. . . .

'But the God of Israel and His Angel of Truth will succour all the sons of light. For it is He who created the spirits of Light and Darkness and founded every action upon them and established every deed [upon] their [ways]. And He loves the one everlastingly and delights in its works for ever; but the counsel of the other He loathes and for ever hates its ways.'[1]

All this is done 'in accordance with the mysteries of God'. Humanly speaking there is no sense in it, and, as Jung saw, God cannot be exonerated from being the source of evil: he is good-and-evil, light-and-darkness, indeed he is Monsieur Ouine, *oui-non*, 'Yes-No', 'both a persecutor and a helper in one, and the one aspect is as real as the other. [He] is not split but an *antinomy* – a totality of inner opposites – and this is the indispensable condition of his tremendous dynamism.'[2] Only Zoroastrian orthodoxy dared to cleave the divine Unity in two, thereby preserving the absolute goodness of God. In his confession of faith the Zoroastrian was bound to declare: 'I must have no doubt that there are two first principles, one the Creator and the other the Destroyer. The Creator is Ohrmazd who is all goodness and all light: and the Destroyer is the accursed Destructive Spirit who is all wickedness and full of death, a liar and a deceiver.'[3] But there is in man a thirst for unity, a thirst for the harmony he thinks he descries in the

1. G. Vermes, *The Dead Sea Scrolls in English* (revised edition, Penguin Books, Harmondsworth, 1965), pp. 75–6.
2. C. G. Jung, *Answer to Job*, p. 10 (*Collected Works*, Vol. 11, p. 369).
3. See R. C. Zaehner, *The Teachings of the Magi*, pp. 22–3.

universe but which has somehow gone all awry in man. This is probably psychologically, even genetically, inborn in him. He cannot rationalize it, but it is there; and the proof of the strength of it lies in the disappearance of the one religion that refused to make God even indirectly responsible for evil at the hands of Islam, a religion that reaffirmed the absolute oneness of God who is both 'the Merciful, the Compassionate' and 'the Wrathful' who is not even beyond deceit (*makr*).

In his *Answer to Job* Jung psychoanalysed Yahweh, but he did not psychoanalyse him out of existence. On the contrary, because he recognized that 'God is a mighty activity in my soul', he must concern himself with him and come to terms with him.[4] He must face the terrible aspect of God before he can understand his love.

Jung, like Teilhard de Chardin, when still a schoolboy, *knew* God in Nature: he was born, one might say, a nature mystic. 'Nature seemed to me full of wonders, and I wanted to steep myself in them. Every stone, every plant, every single thing seemed alive and indescribably marvellous. I immersed myself in nature, crawled, as it were, into the very essence of nature and away from the whole human world.'[5] But this was not by any means all there was to God. In his twelfth year he had a 'revelation' which, as described in his *Memories*, sounds simply grotesque, but which produced in him such a profound sense of liberation that it affected the whole of his life and even the cast of his mind. The occasion for it at first sight looks like just another instance of nature mysticism.

'One fine summer day that same year', he writes, 'I came out of school at noon and went to the cathedral square. The sky was gloriously blue, the day one of radiant sunshine. The roof of the cathedral glittered, the sun sparkling from the new, brightly glazed tiles. I was overwhelmed by the beauty of the sight, and thought: "The world is beautiful and the church is beautiful, and God made all this and sits above it far away in the blue sky on a golden throne and . . ." Here came a great hole in my thoughts, and a choking sensation. I felt numbed, and knew only: "Don't go on thinking

---

4. C. G. Jung, *The Secret of the Golden Flower*, loc. cit.
5. *Memories, Dreams, Reflections*, p. 44.

now! Something terrible is coming, ... something I dare not even approach. Why not? Because I would be committing the most frightful of sins." [6]

For three nights he could barely sleep, wrestling against the unmentionable thought that seemed to be forcing its way, despite all his efforts to resist it, into his conscious mind. 'Sweating with fear, I sat up in bed to shake off sleep. "Now it is coming, now it's serious! *I must think*! ... *Why* should I think of something I do not know? I don't want to, by God, that's sure. But *who* wants me to? Who wants to force me to think something I don't feel and don't want to know? Where does this terrible will come from?"' [7]

The 'terrible will' brought his thoughts right back to the Garden of Eden and he was forced to the conclusion that 'God in His omniscience had arranged everything so that the first parents would have to sin. *Therefore it was God's intention that they should sin.*' This thought immediately released him from his worst anxiety, for if it was God's intention that Adam and Eve should sin, then the 'terrible will' that had oppressed him must be the will of God even though it might be at variance with his formal commandments. ' "Obviously God also desires me to show courage," [he] thought. "If that is so and I go through with it, then He will give me His grace and illumination."

'I gathered all my courage,' Jung continues, 'as though I were about to leap forthwith into hell-fire, and let the thought come. I saw before me the cathedral, the blue sky. God sits on His golden throne, high above the world – and from under the throne an enormous turd falls upon the sparkling new roof, shatters it, and breaks the walls of the cathedral asunder.' [8]

This vision maybe is grotesque, but to the twelve-year-old Jung, it was literally a 'true' revelation of the nature of God. His relief was indescribable. 'Instead of the expected damnation, grace had come upon me, and with it an unutterable bliss such as I had never known. I wept for happiness and gratitude. The wisdom and goodness of God had been revealed to me now that I had yielded to His inexorable command.' A strange way of doing it, you may say, but surely a way that could be easily understood by a twelve-

6. Ibid., p. 47.   7. Ibid., p. 48.   8. Ibid., p. 50.

year-old boy with an unusually religious disposition. The moral that Jung drew from this 'illumination' and on which he was never to go back was that 'in His trial of human courage God refuses to abide by traditions, no matter how sacred. In His omnipotence He will see to it that nothing really evil comes of such tests of courage. If one fulfils the will of God one can be sure of going the right way.'[9]

Certainly Jung's idea of God was to change. The antinomy of God's nature in which love is counterbalanced by a terrible wrath is also present in man himself. Since God became man in Christ, man and God are inseparable. But although Jesus says in the New Testament, 'No one is good but God alone', and St John in his Gospel and Epistles teaches that God is love and that Satan, the 'father of lies' and a 'murderer from the start', is the source of all evil, the fact remains that the New Testament ends with the Apocalypse, traditionally written by the same John, thus bringing the Bible to an end with an appalling revelation of the reality of God's wrath. So too, Jung, now an old man, can still write towards the end of his *Answer to Job*:

'Since the Apocalypse we now know again that God is not only to be loved, but also to be feared. He fills us with evil as well as with good, otherwise he would not need to be feared; and because he wants to become man, the uniting of his antinomy must take place in man. This involves man in a new responsibility. He can no longer wriggle out of it on the plea of his littleness and nothingness, for the dark God has slipped the atom bomb and chemical weapons into his hands and given him the power to empty out the apocalyptic vials of wrath on his fellow creatures. Since he has been granted an almost godlike power, he can no longer remain blind and unconscious. He must know something of God's nature and of metaphysical processes if he is to understand himself and thereby achieve gnosis of the Divine.'[1]

This makes sense to a generation that has seen the 'wickedness of evil' in Hitler's Germany, the concentration camps, the mass extermination of the Jews, the dropping of the atom bomb on

---

9. Ibid., p. 51.
1. *Answer to Job*, pp. 163-4 (*Collected Works*, Vol. 11, p. 461).

Hiroshima and Nagasaki, not to mention Vietnam, the Chinese rape of Tibet, the Russian suppression of the 'human face' of Communism in Czechoslovakia; and now the horrors that forced some ten million wretched people out of East Pakistan. But it takes the insight of a Jung and the faith of a deeply convinced Christian like Bonhoeffer to see the wrath of God as the necessary obverse of his grace. 'Never', writes Bonhoeffer, 'have we been so plainly conscious of the wrath of God, and that is a sign of his grace.'[2]

It takes the vision of a saint to see this; and there is no doubt that Bonhoeffer must always remain a symbol of Christian fortitude in the face of intolerable evil. But to the youth of today Bonhoeffer is little more than a name and his sacrifice is forgotten. That evil is still rampant in the world is, of course, painfully obvious, but with luck, in spite of the complete cynicism and lack of principle that characterize the present shifts in great power politics, we may still avoid the final holocaust. In that case we may find ourselves dropped into a 'peace which passeth all understanding', the silent peace of Monsieur Ouine, the peace of spiritual disintegration and moral decay.

2. D. Bonhoeffer, *Letters and Papers from Prison*, p. 146.

6

SALVATION THROUGH DEATH

In the First World War two men were serving in the ranks of the French Army who were later to achieve a world-wide reputation: one was Bernanos, the other Pierre Teilhard de Chardin, a Jesuit priest. The first served in the Dragoons where he found more natural nobility among the horses than among the men; the second, as befitted his ecclesiastical calling, served as a stretcher-bearer. Both men were visionaries of a quite exceptional order, but their respective visions could scarcely have been more different. For Bernanos the war was an obscenity unleashed and mismanaged by imbeciles and liars, for Teilhard it was a sign of almost supernatural hope, the birth pangs of a world about to be reborn. Certainly, both men despised the faceless men who directed and misdirected the holocaust from behind the lines and the hypocritical patriotism of those who, from positions of safety and relative comfort, extolled the virtues of the common soldiers wallowing in the mud and dying daily in their thousands 'for their country'. For Bernanos, the senseless carnage of the front was essentially a defilement of the earth: 'The earth is not so much turned upside down as irreparably befouled.... What is impure in war [now] stands revealed to all eyes.'[3] There is no renewal here, only impurity and decay: 'How grey, how *dirty* it is today – this Picardy sky. Already the colours are fading, already life is withdrawing from the world.'[4] How different was Teilhard's experience when he returned to the front from a brief spell of leave:

'During those days of unforgettable confusion in the citadel at Verdun where, in the dust and among the cries, rations, fuses, and grenades were being distributed to those who were to be in on the big act – and then, a few hours later, during that interminable night

---

3. G. Bernanos, *Correspondance*, Vol. 1, 1904–1934 (Plon, Paris, 1971), p. 122.
4. Ibid., p. 117.

march, above Belleville and Froideterre, I observed in myself that agonizing yet victorious loosening up, followed at last by peace and exaltation in the more than human atmosphere to which the soul had once again adapted itself.

'It was the soul of the front that was being reborn in me. . . .'[5]

Both men saw that the First World War was a 'turning-point (*limite*) in the history of the world'.[6] For Bernanos it was a turning-point for the worse, a senseless sacrifice demanded not by God but by corrupt politicians, the 'imbeciles' and 'imposters' he was to spend so much of his life denouncing – wherever they were to be found, whether on the Left or the Right, among politicians or intellectuals or, what was worse (for this is where the scandal hurt him most), among the higher echelons and the well-fed princes of the Church. 'I do not know what I am defending,' he cries out, 'nor do I know what I may have to die for. What amazing stupidity . . . . But let us see it through simply for the sake of honour and because the fruit of our labours must not be lost.'[7] All that matters is that a man should preserve his integrity, that 'truth' which, as La Rochefoucauld said, was the same in all of us, in the greatest as well as the smallest.[8] 'What so many imbeciles think are hollow clouds – honour, justice, faith – I take to be living things, more living than they. These great abstractions are my friends.'[9] Honour, integrity, justice, and faith: these are the virtues that Bernanos demanded of himself, and which he demanded, uncompromisingly, of his fellow-men. Lose these, he thought, and you will land yourself in the ambiguous and insane world he described in *Monsieur Ouine*.

For Teilhard the front had quite a different meaning. Beneath the mud, the filth, the sordid suffering, and the impersonal violence, he saw (as Jung might have seen) a union of opposites from which a new type of being must emerge – indeed was already emerging –

---

5. P. Teilhard de Chardin, *Écrits du temps de la guerre* (Grasset, Paris, 1965), p. 211.
6. G. Bernanos, op. cit., p. 113.
7. Ibid., p. 102.
8. La Rochefoucauld, *Réflexions diverses*, i (Bibliothèque de la Pléiade, Gallimard, Paris), p. 503.
9. G. Bernanos, op. cit., pp. 112–13.

the 'soul of the front' which was in embryo the 'soul of the world'. It was, indeed, during these war years that Teilhard's whole vision of a world converging upon itself took shape. The carnage of the front, by the mere fact that it was impersonal and 'more than human', pointed to the birth of a higher 'personality' which transcended and in a mysterious way united the warring factions.

'The front', he writes, 'is not only the burning surface (*nappe ardente*) on which the contrary energies accumulated in the enemy masses reveal themselves and neutralize one another. It is still more a link of a specific kind of life in which only those can share who take the risk of going right up to it and then only for as long as they stay in it. Once an individual has been admitted somewhere on to this sublime surface, it seems to him, in the most positive way, that a new form of existence swoops down on him and takes hold of him . . . a higher life in which he will have been baptized. The man who has passed through the fire is a different species of man.'[1]

So you have the two visions: a world in putrefaction, and a world about to be reborn. Which is the more true? Probably there is a little bit of truth in both.

What was real and a scandal for Bernanos was the decline of the virtues which he regarded as being inborn in mankind – honour, justice, self-respect, and truth – being true to yourself and loyal to others. The enemy he combated all his life was subterfuge in all its forms, *false* patriotism, *false* piety, *false* righteous indignation, what he calls 'impurity' in all its forms. This – and the dehumanization of man and his alienation from his very roots by the machine and above all the power of money behind the machine, were what he fought throughout his bitter and tormented life. What he was witnessing, he thought, was the dechristianization of the Western world. In place of compassion, '*souffrir avec*', 'suffering with others', he saw the approach of a creeping paralysis he called '*pourrir avec*', 'rotting with others'.[2] In the short run he was probably right, and no one would have been more passionate than he in his condemnation of what is nowadays called the 'sexual

1. P. Teilhard de Chardin, op. cit., pp. 210–11.   2. Above, p. 142.

revolution' in which not only is sex without love openly advocated but also the production of films showing schoolteachers masturbating for the edification of their charges is considered by some as a basic human right. This kind of *reductio ad absurdum* of sexual licence Bernanos had foreseen and he regarded it as a form of madness. 'After all,' he said, 'what do we know about madness? What do we know about lust? What do we know about the secret connections between them? Lust is a mysterious wound in the flank of the human race. In its flank? No, that's not quite right: at the very source of life. To confuse lust which is peculiar to man with the desire that brings the sexes together is about as sensible as to give the same name to a tumour and the organ at which it eats away, so that the deformed tumour finishes up, frightfully, by reproducing the very form of the organ it devours. The world, aided and abetted by all the prestigious resources of art, goes to a lot of trouble to cover up this shameful wound.'[3] Not now. The once Protestant and puritan countries seem to be displaying a quite shameless rivalry in this little matter of who can exhibit most completely this 'shameful wound' in all its suppurating life. It is only to be feared that when the pendulum swings back it will swing with a violence that might have shocked Bernanos himself. For which is worse: impurity naked and unashamed or impurity leeringly pretending to be pure? Since 'everything is impure to the impure', perhaps it doesn't matter very much. As practically everyone says at some stage in *Monsieur Ouine*: '*il n'y a rien*' – 'nothing whatever is left'.

If the stench of the battlefields remained with Bernanos, on and off, for the rest of his life, it had a very different effect on Teilhard de Chardin. Bernanos was not a mystic, indeed he had a rooted mistrust of cloistered monks whose contemplative prayer, however admirable it might be in itself, necessarily kept them unspotted by the world and therefore unaware of the sheer wickedness of man. Teilhard, right up from boyhood, had a deep feeling not only for God but also, and more so, for the spiritual potential of matter. In 1950, some four years before his death, he wrote:

'I am doing my best, just now, to recapture and to express my

3. G. Bernanos, *Journal d'un curé de campagne*, p. 1126.

feelings as a child, toward what I have called, later on, *la sainte Matière*. A rather delicate and critical point, since it is unquestionably out of these early contacts with the "essence" of the World that my whole internal life has sprung and grown. In this case, at least, nobody can say that I am intruding on the grounds of philosophy or theology. A personal psychological experience: nothing more, but also nothing less.'[4]

As we have seen, many people have had this feeling. They have called it the 'oceanic feeling' or 'cosmic consciousness', and the more sensible ones have been content to leave it at that. From only one such experience the Canadian doctor, R. M. Bucke, was foolish enough to write that he 'saw and knew that the Cosmos is not dead matter but a living Presence, that the soul of man is immortal, that the universe is so built and ordered that without any peradventure all things work together for the good',[5] and that what he had experienced 'shows that death is an absurdity, that everyone and everything has eternal life; it shows that the universe is God and that God is the universe, and that no evil ever did or ever will enter into it'.[6] This, of course, is, from the point of the scientific establishment, 'vitalistic' nonsense, but it is a nonsense that dies very hard.

Teilhard himself was in his later period to make a clear distinction between the mysticism of matter – 'unity at the base, by dissolution' – and the mysticism centred on God through love – 'unity at the top, by ultra-differentiation'. The one he called the 'pantheism of identification, at the antipodes of love: "God is the All",' the other the 'pantheism of unification, beyond love: "God is All in all things." '[7] But he was quite ready to admit that these two 'extreme poles' of mystical experience shared many common characteristics which made them seem terribly alike,[8] so much so that he sometimes thought that God could only be reached through the cosmic vision of matter, much as in the *Katha* Upanishad (3.11: 6.8) the 'Person', that is, God, can only be reached by

---

4. P. Teilhard de Chardin, *Letters to Two Friends, 1926–1952* (Rapp & Whiting, London, 1970, and the New American Library, New York, 1968), p. 214.
5. R. M. Bucke, *Cosmic Consciousness*, p. 10.   6. Ibid., p. 17.
7. P. Teilhard de Chardin, *L'activation de l'énergie*, pp. 231–2. Written in 1950.
8. Ibid.

passing through the 'Unmanifest' (*avyakta*), a term that later became identified with primal, undifferentiated matter. It did not seem to worry him overmuch that matter is of its very nature amoral, 'the combined essence of all evil and all goodness'.[9] Teilhard's 'matter' and Jung's 'God' have much in common.

Usually Teilhard speaks of the 'cosmic sense' (*le sens cosmique*), but occasionally he too speaks of cosmic 'consciousness', and this is clearly what possessed him in the trenches during the First World War and which he then called the 'soul of the front'. Unlike Bucke, he does not jump to unwarrantable conclusions about the impossibility of evil ever entering into the world: he tries to be a little bit more precise, a little bit less silly. 'When one reads', he writes, 'the accounts of certain Christian or pagan mystics or indeed the confidences of many apparently quite ordinary men, one has to ask oneself seriously whether there is not a sort of cosmic consciousness in our soul more diffused than individual consciousness, more intermittent, but perfectly well defined – a sort of feeling of the presence of all beings at once, not perceived as multiple and separate but as sharing in the same unity – at least in some future time . . . . Is this consciousness of the universal a reality, or only the materialization of an expectation or a desire? Well it is up to the psychologists to answer if they can.'[1]

Jung no doubt would answer that this cosmic consciousness is of the very essence of what he calls the 'collective' consciousness of the race reflected in myths of an original innocence when men knew neither good nor evil, 'nothing of loving life, nothing of hating death'[2] – a consciousness prior to the emergence of individual consciousness and therefore most like the consciousness of a very small child. In 1923 Teilhard thought that this experience of the All must necessarily point towards God. 'The All', he then wrote, 'with its attributes of universality, unity, and infallibility (at least relative), could not reveal itself to us unless we recognized God in it – or the shadow of God. – And can God, on his side,

---

9. *Écrits du temps de la guerre*, p. 438: E.T. in *Hymn of the Universe* (Collins, London, and Harper, New York, 1965), p. 60.
1. *Comment je crois* (Éditions du Seuil, Paris, 1969), pp. 75–6. Written in 1923.
2. Above, p. 130.

manifest himself to us except by passing through the All, by assuming the figure, or at least the clothing, of the All?'[3]

This is a rhetorical question expecting the answer 'No' – and it comes oddly from a Christian even though he calls himself a 'pantheistic' Christian. It is not at all what Western Christianity has understood by the Cross, but Western Christianity's understanding of the human sacrifice which was ritually enacted on Calvary was as displeasing and dated to Teilhard as it is to the modern world for whom he claimed to speak. Hence he can write: 'The essential message of Christ, I should say, is not to be sought in the Sermon on the Mount, nor even in the gesture[4] of the Cross; it lies wholly in the proclamation of a "divine fatherhood". . ., in the affirmation that God, a personal being, presents Himself to man as the goal of a personal *union*.'[5]

Teilhard's mysticism, except in his last period when he makes a clear distinction between the mysticism of diffusion and the mysticism of unification, is far more akin to the pantheism of the Upanishads and Zen than it is to the austere and painful 'ascent of Mount Carmel' of St John of the Cross; and it is only when the shadow of death is already beginning to fall on him that he begins to understand what the Zen Buddhists meant by the phrase, 'Die while alive, and be completely dead'. His interpretation of the 'gesture' of the Cross as 'the proclamation of a "divine fatherhood" ' is no interpretation at all. That the 'gesture' needs reinterpreting few would deny, but Teilhard's is not an interpretation, it is not even an explaining away. In another passage, writing about André Gide's novel, *La porte étroite*, he says: '*La porte étroite* is a clever but extremely unpleasant book: this idea of a value of sacrifice and pain for the sake of sacrifice and pain itself (whereas the value of pain is simply to pay for some useful conquest!) is a dangerous (and very "Protestant") perversion of the "meaning of the Cross" (the true meaning of the Cross is: "Toward progress through effort").'[6]

3. P. Teilhard de Chardin, *Comment je crois*, p. 77.
4. *Geste*: the E.T. has 'drama'.
5. P. Teilhard de Chardin, *L'énergie humaine*, p. 193: E.T. *Human Energy*, p. 156. Written in 1937.
6. *Letters to Two Friends, 1926–1952*, p. 187. Written in 1948.

It is no doubt true that the cosmic Christ of the first chapter of Paul's letter to the Colossians, where Christ is described as 'the image of the unseen God and the first-born of all creation, for in him were created all things in heaven and on earth', has been much neglected by modern Christianity, but to emphasize it at the expense of everything else is quite simply heresy in the literal sense of that word, 'choosing' what suits you at the expense of everything else.

Teilhard has been attacked for his glossing over of the problem of evil, and rightly so: he has no more sense of the 'wickedness of evil' than the average nature mystic as represented by R. M. Bucke. In his apprehension of the total indifference of Nature to man and his sufferings Richard Jefferies is far more clear-sighted than Teilhard. Jefferies cared, Teilhard all too often seems not to care at all. His whole vision of a world converging irreversibly on a cosmic 'centre of centres' is based, it seems to me, on his prolonged participation in 'cosmic consciousness' which he had experienced from boyhood but which only became acute in the mire and misery of the First World War. Combining this with a pathetic faith in biological evolution and human progress and pretending that this faith was scientifically based, he succeeded in firing the imagination of many Christians who were sick and tired of the rigidity of the Catholic Church as personified in Popes Pius IX to XII. The vision of course is nothing more than a vision, but his insistence that evolution *must* result in man converging on himself runs very much counter to the evidence of our times, is frequently puerile, and makes a mockery of human suffering. As in the case of the 'gesture' of the Cross he could only attack the traditional doctrine of original sin, he never attempted to interpret it. For him evil is the same thing as multiplicity:[7] it is 'the *inevitable* corollary of the creative act',[8] for 'in this perspective physical suffering and moral faults *inevitably* creep into the world, not by virtue of some defect in the creative act, but by the very structure of shared being (that is to say, as a *statistically inevitable by-product* of the unification of the multiple) they contradict neither the power nor the goodness of God.'[9] Once again the danger-signal is there – the use of italics

7. *Comment je crois*, p. 102.   8. Ibid., p. 101.   9. Ibid., p. 228.

to warn us that something very phoney is going on. When Teilhard speaks as a theologian and scientist at once, you may be quite certain he is not worth listening to.

That the Genesis story of the 'Fall' *can* be explained along evolutionary lines I have tried to show elsewhere.[1] Self-consciousness developing out of group consciousness, what Genesis calls the 'knowledge of good and evil', was certainly almost bound to lead to selfishness and the misuse of the knowledge acquired; and the cure for selfishness can only be selflessness. Hence the teaching of the Buddha concerning the 'not-self', and Christ's 'gesture' on the Cross. Both teach us that we must 'die before we die'. 'Sin' in German is *Sünde*, and *Sünde* is etymologically connected with *Sonderung*, 'sundering': it is an alienation of the human personality from its roots in God. For Teilhard neither sin nor evil present any problem at all: 'It can be said', he writes, 'that the modernization of Christology would simply consist in explaining *sin* in theological and liturgical formulas by *progress*, in fine, smoke by fire. Is that so grave?'[2] No, just trivial – and heartless.

Teilhard, indeed, is not really interested in human beings as such, what interests him is his pipe-dream of humanity converging on itself, and never mind the casualties on the way. 'The world', he says, 'seen by experience at our level, is an immense groping, an immense search, an immense attack; its progress can take place only at the expense of many failures, of many wounds. Sufferers of whatever species are the expression of this stern but noble condition. They are not useless and dwarfed. They are simply paying for the forward march and triumph of all. They are casualties, fallen on the field of honour.'[3] Of course, this might make some sort of sense if we had the slightest idea of where this forward march was leading us. But when Teilhard comes to speak of it at all, he is as banal as the most philistine of humanists. You shall have aeroplanes, radios, movies,[4] television, birth control, euthanasia, the sacrifice of the weak to the strong, and, of course, a totalitarian organization.[5] On the last the French editor remarks:

1. *Concordant Discord*, chapter xvi; *Evolution in Religion*, pp. 60ff.
2. P. Teilhard de Chardin, *Comment je crois*, p. 103, n. 1.
3. *L'énergie humaine*, p. 63: E.T. *Human Energy*, p. 50.
4. *Human Energy*, p. 128.   5. Ibid., pp. 132–4.

'Obviously this adjective is intended to convey a general notion of totality, not a so-called "totalitarian" régime.' Unfortunately this is not at all obvious. Teilhard seems to have admired any form of totalitarianism simply because it seemed to prove his theory of 'convergence'. Whether it was Hitler or Stalin or the early Mao Tse-tung did not seem to worry him very much. From the safety of Peking he wrote to a friend after the collapse of France: 'There is something dreadfully primitive and narrow in the [*sic*] Hitler's religion and ideal. But the Germans had an internal flame, and *this* was too strong for us, much more than the tanks.'[6] And, more astonishing still: 'Just now, the Germans deserve to win because, however bad or mixed is their spirit, they have more spirit than the rest of the world. It is easy to criticize and despise the fifth column. But no spiritual aim or energy will ever succeed, or even deserve to succeed, unless it proves able to spread and keep spreading a fifth column.'[7] And in case you should have any doubts on the kind of convergent world for the emergence of which it is both right and inevitable that many shall be sacrificed on the way, you have only to listen to what the prophet of progress has to say about the dropping of the atom bomb:

'At that moment man found himself hallowed[8] not only with his existing strength but with a method which would enable him to master all the other forces surrounding him. . . . He had discovered, in the unconsidered unanimity of the act which circumstances had forced upon him, another secret pointing the way to his omnipotence. For the first time in history . . . a planned scientific experiment employing units of a hundred or a thousand men had been successfully completed. . . . The greatest discovery ever made by man was precisely the one in which the largest number of minds were enabled to join together in a single organism, both more complicated and more centred, for the purpose of research. Was this simply coincidence? Did it not rather show that in this as in other fields nothing in the universe can resist the converging

---

6. *Letters to Two Friends, 1926–1952*, p. 145.
7. Ibid., p. 146.
8. *Sacré* (the same word used for the 'consecration' of a king): the E.T. has (misleadingly) 'endowed'.

energies of a sufficient number of minds sufficiently grouped and organized.'⁹

From the pen of a Christian these words are well-nigh unbelievable. Not a word of sympathy for the innocent victims of Hiroshima and Nagasaki; only inflated talk about the omnipotence of man which is neither true nor Christian. And the conclusion? 'War will be eliminated at its source ... and now that a true objective is offered us, one that we can only attain by striving with all our power in a concerted effort, our future activities can only be convergent, drawing us together in an atmosphere of sympathy. I repeat, sympathy, because for everyone to be all together ardently intent upon a common object is inevitably the beginning of mutual love.'¹ 'Sympathy, compassion, συμπαθεῖν', I seem to remember Monsieur Ouine saying, 'to "suffer together". Better say to "rot together".'²

Teilhard himself admits that ' "enemy No. 1" of the modern world is boredom',³ and he seems to think that the scientific breakthrough represented by the explosion of the atom bomb will fill us with enthusiasm for the limitless prospects now open before us. How little did he know how bored we would become with the repeated manned landings on the moon, so much so that the mass media did not even give Apollo 15 top-ranking coverage. How much wiser was Professor Monod when he told us that science was in a position to kill not only our bodies but the soul itself.⁴ How hollow does Teilhard's talk of 'amorizing' the universe sound now; for not only have we totally failed to love each other in the shadow of the atomic bomb, not only have our divisions grown more bafflingly complex as one national selfishness tries to outwit the other, but the further we probe into the universe, the more certainly do we realize how terribly and senselessly isolated we are. For what is the sense of talking of a 'cosmic' Christ when this wretched planet of ours to which alone he was sent has been deaf to his message long ago – so deaf indeed that now at last it refuses to listen to priests and pastors, scribes and Pharisees, who

---

9. P. Teilhard de Chardin, *L'avenir de l'homme*, pp. 182–3: cf. E.T. *The Future of Man*, pp. 143–4.
1. Ibid., p. 186: E.T., p. 147.   2. Above, p. 142.
3. *L'avenir de l'homme*, p. 184: E.T., p. 145.   4. Above, p. 22.

Salvation through Death

would have us believe they speak in his name. As to the unification of this planet by love, even in what is perhaps the most attractive of his works, Teilhard himself confesses how greatly he himself had failed to love his fellow-men:

'Once a man has fallen in love with the divine milieu he cannot bear the darkness, tepidity, and emptiness he sees on every side in what ought to be filled with God and pulsating in him. At the very idea of the countless spirits bound to him in the unity of the same world but not yet fully kindled in the fire of the divine presence, he feels himself stiff and cold. . . .

'My God, I confess to you that I have long been and still am impervious to the love of my neighbour. The more ardently I have tasted of the superhuman joy of being broken and lost in the souls to which some mysterious affinity of human love predestined me, the more I feel hostile and closed to the common run of those you bid me love – and that is something I seem to be born with. What is above me or below me in the universe, . . . matter, plants, animals, and then Powers, Dominations, Angels – these I can accept without difficulty and rejoice in feeling myself supported in the hierarchy they represent. But the "other", my God, by which I mean not only "the poor, the lame, the twisted, the plain stupid", but simply the *other*, the other *tout court* – the other who seems to live independently of me in a universe apparently closed to mine and who, as far as I am concerned, shatters the unity and the silence of the world – would I be sincere if I were not to tell you that my instinctive reaction is to fight him off, and that the very idea of entering into spiritual communion with him disgusts me?'[5]

This is at least honest, but it does make nonsense of all Teilhard's talk about 'convergence through love'. Just as with the Zen Buddhists 'it may not be difficult to *talk about* this experience of awakening to "Self-nature" or "True Self" which we have deep at the bottom of our personalities, but to come to this realization experientially as the fact of one's own actual experience, is not

---

5. P. Teilhard de Chardin, *Le milieu divin* (Éditions du Seuil, Paris, 1957), pp. 183–5: cf. E.T., *Le Milieu Divin* (Collins, London, 1960), pp. 137–8; *The Divine Milieu* (Harper, New York, 1960), pp. 125–6.

easy at all',[6] so too is it easy for Christians to talk about the love of God and our fellow-men, but it is quite a different thing not only actually to love them but to be seen to love them. The words love and charity have, in any case, lost all meaning: very often they are regarded as being synonymous with copulation on the one hand and institutionalized 'charity', which could be equally well or better arranged by a computer, on the other.

Teilhard, in his wilder flights of fantasy, said he had little use for the Sermon on the Mount, yet his moving confession of his sheer inability to love the 'other' shows that he knew that in one essential respect he had utterly failed to be a Christian.

'Love your enemies and pray for those who persecute you' had been the impossible demand that Jesus made upon his followers: 'For if you love those who love you, what right have you to claim any credit? Even the tax collectors do as much, do they not? And if you save your greetings for your brothers, are you doing anything exceptional? Even the pagans do as much, do they not?'[7] This is a demand that Bernanos, quite as much as Teilhard, failed to fulfil, Bernanos because he was filled with righteous indignation at the mediocrity, the sickening hypocrisy, and the sheer rottenness he discerned in the dominant élite in Church and State and Press, Teilhard because he was even more absorbed in his cosmic vision of a world converging on itself for which individual suffering was no more than an inevitable by-product. Among the four modern 'prophets' we have briefly discussed it was only Jung and Bonhoeffer who showed real compassion for 'the poor, the lame, the twisted, the plain stupid', because for both of them God was a living and ever present reality – quite as terrible as he was lovable, but known and experienced as the ultimate Good that is beyond all good and evil.

Death is the goal to which we are all moving. For the Hindus and Buddhists, with their belief in endless reincarnations throughout measureless aeons of time, final death – the definitive extinction of all becoming and therefore of all life – could only mean a happy release and freedom of the spirit. For them it is life that is

6. Z. Shibayama, *A Flower Does Not Talk*. p. 105.
7. Matthew 5:44–7.

fraught with sorrow, 'death without rebirth'[8] is the ultimate release. This is true of all the mystics. For the Muslim mystics *fanā*, 'destruction', must precede *baqā*, 'eternity'; that is to say, all purely human characteristics must be annihilated if the divine is to fill their place: 'Die before you die', as an admittedly spurious 'tradition' of the Prophet says. *Fanā*, according to the eleventh-century Muslim mystic, Ansārī, means the 'dissolution of everything except God': its obverse is *baqā*, the 'continued existence in eternity of what has never ceased to be in Truth[9] through the shaking off of what [originally] was not, by obliterating it'.[1] This means the death of the purely 'natural' man and his transfiguration into the divine. The temptation of the mystic is, then, to exalt death above life; for death means to be reunited with the eternal and timeless from which our miserable lives in time can only appear totally insignificant and unreal.

In Christianity, however, the balance is restored, for Christ did not only say: 'Anyone who loves his life loses it; anyone who hates his life in this world will keep it for the eternal life.'[2] He also demands that we should make use of our 'talents', bringing them to fruition and not burying them in the ground.[3] So too the *Ishā* Upanishad says: 'Abandon [the world] and then enjoy.' But surely the perfect formula for the ordering of our life in view of our death and our 'death' in view of our life is Jesus's command that we should 'die before we die' in order to yield a rich harvest of a worthwhile life fulfilled.

> I tell you, most solemnly,
> unless a wheat grain falls on the ground and dies,
> it remains only a single grain;
> but if it dies,
> it yields a rich harvest.[4]

Teilhard's tract *Le Milieu Divin*, which is probably his best as well as his most sober book, might almost be a commentary on this

8. Philip Kapleau, *The Three Pillars of Zen*, p. 45.
9. *Haqq*, 'truth', is also the usual Sufi word for 'God'.
1. S. de Laugier de Beaurecueil, O.P., *Abdallah al Ansārī al Harawī* (Cairo 1962), pp. 104-5 (Arabic text), pp. 129-32 (French translation).
2. John 12:25: cf. Matthew 16:25, etc.   3. Matthew 25:14-30.
4. John 12:24.

text. It is based on the Catholic assumption that God assumed our humanity in order that we might partake of his divinity: hence the first two parts are called 'the divinization of our activities' and 'the divinization of our passivities'. This means that we must make the most of our talents while alive so that when we come to die and our physical being is reduced to nothingness we may yield a rich harvest which we shall be able to offer up to God if he exists, and if he does not, then at least we shall have left this unhappy world enriched, however little, but having been true to ourselves without any selfishness. For each of us has his own part to play which cannot be played by anyone else, for in a sense the whole is dependent on the part almost as much as the part is dependent on the whole. And so, in conformity with his dictum that union diversifies since to love is not to wish for the destruction of the beloved but to wish him to be ever more true to his inmost self, Teilhard says: 'We can only lose ourselves in God by prolonging the most individual characteristics of beings far beyond themselves .... The heart of God is boundless, *multae mansiones*.[5] And yet in all that immensity there is only one possible place for each one of us at any given moment, the one we are led to by unflagging fidelity to the natural and supernatural duties of life.'[6] It is just as the *Chāndogya* Upanishad (6.9.1) said long ago and in a quite different religious atmosphere:

'As bees, dear boy, make honey by collecting the juices of many trees and reduce the juice to a unity, yet those juices cannot perceive any distinction there so that they might know: "I am the juice of this tree", or "I am the juice of that tree", so too, my dearest boy, all these creatures here, once they have merged into Being do not know they have merged into Being.'

If you bury your talents in the ground death will destroy you irrevocably, but if you let the best of yourself flow into what is greater than yourself, just as the juices of various flowers combine to form honey, then you will survive as a flavour in the ocean of

---

5. 'many mansions'. Reference to John 14:2: 'In my Father's house are many mansions' (AV): 'There are many rooms in my Father's house' (Jerusalem Bible).
6. P. Teilhard de Chardin, *Le milieu divin*, p. 142: E.T., p. 106 (pp. 95-6 in U.S. ed.).

Brahman as the Hindus would say or, in Teilhard's words, in the immeasurable heart of God. Whatever we may do and however hard we may try to deceive ourselves, we cannot escape 'that slow, essential deterioration – old age, moment by moment robbing us of ourselves and pushing us on towards the end. ... [And] in death, as in an ocean, all our diminishments, whether sudden or gradual, merge into one another. Death is the epitome and consummation of all our diminishments: it is *evil* itself – purely physical evil in so far as, organically, it is the result of the material plurality in which we are immersed – but moral evil too in so far as, whether in society or in ourselves, this disorderly plurality which is the source of all our setbacks and all corruption, is generated by a wrong use of our liberty.'[7]

For the individual separated from his fellow-men, from all sense of the eternal, and therefore from God, death is the ultimate horror, the ultimate obscenity. That is because we identify ourselves with our everyday ego – that ego the very existence of which the Buddhists deny – and we cannot bear to think that this 'ego', this 'I', with all its absurd pretensions, must for ever disappear. 'Dust you are and to dust you shall return'[8] was God's sentence on our first parents – and it is the sentence the silent, unhearing, uncaring immensity of space-time repeats to us with crushing finality today. We must learn that we, as egos, as individuals, do not matter. If we cannot welcome death with joy, then let us at least accept it with dignity as befits an honourable man. This at least you can do even if you have never been conscious of the eternity within you which is your true self and your real humanity – a 'form of Brahman',[9] as the Hindus would say, the 'ground' of your soul which is rooted in God. And so Teilhard says: 'Let us overcome death by discovering God in it. And then, simultaneously, we will find the Divine ensconced in our own hearts, in that last recess which seemed to be able to evade him.'[1]

And even if he cannot do this, does it matter so very much? In his most sober moments Teilhard did not think so. 'To tell the

---

7. Ibid., pp. 83–4: cf. E.T., pp. 60–1 (p. 54 in U.S. ed.).
8. Genesis 3:19.   9. *Kena* Upanishad, 2.1.
1. *Le milieu divin*, p. 84: cf. E.T., p. 61 (p. 54 in U.S. ed.).

truth', he wrote, 'the problem of personal survival does not worry me much. So long as the fruits of my life are received up into someone Immortal what does it matter to me whether I should selfishly be conscious of them and enjoy them? Quite sincerely, my personal happiness does not interest me. To be happy it is enough for me to know that what is best in me passes on into one who is greater and more beautiful than I – for ever.'[2]

When all is said and done, and however much one may be irritated by his cosmic vision which so often seems to disregard unmerited suffering, Teilhard's greatness lies in the fact that he could be serenely happy in the thought that death, the inevitable climax of his diminishment, could only mean that what was worth saving in him was for ever preserved in someone greater than he.

However much his vision may have been at variance with the traditional doctrine of the Catholic Church, Teilhard remained profoundly Catholic, 'hyper-Catholic'[3] as he put it, because he saw in the Roman Catholic Church the only human institution on and around which humanity as a whole could possibly converge upon itself.

Bernanos, like Teilhard, was a born Catholic and a daily communicant, and again, like Teilhard, he came up against the hierarchy and castigated it in no uncertain terms. Unlike Teilhard, however, he took suffering and evil seriously. The Cross was to him not a 'gesture' but the only way that man could pass triumphantly from this evil and corrupt world to eternal life. What was central to him in Christianity was the agony in the garden of Gethsemane and the utter dereliction on the Cross ('My God, my God, why hast thou forsaken me?').

Jung, it may be remembered, became convinced of the hollowness of the form of Christianity in which he had been brought up by the fact that not only did nothing whatever happen at his first Communion but that obviously nobody had ever expected anything to happen. The experience of the young Bernanos was quite

2. *Comment je crois*, pp. 135–6.
3. *Letters to Léontine Zanta* (E.T., Collins, London, and Harper & Row, New York, 1969), p. 36.

the reverse. He sometimes referred to his first Communion as a 'conversion': and it quite certainly changed his whole outlook on life – and death. From early childhood he had been sickly and the shadow of death was never far from him. At the age of seventeen he wrote: 'I am afraid of death, and unfortunately (perhaps my guardian angel would say "fortunately") I think of it all the time.'[4] Indeed his whole life was orientated towards death, and life and death seemed to him to hang inseparably together. 'At the time of my first Communion', he writes, 'the light began to dawn on me, and I told myself that it was not life that one had to try particularly to make happy and good, but death which is the final end of everything. And I thought of becoming a missionary, and, in my thanksgiving at the end of the Mass of my first Communion, that is all I asked from the Father as my only present.'[5] At the same time he had an acute sense of the presence and reality of God – the God of Pascal – 'God of Abraham, God of Isaac, God of Jacob, not the God of the philosophers and scientists'. This God was, for him, as he was for Pascal himself and for Jung, a God as terrible as he was 'good'. Only by submitting to the will of God and confidently accepting suffering at his hands, could one face death and 'drop into God',[6] the author of one's being, one's suffering, one's despair, as well as one's hope, and finally one's beatitude.

Bernanos had no illusions about the 'goodness' of God: he knew that he inflicted on his elect sufferings to the limit of their endurance, and this is the theme of most of his novels with the notable exceptions of *Monsieur Ouine* and *Un mauvais rêve*. Suffering must be accepted as coming from God, even if it brings you to the brink of despair, indeed particularly if it brings you to the brink of despair, because only if you have had a glimpse of the abyss, can you understand what salvation means and understand that, despite all appearances to the contrary, in death (a 'good' death, that is) 'all is grace'.[7]

Although, to judge from his novels, Bernanos is only interested

---

4. G. Bernanos, *Correspondance*, Vol. 1, p. 75.
5. Ibid.   6. *Monsieur Ouine*, p. 1560.
7. *Journal d'un curé de campagne*, p. 1259.

in saints and the utterly outcast of this world, he realizes that each individual must be true to himself first if he is to be true to God. 'To be happy', he says, 'you must live and die for [God], helping his kingdom to come according to your age, your position, your means, your fortune, and your tastes. And so I will no longer be afraid of that ghastly thing – death.'[8]

But to die well you must not only be yourself to the limits of your being (as Teilhard would have it), you must also recapture the innocence of your childhood before you ate of the fruit of the tree of the knowledge of good and evil. This nostalgia for a vanished innocence returns again and again in the novels of Bernanos. For him adolescence was a 'time of troubles' in which one first became obscurely aware of good and evil and of paradise lost. 'You know', he wrote to a young friend in 1926, 'that I am not particularly enamoured of adolescence, the female time of our lives. Everything is there, good and evil, utterly mixed up. And it's true that impurity only makes headway bit by bit, from the outside to the inside, until it reaches the heart that is still the heart of a child.'[9]

'Happy the pure in heart; they shall see God':[1] and 'Let the little children come to me; ... for it is to such as these that the kingdom of God belongs.'[2] These two texts meant far more to Bernanos than St Paul's grandiose vision of the cosmic Christ that so captivated Teilhard. For the innocence of childhood death held no terrors, for the child is still, if he is lucky, in what Jung calls 'God's world'. The passage from the innocence of childhood to the guilt of adolescence is wonderfully described by Bernanos in *Monsieur Ouine*.

Philippe, the young hero, is up at dawn on the open road, the symbol of hope. 'The magic hour when one's first youth rises up little by little from the depths to which it will never return again, bursts forth like a great venomous flower on to the surface of one's consciousness, rises up to the brain like a poison. The magic hour when the little human animal gives a name that can be understood to his strength, his joy, his gracefulness, and already they no

8. *Correspondance*, Vol. 1, p. 76.   9. Ibid., p. 233.
1. Matthew 5:8.   2. Mark 10:14, etc.

longer exist. Never mind! . . . "For a few more weeks", he said to himself, "perhaps only for a few days, I am my own master . . . ." The road was so fresh, so pure, criss-crossed with shadows, so like the idea he had of himself just then that he would have liked to bathe his hands and head in it and roll in it as if it were limpid water. For the thought of a wholly new life kept coming to him, of a life wholly bright and intact – intact, immaculate – miraculously placed between his hands, to do what he liked with – a life which the lightest caress, the slightest contact would sully for ever – until the image of death – a death as different as possible from anything he had ever dreamt of hitherto – the radiant image of death should burst forth of its own accord, at the summit of his joy.'[3]

This is death as seen in the last hours of childhood before the 'caress' of adolescence shatters its radiance and joy. Meanwhile there is nothing for it but to realize that 'we can only be worth anything at all by sacrificing ourselves and by totally forgetting ourselves for God and his cause, and that the best way we can come to despise death is to offer up our life *and* our death'.[4] Bernanos wrote these words when he was seventeen and he was never false to them. Throughout his life his inspiration was the God 'whom we have learnt to know as a wonderful living friend who suffers in our sorrow, rejoices in our joy, who will share our death agony and receive us in his arms, upon his heart'.[5]

A few months before his death he wrote: 'We really want what He wants; without knowing it, we really want our sorrows, our sufferings, and our loneliness, although we fondly imagine we only want our pleasures. We imagine that we are frightened of our death and run away from it when we really want our death as He wanted His – anyhow our death *is* His. Just as He sacrifices Himself on every altar where Mass is celebrated, so does He begin to die again in the death agony of every single man. We want everything that He wants, but we do not know that we want it. We do not know ourselves. Sin makes us live on the surface of ourselves: we

3. G. Bernanos, *Monsieur Ouine*, pp. 1409–10.
4. *Correspondance*, Vol. 1, p. 79.
5. *Journal d'un curé de campagne*, p. 1051.

only go back into ourselves to die – and it is there that He is waiting for us.'⁶

Sin is the dirt on the 'bright mirror'⁷ and it is the 'light caress' of death that wipes it away 'at the summit of our joy'.

After a life of constant struggle against evil and the dark accomplices of evil Bernanos died a natural death knowing that death meant resurrection. Bonhoeffer was hanged as a traitor to his country, but, as one who was with him in the last days of his life bore witness:

'Bonhoeffer was all humility and sweetness; he always seemed to diffuse an atmosphere of happiness, of joy in every smallest event in life, and of deep gratitude for the mere fact that he was alive. ... He was one of the very few men I have ever met to whom his God was real and ever close to him.'⁸

Bonhoeffer, too, had experienced the wrath of God poured out upon his country as on others, on the righteous as well as the wicked, and he too accepted 'God's wrath and vengeance' as 'grim realities' over the heads of his enemies as well as his own, and it was only so that he came to know 'something of what it means to love [one's enemies] and forgive them'.⁹ For him, too, death was not the end; rather it was 'the beginning of life'.¹ The beginning of life; and herein, I think, all the great religions agree. As Persia's greatest mystical poet Jalālu'd-Dīn Rūmī sings:

> On the day I die and my coffin moves out,
> Do not think, do not think, that my heart is in this world.
>
> Do not weep for me and say, 'Woe is me, ah, woe is me!'
> For you would fall into Satan's trap, and that would be woe indeed.
>
> When you see my hearse, do not say: 'Departed, passed away.'
> For this is the time of meeting and union of Him with me.
>
> When you hand me on to the grave, do not say: 'Farewell, farewell',
> For the grave is the curtain concealing the communion of Paradise.

---

6. *Oeuvres romanesques*, p. liv.   7. Above, p. 158.
8. E. Bethge, *Dietrich Bonhoeffer*, p. 823.
9. D. Bonhoeffer, *Letters and Papers from Prison*, p. 157.
1. E. Bethge, op. cit., p. 830, n. 54.

Salvation through Death

You have seen the downward passing, now look at the rising up.
Both sun and moon must set; how should they suffer harm thereby?

To you it seems a setting, in truth it is a rising.
The tomb seems like a prison, it is the freeing of the soul.

What seed went down in the earth that has not grown again?
Why then are you all doubtful when it comes to the seed of man?

What pail went down to the well that did not come up full?
Why then should the soul which is Joseph complain about the well?

Though your lips are closed to this world, they will open in another;
For your song of jubilation is in a spaceless atmosphere.[2]

A spaceless atmosphere, yes, and a timeless one too. So what does it matter, if, as Einstein feared, God is playing at dice? For behind this deterministic universe of space-time, where, on our miserable bit of cosmic dust, we seem to have been thrown up by pure chance, there must be – unless all the religions lie – another world quite different, untrammelled by space and time, which is the milieu natural to our inmost self as the Hindus never tire of telling us. '*This* is the self, *this* is the real, *this* is what you must try to understand.'[3] Perhaps they are right, and perhaps the Christian overdoes his emphasis on personality. Anything that we may call 'I' in this world, I venture to think, is very different from the 'imperishable self' of the Hindus and the 'spiritual body' of which St Paul speaks. For the risen Christ was so different from the man Jesus who died on the Cross that even his closest associates could not at first recognize him. And if such was the nature of the risen God-man, must we not then too suppose that our own resurrection will have nothing to do with what we here and now call 'I'? Surely it is enough to know that 'what is best in us passes on into one who is greater and more beautiful than we – for ever',[4] for 'death is [indeed] the supreme festival on the road to freedom'.[5]

This surely is the only true Christian hope both for ourselves

---

2. R. A. Nicholson, *Selected Poems from the Dīvāni Shamsi Tabrīz* (Cambridge University Press, Cambridge, 2nd ed., 1952), pp. 94–7.
3. Cf. *Chāndogya* Upanishad, 8.7.1.
4. Above, p. 188.   5. D. Bonhoeffer, op. cit., p. 376.

and for the dead. But it is enough: for death is God's greatest gift to man, a gift we should accept not in fear and trembling but with joy. For we have the assurance not only in Christianity but in all the great religions that what we call death is nothing worse than the breaking up of the husk of our self-love and the release from within us of the sap of a selfless love both human and divine, the Holy Spirit who dwells in the hearts of all.

7

MAKE-BELIEVE

There was a time – it now seems very long ago – when, in a world devastated by two world wars, man, faced with the decay of all traditional moral standards, could look towards one institution which stood as firm as a rock – the rock of Peter, the 'Holy Roman Catholic Church'. From the ruins of the French revolution what was left of the Roman Church had slowly risen like the phoenix from its ashes, and during the pontificate of Pius XII it seemed to be the one abiding fact in a world in violent flux. Hers were the keys of Peter, hers the power to bind or loose, hers the inerrant teaching *magisterium* which, under a Pope now declared infallible, claimed to be the sole guide of mankind to the fullness of Truth. The Roman Church might attract or repel, but it was difficult to ignore it: it still had the power to fascinate by its steady refusal to come to terms with a world 'come of age'. A world come of age? This was Bonhoeffer's dictum, but can we be so sure? Is it not more likely that, reckoning as we now do, in terms of evolutionary time it was a Church on the verge of adolescence: 'everything was there, good and evil, utterly mixed up'. This atom – this *a-tomon*, this 'indivisible' rock – had not been split, and under the austere but dignified and benevolent rule of Pope Pius XII it looked as if it never would be split. 'Modernism' had long since been crushed and it looked as if a docile Church were prepared to accept anything, once Rome had unequivocally spoken. The definition by the Pope of the 'infallible' dogma of the Assumption of the Blessed Virgin Mary 'in body and in soul' met with hardly a protest except from a few intellectuals with ecumenical inclinations. After all what would be the point of gibbing at yet one more 'impossible' dogma since the whole Church, and not only the Roman Catholics, had long ago accepted Christ's resurrection from the dead, his ascension into heaven, and his virgin birth? In those days Catholics accepted their religion as God-given and they accepted the Pope as the successor of St Peter and the Vicar of Christ on earth: they were trained and docile and, like the White Queen in *Alice through the Looking-glass*, had no difficulty in believing in 'as many as six impossible things before breakfast'. The Rock of St Peter stood firm in the restless sea of uncertainty and doubt. Let others desperately swim in search of that bottle bobbing up and down in the waves of a world in flux[6] which they were convinced contained a message of vital importance to the modern world. They reached the bottle: the bottle broke, and nobody even knew whether there ever had been a message in it: in any case they drowned. The people on the Rock looked on with calm disdain.

There were rumblings, it is true, but they rarely came to the surface. An obscure Jesuit, Pierre Teilhard de Chardin, had had his vision of a new type of Christianity based on evolution and of the convergence of the world along the axis of the Roman Catholic Church – for him the only possible axis – towards a cosmic Christ who stood at the end of the road to integrate this widened and now all-comprehensive Church back into his sacred heart. He expounded and refurbished his ideas in endless pamphlets and booklets. Very few of them were published during his life-time, but many were cyclostyled and passed around from hand to hand very much as the underground journal *Samizdat* is surreptitiously passed from hand to hand in the Soviet Union today. Loyally all this material was passed on to his superiors in the Society of Jesus and to the Curial authorities in Rome, and regularly the answer came back forbidding publication. All this took place in the utmost secrecy as was Rome's custom in those days. The Rock would not and apparently could not move, and it was against this immobilism that Teilhard fruitlessly struggled. Yet despite it all he realized that for him, at least, 'outside the Church there was no salvation', and from Rome itself he wrote: 'One of the most powerful spiritual axes of the world is certainly passing here. If only it could be set to move!'[7] As to breaking with the Jesuits, this too seemed un-

6. Above, pp. 155-6.
7. P. Teilhard de Chardin, *Letters to Two Friends, 1926–1952*, p. 189.

thinkable: his problem was '*not* to fight but to transform. On such a battlefield, I can only act *from inside.*'⁸ 'Inside' was what Dr Hans Küng, in his recent and needlessly provocative book, *Infallible?*,⁹ called a 'ghetto'.

Teilhard saw himself as a prophet *within* the Church, but sometimes the existing structures of the Church nearly drove him mad. He saw himself as 'a voice that repeats, *opportune et importune*, that the Church will waste away so long as she does not escape from the factitious world of verbal theology, of quantitative sacramentalism, and over-refined devotions in which she is enveloped, so as to reincarnate herself in the real aspirations of mankind. . . . Of course I can see well enough what is paradoxical in this attitude: if I need Christ and the Church I should accept Christ as he is presented by the Church, with its burden of rites, administration and theology. . . . But now I can't get away from the evidence that the moment has come when the Christian impulse should "save Christ" from the hands of the clerics so that the world may be saved.'¹

These are strong words indeed and have an almost Protestant ring, but they represented even then, in 1929, a real *malaise* that was already felt but rarely expressed in the Catholic world. Teilhard saw the institutional Church as a kind of 'salvation-machine', and that is precisely what it was and is and will continue to be so long as it thinks that it is not exclusively the saints in whom God (and the Devil) is interested, nor 'the poor, the lame, the twisted, the plain stupid' whom Teilhard found it impossible to love,² but also the 'dull, inert mass of those who believe in nothing at all',³ whom Bernanos habitually spoke of as 'imbeciles'. Of course all right-minded people agree with them: there is plenty of stupidity, mediocrity, fanaticism, and pusillanimity in Rome and in the Roman Catholic clergy at large, but these do not have a monopoly of those amiable qualities. You will find them too among the progressives and even outside the Roman Church where they

---

8. Ibid., p. 158.   9. Collins, London, and Doubleday, New York, 1971.
1. P. Teilhard de Chardin, *Letters to Léontine Zanta*, pp. 34–5.
2. Above, p. 183.
3. P. Teilhard de Chardin, *The Future of Man*, p. 76.

flourish in equal profusion in a wild abandon. Charity, of course, you will not expect to find, for Christians who preach a religion of love have a unique ability to hate each other. Just now it has become very fashionable and very avant-garde to love our 'separated brethren' – the heretics of yesteryear – and unctuously hate the Pope. The Roman Church is no longer a 'system' or a 'sect', but is once again truly Catholic,[4] rejoicing in its Catholic liberty to tear itself to pieces.

Teilhard de Chardin, it is true, was very badly treated by the purblind bureaucracy in Rome, and this caused him to pass through 'a rather bad crisis of anti-ecclesiasticism, not to say anti-Christianity'[5] – so do we all – but in the end he came to terms with himself and the old authoritarian Church as she was. 'And then', he writes, 'the pettinesses of my Order and even of the Church affecting me but little, I find myself much more free to appreciate their marvellous treasure of religious experience and their unique power of divinization; and I'm more at peace than ever within them, though at a different level – having had "to give the Fire its share".'[6] Not for nothing did Teilhard describe himself as 'hyper-Catholic'.

To be a Catholic means not only to belong to an ecclesiastical organization, but to be so rooted in its universality, so at one, not only with its saints but perhaps even more with its sinners, as to feel oneself to be a 'cell', however insignificant, in the one Body of Christ, so at one, that to leave it, means to be 'lost' – as lost, as deprived of all sense and value, as was the dying Monsieur Ouine. This Teilhard understood in his bones as did Bernanos. In the terminology of Dr Ivan Illich, one of the most attractive of the Catholic dissidents, however much you may loathe and despise the Church as 'It' – as a faceless and stupid bureaucracy – you cannot stop loving her as 'She' – the Bride of Christ turned whore maybe, but the Bride of Christ none the less.

Bonhoeffer was not a Catholic: and the 'Church' has never meant to Protestants what it means to Catholics. This is obvious,

---

4. Cf. *Letters to Léontine Zanta*, p. 34.   5. Ibid., p. 91.
6. Ibid., p. 98.

for the Catholic ideal has always been unity as its very name implies. Protestants have always laid more stress on private judgment which has, of course, led to the proliferation of Protestant sects. In Bonhoeffer's case the concept of the 'Church' came to have less and less meaning since his own 'Confessing Church', which had broken away from the main body of German Lutheranism on the fundamental issue as to whether one could at the same time serve both Christ and Hitler, represented only a tiny minority in the total Lutheran body. Hence he could ask himself a question that no Catholic could even formulate: 'What do a church, a community, a sermon, a liturgy, a Christian life mean in a religionless world?'[7] For him, as for the impatient young today, the classical divisions of Lutheran versus Reformed, and even Catholic versus Protestant, were now quite meaningless; and the whole concept of 'the Church' no longer made sense to him in a secularized and largely religionless world. He took Protestantism to its logical conclusion, for once the apostolic authority of the Catholic Church had been rejected, then there was no *legitimate* authority that could take its place. The inevitable result had been that Protestantism, in order to survive, had had to appeal to secular power and therefore to submit to it. Under these conditions it became plain that once the authority of the Catholic Church had been rejected, the whole concept of 'the Church' became meaningless. National churches and sects, yes: *the* Church, no. And so Bonhoeffer decided that at last 'we must simply take it that it is so', in other words it was necessary to stop lying to oneself. 'We cannot,' he said, 'like the Roman Catholics, simply identify ourselves with the church.' But, despite this, 'Karl Barth and the Confessing Church have encouraged us to entrench ourselves persistently behind the "faith of the church", and evade the honest question as to what we ourselves really believe. That is why the air is not quite fresh, even in the Confessing Church. To say that it is the church's business, not mine, may be a clerical evasion, and outsiders always regard it as such.'[8] This is a new note in 'orthodox' Protestantism, but it is surely of the essence of the Protestant

7. D. Bonhoeffer, *Letters and Papers from Prison*, p. 280.
8. Ibid., p. 382.

protest against the rigid, 'imperial', centralism of the Roman Church in favour of the individual conscience. It is strange that Bonhoeffer's plea for 'fresh air' should have found its natural response not among his own would-be followers, the 'religionless Christianity' boys in the USA and their like, but in a like-minded spirit miraculously elected to St Peter's Chair in Rome, John XXIII, who inaugurated precisely the kind of *aggiornamento*, the opening of windows to the fresh air outside, for which Bonhoeffer had been calling. In an outline for a book he did not live to write Bonhoeffer had said:

'The church is the church only when it exists for others. To make a start, it should give away all its property to those in need. The clergy must live solely on the free-will offerings of their congregations, or possibly engage in some secular calling. The church must share in the secular problems of ordinary human life, not dominating, but helping and serving. It must tell men of every calling what it means to live in Christ, to exist for others. In particular, our own church will have to take the field against the vices of *hubris*, power-worship, envy, and humbug, as the roots of all evil. It will have to speak of moderation, purity, trust, loyalty, constancy, patience, discipline, humility, contentment, and modesty. It must not under-estimate the importance of human example (which has its origin in the humanity of Jesus and is so important in Paul's teaching); it is not abstract argument, but example, that gives its word emphasis and power.'[9]

What did Bonhoeffer understand by the Church in this passage? Surely not his own exiguous Confessing Church whose very *raison d'être* ceased to exist with the crushing of the Nazi tyranny. He can scarcely have been thinking of the Roman Catholic Church whose '*hubris*, power-worship ... and humbug' must have been obvious to him, if less *painfully* obvious than it was to Bernanos who suffered the whole immeasurable scandal from within. Yet it was in fact in the Catholic Church that the long desired opening out was to take place.

On 28 October 1958 the cardinals of the Holy Roman Church

9. Ibid., pp. 382–3.

designated a former peasant boy from the village of Sotto il Monte near Bergamo to be the supreme Pastor of the universal flock of Jesus Christ: Angelo Giuseppe Roncalli, later to be known and loved as Pope John XXIII, whose short pontificate was to transform the Roman Church out of all recognition from a bastion of solid conservatism, disdainful of the passing fashions of an ephemeral world, into a wasp's nest of jangling opinions of men who were, incredibly, being asked to think for themselves. The Rock of Peter moved.

The Rock of Peter moved: or rather it transformed itself into a highway along which the 'pilgrim' Church was henceforth to travel. The Rock and the ideas it symbolized have gone for ever, for the embattled citadel of the Church militant, fighting a losing battle against the chaotic turmoil of our times, has collapsed like a pack of cards, and the Catholic now finds himself hobbling along the broad highway opened by the charity of a great and humble heart to all who may care to take this particular road from the swirling flux of this world to the perfect peace of Nirvana, 'moving slowly towards him, as if he stood waiting with outstretched arms'.[1] The road is fresh and pure but it is also 'criss-crossed with shadows'[2] and not everyone on it is pure. There is plenty of squabbling on the road and much jockeying for position. How could it be otherwise, since even when Christ Jesus was alive his disciples were for ever asking him who should be the first in the kingdom of heaven? They too had to learn the hard way that 'the first shall be last and the last shall be first'.

So it was with John. He knew perfectly well that in the ebb and flow of a papal election he, at the age of seventy-seven, had no chance of succeeding to the throne of Pius XII, his imperious and imperial predecessor, who had none the less done more than most to restore the dignity of the Catholic Church as a bastion of stability in a world in flames, except as a 'provisional and transitional Pope',[3] a nice old buffer whom it would no doubt be easy to manipulate. The cardinals made a mistake, for they had elected

1. Pope John XXIII, *Journal of a Soul* (Geoffrey Chapman, London, and McGraw-Hill, New York, 1965), p. 306.
2. Above, p. 191. 3. *Journal of a Soul*, p. 303.

a genuinely humble man, and humility is a virtue that, contrary to all expectations, can set the world ablaze, not with the blaze of war but with the living flame of love. What Pope John set out to do was exactly what Bonhoeffer had thought the Church as a whole must do. In 1959, in the first year after his election, he wrote:

'Since the Lord chose me, unworthy as I am, for this great service, I feel I have no longer any special ties in this life, no family, no earthly country or nation, nor any particular preferences with regard to studies or projects, even good ones. Now, more than ever, I see myself only as the humble and unworthy "servant of God and servant of the servants of God". The whole world is my family. This sense of belonging to everyone must give character and vigour to my mind, my heart and my actions.'[4]

'Happy the gentle: they shall have the earth for their heritage',[5] Jesus had said. John was lowly and gentle, and the world indeed was his heritage – his family which looked to him not so much for guidance as for goodness. John knew this, and he knew, as popes had rarely known before, that since the faithful called him 'Holy Father', holy he must be. At the age of eighty he knew that his time must be running out and that he must be prepared to die a holy death or lead a holy life, whichever way the Lord should decide. To be holy, oddly enough, also means to be happy: and 'to be happy', Bernanos had said, 'you must live and die for [God], helping his kingdom to come according to your age, your means, your fortune, and your tastes'.[6] Very much in this spirit this unforgettable man wrote:

'I must always hold myself ready to die, even a sudden death, and also to live as long as it pleases the Lord to leave me here below. Yes, always. At the beginning of my eightieth year I must hold myself ready: for death or life, for the one as for the other, and I must see to the saving of my soul. Everyone calls me "Holy Father", and holy I must and will be.'[7]

What was the secret of Pope John? Surely it was that right up

4. Ibid., pp. 298–9.
5. Matthew 5:4 (see also note d. in the Jerusalem Bible).
6. Above, p. 190.   7. *Journal of a Soul*, p. 303.

to his death at the ripe old age of eighty-one he never lost the innocence and purity of childhood, the loss of which so greatly embittered Bernanos's life. For it is not years that make a man young or old, since 'youth and old age are a matter of temperament or, if you prefer it, of soul';[8] and it is rather silly to talk so glibly about the 'generation gap' as we all tend to, for there are old men aged eighteen and young men aged eighty. The scandal of John was that he was a young man in an old man's body moving among a hierarchy that was genuinely old, many members of which had had all the youth (if they ever had any) crushed out of them in the corridors of their antiquated seminaries. John brought the spirit of childhood and purity into a world grown old and utterly corrupt. 'I have always thought', Bernanos said in one of his more cheerful moments, 'that the modern world has sinned against the spirit of youth and that this crime would kill it. It is clear that the word of the Gospel, "you cannot serve God and money", has its naturalist equivalent in: "You cannot serve both the spirit of youth and the spirit of avarice".'[9] John almost was the spirit of youth, but the spirit of avarice, the spirit of holding on to what you have got – what the Roman Church dignifies by the name of prudence – was all the time breathing down his neck.

John was convinced that his decision to call an ecumenical council was inspired by the Holy Spirit and that a new outpouring of that same Spirit was already at hand to breathe life into the stiff joints of the Roman Church. No doubt he was right, for at the first Pentecost the Holy Spirit manifested itself not as a dove but as a rushing, mighty wind and tongues of fire. The first Pentecost can be seen as the baptism of the infant Church: the second, if that is indeed what Vatican II was, must then be the Church's confirmation, the rite of adolescence in which everything, good and evil, is 'utterly mixed up'.[1]

Pope John did not live to see the Council through to its end. His successor Paul VI, formerly Cardinal Giovanni Battista Montini, Archbishop of Milan and then the darling of the liberal and ecumenical wing of the Church, proved to be a man of a very

---

8. G. Bernanos, *Les grands cimetières sous la lune* (Plon, Paris, 1938), p. 250.
9. Ibid., p. 265.   1. Above, p. 190.

different character. Quite obviously he has neither the manifest goodness nor the childlike humility of John. Despite his hectic flights to the uttermost ends of the earth he has not got the common touch which endeared Pope John to the entire world. He is not so much *amletico* ('like Hamlet', as John is reported to have said), rather he is like Cordelia: his intentions are pure, but he has a wonderful propensity for saying the wrong things at the wrong time. To his undoing he also has principles in which he passionately believes. Among these are a strongly held belief in the value of chastity which hardly endears him to our pornographic age. This had led him to act on his own initiative in the matter of both birth control and the celibacy of the clergy. That he has been tactless and heavy-handed on both issues few will deny; but on neither is there any justification for questioning his integrity. Nor is there any reason to suppose that Pope John would have taken a different line; for on 11 August 1961 he wrote in his diary: '*Sins*. Concerning *chastity* in my relations with myself, in immodest intimacies: nothing serious, *ever*.'[2] Certainly his *manner* would have been different, but in this *matter* of chastity he might well have taken as tough a line as his successor but scarcely with the authoritarian overtones that have so distressed the progressives.

That both the timing of his long-delayed encyclical *Humanae vitae* and the wholly outdated arguments from so-called natural law he used in its defence were deplorable seems scarcely debatable. In the celibacy issue he did well to exalt the celibate status of the Latin priesthood, particularly in the missionary field, since not only is a priest a man set apart to administer the sacraments, he is also (or should be) wholly dedicated to the service of Christ and his Church, not to the bringing up of a family. What Paul VI was asking of his clergy was that they should prove their worth by renouncing for Christ what is in fact the normal state of man – marriage. Before Vatican II priests had done this as a matter of course. Why the outcry afterwards? That many priests should have left the Church on this issue may be no great loss; but even if it were, can Pope Paul be wholly blamed for holding views similar to those of St Paul, St Augustine, and John XXIII himself?

2. *Journal of a Soul*, p. 304.

'Renounce', the combined voices of both Hindus and Buddhists ring in our ears, but the fattened materialist West, which includes much of what still flatters itself that it is Christian, no longer knows what the word means. The words of Pope John they have either never read or, reading, they have not understood. For himself he asked only 'total detachment from everything, with absolute indifference to both praise and blame, and to any grave event that may happen in this world, as far as it affects me personally':[3] and again, 'Always acknowledge my own nothingness.'[4] 'Renounce, and then enjoy': that is what the Upanishad said. Pope John did just this, and in that lay the secret of both his holiness and his happiness.

Of course the matter of celibacy may appear quite differently to some future pope since it is a matter of ecclesiastical discipline which has changed in the past and may well change in the future. How do things stand with that little matter of birth control which roused such vehement feelings on either side? Here it seems to me the pass had already been sold by Pius XII who sanctioned the use of the so-called safe period. The *intention* of a married couple who make use of the safe period must obviously be to 'close the marital act to the transmission of life'. Admittedly, they are taking a risk, but if their intention was not to prevent conception, then they would not presumably bother about the safe period at all. Their risk is greater than that run by users of the 'pill', but the intention remains the same. To anyone who is neither a theologian nor a lawyer it would seem that the whole matter is best left to the casuists. They managed the awkward business of usury very competently in earlier times. The same technique is open to them now. *No* contraceptive, as far as I know, is entirely safe any more than any investment is entirely safe. Would it not be more sensible as well as more honest to say that Holy Church in her wisdom forbids the use of any device which is absolutely one-hundred-percent sure to prevent conception? Then perhaps married couples might feel free to follow St Augustine's advice to 'love, and do what you will'. It is all very reminiscent of that other little matter of Friday abstinence. For centuries Catholics had been told that it

3. Ibid., p. 307.   4. Ibid., p. 311.

was mortal sin to eat 'flesh meat' on Friday: that means, in ordinary English, that if you eat meat on Friday without having confessed, or at least internally repented of this sin, and death overtakes you suddenly, you go to hell. Overnight the rule was abrogated, and now not to abstain on Friday is no sin at all. So, too, deliberate failure to 'fast' before the reception of Holy Communion was previously a mortal sin. Now you can eat as much as you like before Communion and take the sacrament without any qualms whatever. There is nothing new in these sudden reversals in the Church's view of what is sin and what is not. Is it then surprising that the 'separated brethren' should consider the self-styled 'people of God' a bunch of hypocrites?

That this particular issue of birth control which seems so easily soluble should have developed into a crisis of authority within the Roman Church seems a trifle ridiculous. Of course it is a pity that the present Pope has not made 'collegiality' a reality and that he still relies far too heavily on the Roman Curia, but you cannot expect a former Under-Secretary of State to so curially-minded a pope as Pius XII to change his spots overnight. The Holy Spirit is indeed blowing at gale force within the Catholic Church today. Perhaps if all concerned were to bring themselves to recognize, if not their own 'nothingness', then at least their mediocrity, much might be gained. For once the 'imbeciles' whom Bernanos so soundly berated could say to themselves: 'Lord, I am mediocre, help thou my mediocrity', then the storm of the Holy Spirit might subside into a more gentle breeze the words of which might be audible even to the deafest ears in Rome. The days seem to be over when the Pope spoke with authority and not as the scribes. Now the scribes, both among the conservatives and the progressives, want it all their own way – canon lawyers, professors of theology, maybe even professors of languages and comparative religion too, like myself and Monsieur Ouine – the whole lot. And the result: we have neither authority nor collegiality. We are still 'in an indeterminate sphere, among the stones and the rafters, in the rain'.

The Church is in a mess all right. But the mere fact that there are tensions in the Church means that it is at least alive and moving – far too fast for some, much too slowly for others: but that is not important. What *is* important is that it seems to have lost all sense of direction; and if it does not know itself where the great highway is leading it, how can it guide others? How can it allay the unrest of our youth – our embryo mystics and prophets, the drop-outs and the revolutionaries, both of whom are in revolt against a materialist and mechanized society which seems to offer them nothing. No doubt what they all want is what Marx wanted, an association in which 'the free development of each will be the condition for the free development of all'. But how is each to develop freely in a society in which most of us are tied to jobs that are wholly without interest? 'Dropping out' is in itself not enough. Unless we have a considerable private income or 'mediocre' parents indulgent enough to help us when the dropping out catches up with us and we are faced with the grim reality of earning our own living, sooner or later we will have to face the ugly facts of modern life. When that awful day comes it would be well to 'acknowledge one's own nothingness'.

At last, in America at least, the young seem to be waking up to their religious heritage, but this does not take the form of a return to past allegiances to the various organized Churches, but to a spontaneous expression of religious enthusiasm centred on the person of Jesus. The religious authorities, in their heavy prudence, would be foolish to frown on this new-found enthusiasm, however much it may irk their respectable, mediocre hearts; for it seems that these young people may have found in the love of Jesus and, astonishingly, in a willingness to obey his commandments, a more satisfying cure for their boredom than the artificial paradises supplied by LSD. The Catholic authorities would do well to harness this spiritual energy, which, in its own way, seeks to break out of time into eternity, to the central rite of their faith – the Mass, in which time and eternity allegedly meet. Is it really beyond our prelates and pastors to rediscover a little of the 'spirit of youth' within themselves or are they so irrevocably old that they must needs cling on to the 'spirit of avarice' and hug to themselves those traditional wares they can no longer sell?

If that is indeed so, then the Zen Buddhists are right, and in this respect at least Dr Leary is right too, and the youthful 'Jesus people'[5] in the USA are right. Nothing can be done until religion ceases to be a formality and becomes a vital experience. The Roman Church, no doubt, is doing its best in trying to bring the liturgy to the people in a form they can understand, but it is sometimes a stupid best, for surely at the moment when the God-man Christ is supposed to become incarnate again in the form of bread and wine, we should be allowed to enter into this mystery in silence, which alone is appropriate when eternity enters time. What the Catholic Church needs is not more Protestantism, not more 'ministry of the word' (we are deluged with words as it is), but a little more silence, a little more Buddhist silence in which we can 'die while alive and be completely dead'.

'Suppose a drop of plain water, thrown into an ocean of orange-flower water, were alive and could speak, ... would it not cry out in great joy: "True, I am living, yet it is not myself who lives, but this ocean lives in me, and my life is hidden away in its depths." The soul that flows into God does not die, for how could she die through being drowned in life? Rather, she lives by not living in herself.'[6]

That is from St François de Sales, and he says something that any Buddhist or Hindu could understand, but it is something that only one in a thousand perhaps will ever experience. But it is surely central to the Christian and Catholic faith, for in baptism we are baptized in Christ's death,[7] the fixed, still state of Nirvana which destroys and negates all the worries and ephemeral joys of life because it destroys *you* or what you have always taken to be you – the acquisitive, status-seeking, complacent little caterpillar that most of us are – mediocre 'imbeciles' which the young dread that they too will become one day. And no doubt they will. Even LSD is helpless against old age and, even on the admission of its most fervent advocates themselves, it is no solution in the long run, for even if it produces ecstasy, then you will be dependent on it for

5. See *Time* magazine of 21 June 1971, pp. 32–43.
6. St François de Sales, *Traité de l'amour de Dieu*, 6.12.
7. Romans 6:3.

more ecstasy just as the sex-addict must always have more sex, regardless of the damage he may be doing to others. In either case you will not be free. And as Dr Leary rightly says: 'You can't free others until *you* are free.'[8] And if you are dependent on a drug, then, obviously you are *not* free.

Catholicism is, or should be, based, not on the ministry of the word, not on sermons and theology and law ('Alas for you lawyers', Jesus said, 'who have taken away the key of knowledge! You have not gone in yourselves, and have prevented others going in who wanted to'[9]), but rather on the sacraments which do not speak: Baptism which kills your ego with Christ in the tomb; the Eucharist which raises you up with Christ, not as yourself but as what you eternally are in the sight of God, what Mahayana Buddhists call the Buddha-nature that is in all of us; Penance, the sacrament that must decapitate your many-headed ego again and again; and at the end, Extreme Unction, the royal anointing which is at the same time your Gethsemane and your Calvary, but which, beyond the agony, confers on you the spiritual royalty of which the *Chāndogya* Upanishad speaks: for now you are an 'independent sovereign, enjoying freedom of movement in every state of being', 'having pleasure in "God", playing with "God"':[1] you are a Buddha, one who has 'woken up' from the bad dream of this world, 'moving slowly towards Him, as if He stood waiting with outstretched arms'.[2]

But, you will say, as Dr Leary says, this simply isn't true. Most people are quite as egotistical after baptism as before, quite as testy and unreasonable after receiving Holy Communion as before, Of course they are, for sacraments are symbols: they are, if you like, make-believe. But with luck and quite a lot of grace, you may actually come to believe, for they work not on the surface of our soul but in that inner self which reveals itself in death. That is why all the other sacraments are, superficially at least, make-believe, for we are not conscious, or only vaguely so, of their working, while the Last Anointing, as any priest will tell you, works, is

---

8. T. Leary, *The Politics of Ecstasy*, p. 250.
9. Luke 11:52.   1. Above, p. 65.   2. Above, p. 201.

seen to work, and is known to work, by the soul in agony which can then cry out with the crucified Christ: 'It is finished.' But it isn't: it is really 'the beginning of life'[3] and 'the supreme festival on the road to freedom'.[4]

The message is always the same: die to self so that you may live in God, so that you may find the Buddha-nature within you. Once you have done that (and you will almost certainly not do it until you are dead), you will be free – free from all those senseless immensities of space-time, from necessity and chance, which we had thought made life meaningless: and once freed yourself, you may even bring release and relief to others.

This is the goal of both Mahayana Buddhism and Christianity; but in Jesus, God became man not to save man from the world but to sanctify man *in* the world: to sanctify man's frustration and suffering and failure by the example of his own frustration and suffering and failure. But God did not just become man, the Eternal did not enter the temporal so that man should drop out of the temporal: he became Jesus of Nazareth, the sort of man who, in his humility and compassion, his spontaneity and hatred of cant and all self-righteousness, in his acceptance of suffering and his experience of dereliction and despair, showed us the sort of man God wants us to be. His is a harsh way, and because it is harsh, it is probably *not* make-believe. His 'way' is the highway of the Church – both the Church as 'It', the impersonal 'sacrament machine' which thrives on the law and theology and which is run for the most part by mediocre scribes whose ridiculous self-importance Christ so scathingly denounced, and the Church as 'She' who is at the same time the Bride of Christ and the Whore of Babylon, the Church of sinners even more than the Church of saints, sinning, sinning, and sinning again, like her children, but always rising again, reaching out in hope towards the 'summit of her joy'. Because Pope John showed us the way of open-hearted love so clearly, and because the fruits of the Council he summoned have so often proved bitter, because Pope Paul seems to many to be shutting again the windows which John had opened, some have

3. E. Bethge, *Dietrich Bonhoeffer*, p. 830, n. 54.
4. D. Bonhoeffer, *Letters and Papers from Prison*, p. 376.

hated and despised her so much that they have left her and denounced her. That is because they have only seen 'It': they have not seen the Bride of Christ beneath her shabby-genteel wedding attire. They are right to denounce but they are foolish to 'drop out'. Bernanos denounced her more bitterly than they are even capable of doing, for Bernanos, with all his faults, was neither mediocre nor an imbecile. He knew that he was what he was through her and that nothing could touch him except through her, and yet it was she (or rather 'it') who had succeeded in wounding him in what was most living in his soul, that part of it from which hope itself springs forth.[5] Always tempted to despair, he did not despair: he refused to be totally disgusted by the Church's adolescence, the 'female time of her life'.[6] For the adolescent Church is still liable to infantile diseases: if she hasn't got the measles she will probably have whooping-cough, and if she hasn't got whooping-cough she will probably have the mumps. What he feared more than all, but would never believe, was that she might succumb to a cancer and rot away into nothingness like his own hallucinatory creation, Monsieur Ouine, boasting to the last, in his final disintegration, that he too had once been a professor of *living* languages, *professeur de langues vivantes*.[7] Even this horror Bernanos could face without flinching, for he must have known, like Teilhard, that the Holy Spirit who works in evolutionary time has scarcely begun his work and the goal of salvation is still a long way off, for though Christ died and rose from the dead *we are not saved yet*. For, as St Paul says: 'We must be content to hope that we shall be saved – our salvation is not in sight, we should not have to be hoping for it if it were – but, as I say, we must hope to be saved since we are not saved yet – it is something we must wait for with patience.'[8]

The Church is a pilgrim Church, and as a pilgrim she can offer hope – the hope of the broad highway that can only end in eternity – and a little faith maybe. Can she offer charity? In the world of

---

5. Cf. G. Bernanos, *Les grands cimetières sous la lune*, p. 115.
6 Above, p. 190.
7. G. Bernanos, *Monsieur Ouine*, pp. 1546, 1549.
8. Romans 8:24–5.

today and with the currency of the word so miserably debased, to speak of charity smacks of humbug; and I seem to remember one who said, not once but six times: 'Woe unto you, scribes and Pharisees, hypocrites.' That is, I think, what the young are saying to us today.

INDEX

References to important passages appear in **bold** type

Aaronson, B., and Osmond, H., 88ff.
Absolute, the, 78, 80, 83, 89, 123, 124, 126, 148, 159, 162, 163
Abu Sa'īd ibn Abi'l-Khay, 82
Adam, 169
adolescence, 152, 190, 191, 195, 203; of Church, 210
advaita ('non-dualism'), 91. *See* monism
Ahriman, 166
Ahura Mazdāh, 166
Albania, 144
alcohol, 48, 49
Alice through the Looking-glass, 196
alienation, 20, 21, 136, 155, 160, 174, 180
All, the; and God, 176, 177-8; as One, 114, 127; becoming —, 47, 50, 87; being —, 51, 70, 93, 125, 127; expansion into, 93; transcendence of, 50
Allah, 47, 71
America, 75, 76, **84**, 85, 87, 207. *See also* USA
Ansārī, 185
Anthony, St, 82
anti-Christianity, 198
anxiety (*Angst*, disquiet, etc.), 26-7, 30, 118, 120, 126, 137; Buddhist *dukkha*, 46
Apocalypse, 170
Aquinas, St Thomas, 36
Arahat, 122
Arberry, A. J., 79
Arjuna, 163
ascension, 195
asceticism, 41, 64; and chemical changes in body, 81; excess in, 81-3; Jefferies on, 57
Assumption, dogma of the, 195
atom bomb, 170; Teilhard on, 181-2
Augustine, St, 36, 68, 78, 82, 83, 106, 107, 125, 134, 204, 205; his experience at Ostia, 109-10
Aurobindo, Sri, 27
authentic(ity), 22, **29**, 32, 33, 34, 115
authority, 206
avarice, 203, 207

Bach, J. S., 84
Bangla Desh, 142
baptism, 203, 208, 209
baqā, 185
Barth, Karl, 39, 40, 199
Beatific Vision, 40, 41, 108
becoming, 41, 43, 93
bees, 54, 186
Being, 82, 90, 109, 154; and becoming, 41, 43, 93; boundless, 42, 43, 46; ground of, 101, 105; merging into, 54, 105, 186
Belgium, 143, 144
Bergson, Henri, 20, 71
Bernanos, Georges, 13, 22, 141, **142-61**, 172-3, 174-5, 184, 197, 198, 202, 206; and suffering, 189; and the Church, 200, 211; and the Cross, 188; and the hierarchy, 188; his first Communion, 188-9; on spirit of youth, 203; on World War I, 172. *See also* Ouine.
Bhagavad-Gītā, 66, 72, 78, 104, 158; and ascetic excess, 81-2; God of, 109; on Brahman and God, 102; quoted, 81, 102, 127, 159, 163
Bible, 36, 43, 50, 170
biblical realism, 85
birth control, 180, 204-5, 206
Bodhisattvas, 122-3; definition of, 122; their compassion, 123; their wisdom, 123
body; affirmation of, 57, 64; condemnation of, 68
Bonhoeffer, Dietrich, 24, 35, 36-7, 39,

Bonhoeffer (*Contd.*)
42, 76, 137-8, 141, 144, 147, 163, 171, 184, 192, 195, 200; and the Church, 198-9, 200, 202; on death, 192; on existentialism and psychotherapy, 138; on 'God' and God, 137; on religion and religious people, 75

boredom, 139, 140, **142-3**, 149, 182

bourgeois(ie), 21, 84, 136, 137

Brahmā Sahampati, 121

Brahman, **43**, 50, 57, 80, 163; a form of —, 187; becoming—, 102; being —, 47, 89; city of, 46, 58; 'does not speak and has no care', 162; indifferent to good and evil, 162, 165; merging into, 43, 46, 49, 105; principle of eternity, 43, 162

Brahmasūtras, 78

Brethren of the Free Spirit, 86

Brihadāranyaka Upanishad; quoted, 44, 47, 51, 54, 64

British, 144

Brunner, Emil, 39

Buber, Martin; on experience of absolute unity, **90**, 91, 101

Bucke, R. M., 50, 63, 71, 88, 89, 92, 101, 176, 177, 179; and 'cosmic consciousness', **60-2**

Buddha, 38, 45, 117, 120, 132, 180, 209; 'all men are the —', 113, 126; and ascetic excess, 81-2; as surgeon, 119; his compassion, 121-2, 123; his temptation, 121; his wisdom, 123; transformed into a Trinity, 123

Buddha-nature, 116, 117, 126, 132, 133-4, 158, 159, 209, 210

Buddhism, Buddhist, 38, 39, 42, 46, 50, 69, 103, 112, 118-27, 132, 147, 154, 158, 160, 162, 184, 187, 205, 208; advent of Mahayana, 122; and evil, 165; early, 72, 79; mysticism, 40; Tantric, 66; Tibetan, 108. *See also* Mahayana, Zen

Bultmann, Rudolf, 39

Calvary, 178, 209
Canaanites, 163
'canned' society, 84
casuists, 205
Catholic Church (Roman), 14, 15, 36, 37, 173, 179, **195-212**; adolescent, 211; as Bride of Christ, 198, 210, 211; as 'It', 198, 210, 211; as 'She', 198, 210, 211; as whore, 198, 210; hypocrisy of, 206; Leary on, 87; militant, 201; on man partaking of divinity, 186; pilgrim, 201, 211; 'Rock of Peter', 195, 201; sinning, 210; Teilhard and, 141, 188, 198

celibacy of clergy, 135, 204, 205

Cénabre, Abbé, 161

centre of centres, 179

chance, **19**, 20, 21, 24, 26, 28, 33, 36, 193, 210

Chāndogya Upanishad; quoted, 43, 46, 54, 57, 58, 65, 186, 209

charity, 35, 184, 198, 211-12; in Zen, 118. *See also* love

chastity, 204

child(hood), 147, 151, 152, 154, 160, 177, 190, 191, 203, 204

China, 40, 124ff

Christ, 16, 86, 104, 135, 136, 144, 145, 156, 170, 178, 180, 185, 197, 199, 201, 204, 208, 209, 210, 211; and DNA code, 74; as bridegroom, 68, 135; body of, 198; bride of, 198, 210, 211; cosmic, 179, 182, 196; in suffering and death, 191-2; living in, 200; the risen —, 193; Vicar of, 196; visions of, 83. *See also* Jesus, God-man

Christian atheism, 37, 42

Christianity, 14-15, 17, 21, 36, 37, 38, 40, 82, 103, 132, **137**, 144, 179, 184, 185, 188, 194, 196, 210; and LSD, 85, 113; and spiritual evil, 165; Bernanos on contemporary —, 143; Bonhoeffer on contemporary —, 75; irrelevance of, 87; Jung and, 164-5; pantheist —, 178

Chuang Tzŭ; quoted, 130, 152

Church(es), 14, 138, 145, 198-200, 202, 207

Clear Light of the Void, 77, 108, 109, 146. *See also* Emptiness, Void

cold, 153, 159; absolute, 146, **154**

collegiality, 206

Communism, 142; with a human face, 144, 171

Communist Manifesto, 21

compassion, 130, 142, 174, 182, 210; Buddhist, 121, 123, 148, 157
Confessing Church, 199, 200
confirmation, of Church, 203
Confucian(ism), 127, 128-9; virtues, 127, 129, and their degeneration, 129
conscience, 13, 28, 129, 154, 200
consciousness, 18, 19, 24, 54, 57, 74, 89, and *passim*; altered, 97; and Nature, 57-8, 59-60; expanded, 42, 47, 65, 67, 68, 72, 73, **98-9**, 115, 132, 133; forms of, 49; group —, 180; heightened, 81; loss of, 159. *See also* cosmic consciousness, self-consciousness
contemplation, 100, 133; infused, 78; of young men, 100, 101
convergence, 141, 174, 179, 180, 181, 182, 184, 188, 196
Copernicus, 16
Cordelia, 204
corruption, 147, 152. *See also* decay, rottenness
cosmic consciousness, 42, 43, 47, 50, **60-1**, 71, 89, 96, 101, 107, 109, 114, 119, 176, **177**
Cross, 15, 156, 180, 193; Bernanos on, 188; Teilhard on, 178, 179
crucifixion, 125
Curia (Roman), 141, 196, 206
Czechoslovakia, 13, 144, 171

damnation, 145-6, 155, 169
'dark night of the senses', 99
'dark night of the soul', 99, 132
Dead Sea Scrolls, 166; quoted, 167
death, 15, 16, 17, 51, 125, 149, **184-94**, 209; an impossibility, 42, 44, 45-6, 52, 61, 93, 130, 176; and grace, 189; beginning of life, 192, 210; Bernanos and, 190; Christ's, 208; conquest of, 38, 44, 46; 'die before you die', 82, 180, 185; 'die while alive', 132, 148, 178; fear of, 45; God in, 187; God's gift, 193; hatred of, 130; is evil, 187; joy in, 191, 194; 'only youth knows —', 152; of ego, 43, 132; re-entry into the timeless, 185; the Great —, 132; transcendence of, 44, 46, 63; without rebirth, 185.
See also Māra
'death of God' theology, 37, 42
'death-rebirth sequence', 104, 116, 132
DeBold, R. C., and Leaf, R. C., 88, 99, 105
decay, 154, 156, 172; moral, 143, 171. *See also* corruption, rottenness
democracy, 33
Denmark, 144
Descartes, 30
despair, 22, 24, 125-6, 138, 139, 142, 143, 189, 210, 211
detachment, 57, 118, 132, 205; attachment to, 132; detachment from, 157
Devil, the, 146, 197; a spiritual reality, 166; apes God, 156; his icy hatred, 157; in St John, 166; murderer and liar, 166. *See also* Evil Spirit, Māra, Satan
Dharmakāya, 123
dialectical materialism, 21, 22, 24, 31, 71
dignity of man, 143, 156
DNA code, 71, 74, 87; and Christ, 74. *See also* genetic code
Dogen, 116
'drop out', 39, 40, 41, 117, 122, 125, 128, 130, 164, 207, 211
Drug Movement, *see* psychedelic cults
dualism, 58; Christian, 146; Manichaean, 146; of spirit and matter, 72, 79; Zoroastrian, 146, 166
duality, 34, 106, 124

East Pakistan (Bangla Desh, q.v.), 13, 171
Eckhart, Meister, 41, 52, 101, 106
ecstasy, 40, 47, 57, 58, 65, 68-9, 72, 100, 101, 110, 208-9; diabolic, 146; false, 111; sensual, 69. *See also* rapture
ego, 65, 73, 98, **187**, 209; death of, 43, 96, 132, 157, 161, 187; is illusory, 120, 187; loss of, 42, 69, 89, 96, 105, 133, 163
egoism, 133. *See also* selfishness
Einstein, Albert, 20, 193
Emerson, Ralph Waldo, 62
Emptiness, 124, 146, 148; 'evil' —, 148, 155-6. *See also* Void

Engels, Friedrich, 18, 20, 21, 22, 23, 28, 30-1, 32, 71, 141
enlightenment (Buddhist), 38, 45, 82, 96, 117, 118, 121, 122; attachment to, 98; instant, 115; Zen, 113-14, 125
Enomiya-Lassalle, Fr H. M.; on Zen monks, 117-18
entropy, 37, 159; spiritual, 142, 148, 155, 160
'ethic of knowledge', 30, 32-4
ethics, 35, 165; J. Monod on, **28-34**, 58
Ethiopia, 144
Eucharist, 209. *See also* Holy Communion
euthanasia, 180
Evangelicals, 76
Eve, 169
evil, 35-6, 46, 61, 62, 143, 145, 147, 149, 154, 159, 164, 166-8, 170-1, 192; absolute zero, 161; as deprivation of good, 36; 'beyond any name', 148; equated with matter, 165; God and, **162-3**; impossibility of, 61, 177; is death, 187; is multiplicity, 179; masquerades as good, 161; spiritual, 143, 165; Teilhard on, 179-80. *See also* good and evil
Evil (Destructive) Spirit, 146, 166, 167
evolution, 18ff., 71, 87, 179, 180, 196; and God, 74-5; evolutionary time, 141, 195, 211; of ideas, 25
existentialism; Bonhoeffer on, 138
'expansion', 98, 109; of the mind, 114, 115. *See also* consciousness (expanded).
Extreme Unction, **209-10**

faith, 15, 16, 28, 86, 104, 112, 171, 173, 211; biblical, 86; of the Church, 199
Fall, the, 85, 180
fanā, 185
fifth column; Teilhard on, 181
flux, 120, 121, 124, 147, 195, 196, 201
France, 142, 147; collapse of, 181
François de Sales, St, 82, 208; on *holy* ecstasy, **110-11**; on spiritual and carnal rapture, 68-9
French Revolution, 195

Freud, Sigmund, 42, 50, 89, 101
Friday abstinence, 205-6

Garden of Eden, 169
Gāthās (of Zoroaster), 146, 166
'generation gap', 13-14, 203
Genesis, Book of, 122, 180
genetic code, 18-19, 22, 23, 26, 33, 74. *See also* DNA code.
genocide, 27, 163
Germans, Germany, 170; Péguy on, 39; Teilhard on, 181
Gethsemane, 188, 209
Ghazālī, Al-, 100
Gide, André, 178
God, 33, 37, 38, 42, 78, 80, 85, 99, 105, 106, 108, 137, 139, 146-7, 156, 166, 173, 176-80, 183, 197, 208, 209, 210; a 'dirty word', 74; and evil, 162-3, 166-7; arms of, 147, 201, 209; as *deus ex machina*, 75; as devouring maw, 159; as DNA code, 71, 73; as energy process, 73; as lover, 68-9, 87; as man, 20, 64, 89 ('I am the Truth'); as Nature, 20, 50, 70; as sex, 64; as state of being, 112; as universe, 20, 61, 176; beyond the One, 93, 116, and Being, 109; beyond good and evil, 164, 170; body of, 66; Christian, 53; creates light and darkness, 167; dropping into, 189; falling into, 160; goodness of, 149, 163, 166, 167, 168, 169, 179, 189; heart of, 186, 187, 191; his wrath, 164, 170, 171, 192; image of, 54; in death, 187, 191; in Nature, 168; in the All, 177-8; indwelling, 71; is love, 170; Jung's, 164-5, 168-70; kingdom of, 41, 65, 71, 190, 202; Leary on, 70-3; life in, 208, 210; love of, 93, 94, 101, 102, 104, 110-11, 127, 170, 184, 186; made man, 87, 170; New Testament —, 71; Old Testament —, 50, 59, 60, 65, 71, 76, 86, 163, 164-5; of Islam, 168; of the Bible, 43, 50; of the Koran, 43, 50, 86; omnipotent, 163, 170; omniscient, 169; 'out there', 39, 41; pantheistic, 50, 64, 65, 127; Pascal's, 106, 109, 189; personal, 19, 43, 49, 73, 86, 89, 112, 116, 127,

163, 178; 'plays at dice', 20, 193; seeing —, 190; Son of, 74, 104; terrible, 127, 159, 169, 170, 184, 189; the Father, 71, 178, 189; the psychedelic, 74, 76; the Son, 71; true self in —, 155, 160; union with, 69, 78, 83, 96, 100, 102, 134, 192; unjust and amoral, 165, 167; will of, 170; wisdom of, 169; within, 75, 101; Word of, 73, **86**
Godhead, 69, 72, 101, 162; beyond God, 163
God-man, 87, 104, 156, 193, 208. *See also* Christ, Jesus
'God's world', 56, 112, 117, 164, 190
golden age, 128
good and evil, 59, 127, 143, 149, 157, 195, 203; beyond —, 86, 93, 125, 146, 148, 154, 161, 177, 184; consciousness of, 154; derive from God, 60, 86; tree of the knowledge of, 128, 154, 180, 190; Zoroastrian ideas on, 166
Good Friday, 104
goodness, 36, 37, 75, 117, 118, 129, 202, 204; 'all is good', 125; of God, 163, 167; spontaneous, 127
grace, 41, 123, 169, 171, 209; and death, 189
Graham, Dr Billy, 76
gratitude, 37, 96, 98, 106, 169, 192

hālāt, 78, 80, 92, 101
Hallāj, Al-, 89
Hamlet, 204
Harada Roshi, 98
harmony, 35, 66, 73, 128, 167
hashish, 40, 100
hatred; supernatural, 161
heaven, 157; kingdom of, 131, 201
Hebrews, Epistle to the; quoted, 74
Hegel(ian), 18, 28, 31, 40
hell, 87, **155**, 169, 206; is the Cold, 154, 157
Heraclitus, 148
heresy, heretic, 37, 179, 198
'higher than deity', 53, 54, 59, 60, 102
Hindu(ism), 47, 62, 76, 80, 103, 106, 112, 126, 148, 154, 159, 160, 184, 193, 205, 208; and evil, 162-3, 165; its comprehensiveness, 71-2; mysticism, 40, 109; Tantric, 66, 114, 134
hippies, 127, 128, 130, 131
Hiroshima, 170, 182
Hitler, 33, 144, 170, 181, 199
holiness, 202, 205
Holland, 144
Holy Communion, 87, 206, 209
Holy Spirit, 133, 146, 166, 194, 203, 206, 211
Homo sapiens, 27
honour, 143-4, 173, 174
hope, 19, 36, 172, 189, 190, 193, 210, 211
Hsün Tzŭ; quoted, 129
Hui Nêng, 125; quoted, 132
Humanae vitae, 204
humanism, 33, 137, 180
humility, 96, 106, 200, 202, 204, 210
Huxley, Aldous, 40-1, 48, 63, 77, 81, 97, 105, 110, 113, 163; his last thoughts, **108-9**

'I and mine', 102, 120
Ibn 'Arabī, 77, 83
identity, 70, 176; in distinction, 64; with Absolute, 89-90
Illich, Dr Ivan, 198
'imbeciles', 75, 172, 173, 197, 206, 208, 211
immortality, 16, 44; experience of, 45, 63, 132
impurity, 57, 158, 172, 174, 175, 190
India, 135, 136
indifference (holy), 101, 118, 205
individuality; is illusory, 120; loss of, 42, 43, 46. *See also* personality
individuation, 96, 108
Indra, 162
innocence, 151, 160, 190, 203; original, 177
intellectuals, 138, 148, 154, 173
intention, 205
interconnectedness, 60, 63, 66, 74, 117
intoxication, 48; mystical, 48, 100-1
Iran, 144
Isaiah, 163
Ishā Upanishad; quoted, 80, 92, 136, 185
Islam, 40, 78, 86, 103, 168; and evil, 165-6. *See also* Muslim

isolation, of spirit from matter, 57, 80, 87, 89; of spirit from God, 89
Israel, 163

James, William, 40, 42, **48-50**, 58, 61, 63, 88, 138
japa, 47
Japan(ese), 115, 116, 117, 144
Jefferies, Richard, **50-60**, 61, 63, 64, 65, 80, 84, 92, 102, 107, 127, 132, 179; his communion with Nature, 51-3; on eternal Now, 54-5; on objective Nature, 59-60; on physical beauty, 57
Jeremiah, 39, 142
Jericho, 163
Jesuits, 141, 196
Jesus, 83, 136, 163, 166, 170, 184, 193, 201, 202, 207, **210**; his 'outstretched arms', 201; humanity of, 210; on lawyers, 209; on little children, 131; Society of, 196. *See also* Christ, God-man
'Jesus people', 208
Jew(ish), 21, 170. *See also* Judaism
Job, Book of, 165, 166
John XXIII, Pope, 15, 36-7, 75, 133, 134, 136, 144, 200, **201-3**, 204, 205, 210; on death, 202
John, St, 73, 166, 170; quoted, 185
John of the Cross, St, 99, 132, 178
Joseph, 193
joy, 37, 44, 47, 61, 62, 63, 65, 80, 91, 93, 95, 98, 103, 106, 114, 146, 187, 190-1, 192, 208, 210; in death, 191
Judaism, 166; and evil, 165. *See also* Jew(ish)
Junayd, Al-, 90
Jung, C. G., 20, 41, 42, 46, 56, 59, 86, 96, 99, 101, 108, 109, 115, 117, 133, 141, 163, 164, 171, 173, 184, 189, 190; his *Answer to Job*, 164-5, 168, 170; his experience of God, 168-9; his father, 112-13; his first Communion, 164, 188; his God, 164-5, 170, 177. *See also* 'positive inflation', 'God's world'

Kaiser (Wilhelm II), 143
Kapleau, Philip, 126
Katha Upanishad, 176-7

Kaushītakī Upanishad; quoted, 162-3
Kena Upanishad; quoted, 187
'kick', 133; Catholic —, 87; defined, 87
Koran, 43, 78, 86; quoted, 86
Kraemer, Hendrik, 85
Krishna, 81, 102, 127, 163
Krishnamurti, 133; on drugs, 114-15
Küng, Hans, 197

La Rochefoucauld, 173
Lamentations, 60; quoted, 163
lawyers, 206, 209
League for Spiritual Discovery, 115
Leary, Dr Timothy, 63, 66, **70-4**, 81, 83, 84-5, 87, 97, 100, 112, 113, 115, 116, 122, 132, 133, 208, 209; a Hindu, not a Buddhist, 79-80; and Catholicism, 86-7; on alcohol, 48-9; on God, 70-1, 73, 76; on LSD and sex, 67, 114; on Protestantism, 87; on religion, 72-3; on Teilhard, 74
leisure, 139, 140
liar, lies, 20, 146, 151, 163, 166, 167, 172, 199; personified, 166
'liberation', 96, 118-19, 120, 154, 160, 168; and laughter, 160; as second birth, 82
life, 15, 19, 104, 117, 208; and death, 120, 152, 153, 177, 184-5, 189, 191, 202, 210; eternal, 61, 176, 185; higher, 174; love of, 130
light, 153, 166, 167; eternal, 110
Logos, 67
love, 34, 68, 91, 93, 103, 104, 170, 176, 182, 194, 198, 205, 210; cosmic, 62, 63, 92, 94, 107; divine, 40, 49, 94, 100, 102; infinite, 106; living fire of, 158, 202; of neighbour, 104, 183-4, 192; of Shiva and Shakti, 67; psychedelic, 94-5, 104-5, 106-7; sexual, 66, 68, 100. *See also* God (love of)
LSD (*lysergic acid diethylamide*), 41, 42, 44, 48-9, 60, 65, 76, 83, 88, 108, 113, 132, 135, 137, 207, 208; and Christianity, 85, 86-7; and kicks, 87; and sex, 67-8, 70, 114, 134; and Sufism, 100; and Zen (*see* Zen); experience(s), 72, 93, 94-5, 96, 99, 107; sensory aids used with, 99-100; summing up, **133-4**

Index

lust, 175
Lutheranism, 199

madness, 132; and lust, 175; and mysticism, 52, 92
Mahayana Buddhism, 66, 106, 113, 148, 209, 210; advent of, 122; its innovations, 122-4. *See also* Zen
Maitrī Upanishad, 55
ma'jūn, 100
make-believe, 15, 16, 28, 31, 209, 210
Mammon, 139
Manichaean(ism), 68, 134; dualism, 146
mantra, 47
Mao Tse-tung, 33, 40, 181
maqāmāt, 78, 80, 92
Māra, **120**
Marcion, 59
Marcuse, Herbert, 40
marriage, 68, 204, 205
Marx, Karl, 21, 39, 40, 71, 136, 141, 207
Marxism, Marxist, 18, 20, 26, 39, 136
Mass (Catholic), 76, 86-7, 189, 191, 207
Masters, R. E. L., and Houston, J., 77, 79, 83, 84, 94, 96-8, 104, 107, 113; on 'authentic' psychedelic experience, 96-7; on LSD and asceticism, 81; on psychedelic 'love', 94-5
materialists, 142, 205, 207
matter, 53, 140, 175, 183; and spirit, 56, 122; equated with evil, 165; 'holy', 176-7
mediocrity, 115, 184, 197, 206, 207, 208, 210, 211
meditation, 101, 102, 114; and love, 115; and psychedelic experience, 114-15, 133; sitting (*zāzen*), 93; Zen, 117, 123
Merton, Thomas, 160
mescalin, 41, 105
'Miracle of Marsh Chapel', 88-9, 103-104
mirror, 125, 158, 192
modern world, 136-7, 142-3, 145, 149, 182, 196, 203
'modernism', 195
money, 139, 174
monism, 49, 50, 80, 91

Monod, Jacques, **18-34**, 43, 58, 60, 71, 72, 74, 76, 84, 139, 140, 182
mortification, 82
Muhammad; vision of, 77, 83
Mundaka Upanishad; quoted, 64
Muslim(s), 40, 47, 48, 80, 99. *See also* Islam, mysticism, Sufism
Mussolini, 144
mutation(s), 19, 20
mysticism, 30-1, 39, 40, 43, 51-2, **85-134**, 141, 161, 162; and absolute good and evil, 161; and alcohol, 48; and detachment, 132; and drugs, 48-50, **66-111**; and Satan, 146; and science, 30-1, 58; and sex, **66-70**; and visions, 77-8; as way of life, 78; blurs differences, 86; 'canned', '84; Christian (Catholic), 38, 40, 49, 50, 66, 68ff., 78, 82, 87, 104, 158; Christian criticism of, 86; Eastern, 76, 113, 164; experience, 41, **51-2**, 61, 77, 78, 80, 96 ('genuine'), 108; interpretation of, 61-2, 77, 78, 79; Muslim, 48, 49, 66, 77, 78, 104, 185; of matter, 176; psychedelic, 65, 66-110; spontaneous, 88, 93, 96; typology of, 89-93; varieties of, 79, 103; William James on, 48-50. *See also* nature mysticism

Nāgārjuna, 123, 126
Nagasaki, 170, 182
Native American Church, 83
natural law, 204
Nature, 19, 54, 63, 128; and man, 20, 24, 35, 57, 60, 129-30, 179; as God, 50, 71; contemplation of, 46, 47, 50; fusion with, 127; identity with, 52, 113, 114, 128, 130; Jefferies on, 57-8; Jung on, 168; objectively seen, 50, 59-60
nature mysticism, 43, 45, 46, 47, 50, 52, 58, 60, 62, 64, 65, 70, 72, 76, 78, 80, 87, 117, 127, 132, 146, 168, 179
Nazareth, 83, 210
Nazi(s), 35, 200
Neanderthal man, 27
'negative dialectic', 124
Neo-Confucians, 148, 161
Neo-Platonism, 78

New Testament, 71, 78, 86, 156, 164, 170
Nietzsche, 20
Nirmānakāya, 123
Nirvana, 42, 50, 82, 83, 158, 161, 164, 201, 208; and *samsāra*, 122, 123-4; definitions of, **118-19**, 147; diabolical caricature of, 155, 159, 164; identical with *samsāra* (Mahayana), 123-4, 126
'noosphere', 23, 25, 34, 140, 141
Norway, 144
'nothing', 155, 156, 157, 160, 175
nothingness, 17, 105-6, 139, 146, 147, 186, 205, 206, 207, 211
'not-self' (Buddhist), 118, 123, 180
Now, eternal, 52, **54-5**, 56, 59, 60, 102, 109, 112

'oceanic feeling', 42, 89, 101, 113-14, 176
Ohrmazd, 166, 167
Old Testament, 86, 163, 164
'Omega point', 74
One, the, 20, 50, 80, 127; and many, 124; as All, 114; being —, 98; contraction into, 93; merging into, 50; reconciles opposites, 63. *See also* unity
Oneness, *see* unity
opposites, 124, 125; in God, 167; reconciliation of, 40, 49, 63, 64, 66; union of, 148, 173
original innocence, 131
Ostia, 83, 109
Otto, Rudolf, 91
Ouine, Monsieur, 145, **147-61**, 164, 171, 173, 175, 182, 190, 198, 206, 211; as intellectual, 148, 154; his ambiguity, 151; his curiosity, 152; his 'detachment', 157; his 'love', 153, 154, 157; is cold, 153-4; on the soul, 159-60; *'oui-non'*, 148

Pahnke, Dr Walter N., 88, 91, 93, 94, 95, 96, 99, 103, 105, 107, 119
pantheism, 20, 50, 66, 72, 76, 83; Christian, 178; sexual, 79; two types of, 176
paradox, 92, 95, 103
Pascal, 16-17, 91, 92, 106, 109, 138-9, 189; on dangers of leisure, 139; on nature of man, 161-2
Paul VI, Pope, 135, 203-5, 210
Paul, St, 71, 78, 190, 193, 200, 204; quoted, (Colossians) 73, 179, (Ephesians) 143, (Galatians) 104, (Romans) 211
peace, 91, 93, 103, 106, 116, 118, 122, 146, 158, 173, 201; Satanic, 147, 153, 155, 171
Péguy, Charles, 39, 79
Peking, 181
Penance, 209
Pentecost, 203
'people of God', 206
perdition, **146**, 148, 150, 159-60, 198
'performance value', 25, 27
personality, 126, 180, 183, 193; higher, 174; is illusory, 120; loss of, 42, 46, 161; second, 46, 55-6, 164
Peter, St; Rock of, 195, 196, 201
Pharisees, 38, 75, 139, 182, 212
Picardy, 172
'pill', the, 205
pity, 147, 149, 157
Pius IX, Pope, 179
Pius XII, Pope, 179, 195, 201, 205, 206
Platform Scripture, 158
Plato, 41
Poland, 144
Pope, the, 196, 198, 206
'positive inflation', 96, 97, 99, 101, 109, 115
'pot', 40, 100
prayer; Jefferies on, 52-3
pride, 18, 102, 145; intellectual, 17; spiritual, 97
'principle of objectivity', 24, 25, 28, 29, 30, 31, 33, 76
progress, 179, 180, 181
progressives, 37, 197, 204, 206
promiscuity, 134
prophecy, prophets, 39-40, 111, 137, 144, 184, 207
Protestant(ism), 14, 39, 50, 87, 88, 163, 175, 178, 197, 198-9, 208; and LSD, 85; and mysticism, 85; Jung and, 164; sects, 199; work culture, 76, 85

Proust, Marcel, 52, 56, 63, 92, 126; his mystical experiences, **44-6**
prudence, 203, 207
Prussia, 144
Pseudo-Dionysius, 78, 106
psilocybin, 88, 105
psychedelic cults, 66, 67, 85, 94, 97, 115, 134
psychedelic drugs, 38, 40, 44, 48-50 (nitrous oxide), 58, 61, 63, 74, 76-110, 113, 115; beneficial effect of, 107, 114; danger of, 133, 161; opposition to, 84-7; varieties of — experience, 79, 102. *See also* LSD, mysticism (psychedelic)
psychiatry, 84-5, 137, 140
psychoanalysts, 133
psychotherapy; Bonhoeffer on, 138
Puritanism, 68
purity, 151, 158, 190, 200, 201, 203, 204

qualitative leap, 18
Qushayrī, Al-, 97, 115; on expanded consciousness, 98-9, 133

radical Left, 39-40, 144
Rāmānuja, 66
rapture, 66, 95, 111, 147; spiritual and carnal, 68-9
Reid, Forrest, 47, 48, 50
reincarnation, 184
religion, 14, 19, 36ff, 71, 72, 140, 208; Leary on, 72-3, 76; prophetic and mystical, 39; synthetic, 84; what it is about, 44, 85
'religionless Christianity', 200
renunciation, 26, 135, 136, 205
responsibility, 164, 170
resurrection, 192, 193
Robinson, Dr John, 39, 41
Rome, 76, 195, 197, 198, 200, 206
rosary, 47
rottenness, 143, 147, 148, 155, 159, 174, 182, 184, 211. *See also* corruption, decay
Rousseau, J-J., 14, 35
Rūmī, Jalālu'd-Dīn, 192

sacramentalism, 197
sacraments, 204, 209

safe period, 205
salvation, 146, 156, 157, 160, 189, 211; -machine, 197, 210. *See also* 'liberation'
samādhi, 126
Sambhogakāya, 123
Samizdat, 196
samsāra, 120, 122, 123-4, 147; and right action, 165; identical with Nirvana (q.v.), 123-4, 126
Sangha, 122
Sānkhya(-Yoga), 72, 87, 89, 91
Sat Chit Ananda, 41, 108
Satan, 135, 143, **146**, 147, 162, 192; counterfeits Nirvana, 147; father of lies, 170; his laugh, 161; imitates God, 147; Prince of this world, 145; vision of, 145-6. *See also* Devil
satori, 40, 92, 115, 117; not for all, 116. *See also* enlightenment
science, 17, 18-34, 57, 84, 130, 139, 142, 145, 182; and ethics, 27; and mysticism, 58; as scapegoat, 36; limitations of, 24, 140
scribes, 15, 38, 75, 76, 139, 182, 206, 210, 212
Self, 63, 132, 187, 209; Hindu, 43, 46, 54 (as Inner Controller), 64, 65, 70, 96, 157, 159, 162, 193; in all beings, 80, 126; in Zen, 81, 116, 117, 126, 158, 160, 183; Jungian, 46; realization of, 161; two selves, 126; union with, 64, 65
self-consciousness, 47, 114, 128, 180
self-hatred, 151, 157
self-hypnosis, 47
selfishness, 133, 180, 186; national, 182. *See also* egoism
selflessness, 130, 180, 194
self-love, 194
self-righteousness, 129, 136, 210
self-sacrifice, 14, 32-3
self-transcendence, 32, 33, 42, 105
'separated brethren', 37, 198, 206
Sermon on the Mount, 178, 184
'set and setting', 83, 84, 88, 99, 103
sex, 40, 63, 64-5, 76, 175, 209; and God, 74; and LSD (q.v.), 134; and mysticism, **66-70**, 100, 134-5; cosmic, 70, 114; in psychedelic ex-

sex (Contd.)
perience, 67; sexual revolution, 13, 68, 174-5
'shadow' (Jungian), 164
Shakti, 67, 134
Shibayama, Abbot Zenkei, 81, **115-17**, 125-6, 133; on drugs, 115, 126
Shiva, 64, 66-7, 72
Shun, 128
Simeon Stylites, St, 82
simplicity, 131, 152
sin, 150, 169, 191, 192, 210; as alienation, 180; mortal, 206; original, 179
Smith, Huston, 79
'sobriety', mystical, 48, 82, 101
socialism, 31, 32
solipsism, 94, 134, 135
Song of Songs, 68, 78
soul, 140, 155, 159, and *passim*; absorption into, 157; and body, 56-7, 64; disintegration of, 155-61; Jefferies on, 53, 54-5, 56; of the front, 173, 174, 177; passing beyond, 110; timeless, 80, 89; undifferentiated unity of, 89
'Soul of the All (world)', 90, 174
Soviet Union, 13, 196. *See also* USSR
space-time, 17, 36, 193, 210
Spinoza, 50, 60, 70
spirit, 56, 63, 122; spirits of truth and falsehood, 167
'spiritual body', 193
spiritual marriage, 68, 83, 87, 127
spontaneity, 125, 127, 131, 133, 210
Stace, W. T., 79, 91, 93, 95, 103, 113
Stalin, 33, 181
'Suchness', 124
suffering, 114, 118, 119-20, 142, 178, 179, 180, 182, 184, 188, 210; acceptance of, 189; Bernanos and, 189; of God, 191
Sufi(sm), 89-90, 99; asceticism, 82; development of, **100-1**; sensory aids used in, 100-1. *See also* mysticism (Muslim)
Suso, Heinrich, 78
Suzuki, D. T., 125

Tao (the 'Way', q.v.), 124, 127, 129, 152; human —, 128
Tao Tê Ching; quoted, 124, 128, 130

Taoism, Taoist, 37, 57, 73, 124, 125, 127-31
technology, 84, 97, 130, 139, 140, 142
Teilhard de Chardin, Pierre, 18, 20, 22, 23, 24, 25, 27, 28, 30, 34, 58, 71, 138, 140-1, 162, 168, **175-84**, 185, 187, 190, 211; and the Roman Church, 196-8; his heresy, 179; his mystical typology, 74; 'hyper-Catholic', 188, 198; Leary on, 74; on atom bomb, 181; on cosmic consciousness, 177; on evil, 179-80; on Germans and fifth column, 181; on *la sainte Matière*, 176; on love of one's neighbour, 183; on personal survival, 188; on sin, 179-80; on the Cross, 178; on unemployment, 140-1; on World War I, 172, 173-4
Tennyson, 42, 43, 46, 56, 63, 130
Teresa, St, 77, 78, 83
theologians, theology, 37, 39, 41, 75, 165, 197, 206, 209, 210
Theosophical Society, 114
Tibet, 171
Tibetan Book of the Dead, 146
Tillich, Paul, 106
time, 109, 122; Jefferies on, 55-6
timeless state, 44, 46, 55, 63, 70, 74, 78, 80, 83, 89, 93, 106, 108, 112, 119 (Nirvana), 126, 146, 157, 185, 193
Tokugawa, 125
totalitarianism, 180-1
Traherne, Thomas, 56, 57
trance, 42, 47, 50, 134
transcendence, 33, 38; of death, 44, 63; of ego, 105; of reason, 69; of space and time, 42, 52, 53, 63, 91, 93, 95, 96, 102, 103; of the All, 50. *See also* self-transcendence
Trinity; Christian, 29, 77, 101; Jacques Monod's, 29, 34

Ultimate Reality, 106
unification, 183; of the multiple, 179
union, in diversity, 141, 186; personal, 178; with Nature (q.v.), 51. *See also* God (union with)
unity (Oneness), 49, 54, 89, 91, 95,

106, 112, 117, 130, 167-8, 177, 183, 186; absolute, 90, 93, 101; by dissolution, 162, 176; Catholic, 199; external and internal, **89-91**, 103; in multiplicity, 116; of the soul, 90; two types of, 176

'Unmanifest', the, 177

Upanishads, 46, 49, 50, 51, 54, 55, 57, 62, 64, 65, 66, 73, 87, 89, 178, 205; pantheism of, 72, 80. *See also Brihadāranyaka, Chāndogya, Ishā, Katha, Kaushītakī, Mundaka*

Upper Clyde Company, 140

USA, 137, 142, 200, 208. *See also* America

USSR, 137, 144. *See also* Soviet Union

usury, 205

Vatican II, 203, 204, 210

Vedanta, 38; neo-, 20, 112

Vietnam, 13, 142, 170

violence, 149, 150, 173

virgin birth, 195

Vishnu, 72

visions, 172, 174; ocular and intellectual, 77-8; of Christ and Muhammad, 83; peripheral to mysticism, 77-8; prophetic, 111; psychedelic, 108, 114, 115

vitalism ('animism'), 22, 26, 29, 30, 31, 32, 43, 50, 71, 72

Void, the, 124, 157, 159; Buddhist, 124, 147, 148, 157; 'Satanic', 147, 148, 157, 162; Taoist, 124. *See also* Emptiness

war, 182, 202

Watts, Alan, 77, 97, 113

Way, the (Taoist), 124, 131. *See also* Tao

Whitman, Walt, 57, 61, 64-5, 70, 74, 79, 80, 83

wholeness, 76, 97

wisdom, 35, 72, 74, 83, 95, 116, 118, 123, 129, 130, 131; and compassion, 123, 148, 157; balanced by love, 110; eternal (perfect), 110, 126, 158; reverse of cosmic consciousness, 118-19; too much, 109

Word (of God), abides in itself, 110; made Book, 86; made Flesh, 82

'world come of age', 137, 144, 147, 195

Yaeko Iwasaki; Zen experience of, 98

Yahweh, 21, 65, 164, 168; Jung's impression of, 165

Yoga, Yogi, 56, 81, 82; claims to omnipotence and omniscience, 96; LSD and, 72; philosophy, 89; techniques, 80, 93

youth, 152; spirit of, 31, 203, 207

zāzen, 93, 98

Zen, 20, 37-8, 45, 46, 81, 83, 92, 112-18, 123-7, 132, 178; and psychedelic drugs, **113-17**, 126, 132-3; as understood by Zenkei Shibayama, 116; 'beat' —, 42; Buddhism, 40, 57, 66, 69-70, 97, 115, 116, 126, 133, 148, 158, 178, 183, 208; difficulty of, 81, 125-7; — experience, 126; — illness, 98; neo-, 112; Soto, 116; techniques, 127

Zoroaster, 146

Zoroastrian(ism); Devil, 146; its spiritual dualism, 146, 166, 167